Criminal Woman, the Prostitute, and the Normal Woman

by Cesare Lombroso

and Guglielmo Ferrero.

Translated and with a

new introduction by

Nicole Hahn Rafter

and Mary Gibson

Duke University Press

Durham and London

2004

Printed in the United States of America on acid-free paper • Typeset in Galliard by Tseng Information Systems, Inc.
Library of Congress Cataloging-in-Publication Data appear on the last printed page of this book.

Nothing too severe can be said of Lombroso's lack of critical judgment and historical insight and accuracy; one forgives it all because he has opened up so many new lines of investigation and set so many good men to work.

HAVELOCK ELLIS, in an 1892 letter to John Addington Symonds

Scientific discoveries carefully choose their discoverers, and not the opposite.

LUIGI GUARNIERI, *L'atlante criminale: Vita scriteriata di Cesare Lombroso* (Criminal atlas: The hair-brained life of Cesare Lombroso)

In memory of Anne Barbara Gibson

Contents

PART III Pathological Anatomy and Anthropometry of Criminal Woman and the Prostitute

PART IV Biology and Psychology of Female Criminals and Prostitutes

List of Tables

Note: Lombroso did not usually title his tables, especially when they were short. We have added brief titles for clarity and ease of reference.

List of Illustrations

Note: For information on Lombroso's original captions, see Appendix 2.

Acknowledgments

When we began working on this project in the early 1990s, fewer than half a dozen people worldwide had close familiarity with Lombroso's major works, which had become nearly inaccessible; and yet nearly everyone familiar with Lombroso's name confidently dismissed him as a figure of scientific fun. Thus our initial task was to persuade people that new translations of his criminological works would prove worthwhile. Peter Becker of the European University Institute in Florence, Piers Beirne of the University of Southern Maine, and Frances M. Heidensohn of Goldsmiths' College, University of London, immediately understood the value of our project and spent long hours explaining it to others. Without them, this book might have never seen publication. Frances Heidensohn also contributed valuable material to the introduction on Lombroso's influence on British criminology in the 1960s and 1970s. Bernard Cohen, Simon Cole, Steven Hughes, Dario Melossi, and Graeme Newman similarly encouraged us, endorsing our odd project vis-à-vis unbelieving others. Once we found him, Raphael Allen, our editor at Duke University Press, quickly grasped the significance of Lombroso's work and its relevance for a variety of audiences. His faith in our concept and our scholarship, and his old-fashioned vision of what an editor should be and do, sustained us—sometimes when we weren't even aware of his efforts on our behalf. There is still an ideal editor in the world, and his name is Raphael.

Tamar Pitch, professor of sociology of law at the University of Camerino, illuminated obscurities in Lombroso's writings that no dictionary could penetrate. We very much appreciate her agreeing to serve as our formal advisor on matters of the Italian language. We are similarly grateful to Maria Grazia Rossilli, sociological consultant to the European Union, for helping informally with problematic passages of the text. Paul Arpaia of Baruch College, organizer of the Italy section of the H-Net listserv, helped with one of our most difficult translation dilemmas by broadcasting our request for an English equivalent of *fusche*. Others who contributed to this project include Massimo Bacigalupo, Nancy Egan, Joe Farara, Vita Carlo Fedeli, Marina Graziosi, Randall Grometstein, Edward Hanlon, Linda Kramer, Bonnie Nelson, Dr. Larry Sullivan, Steve Turner, and Daniel Mark Vyleta. Fernando Azevedo of the Graduate Center at City College of New York reproduced Lombroso's images.

The Bogliasco Foundation of New York and its Liguria Study Center for the Arts and Humanities provided fellowship support to Nicole Rafter for part of this project, as well as delightful quarters on Italy's northern coast in which to write.

According to Lombroso, women, being naturally weak, need male support. Although we are unaware of gender debilities, we are nonetheless immensely grateful to Robert Hahn and James Cohen for the many ways in which they came to our aid during the preparation of this book.

Criminal Woman, the Prostitute, and the Normal Woman

Editors' Introduction

This volume offers a new translation of Cesare Lombroso's *La donna delinquente—Criminal Woman*—a work coauthored with Guglielmo Ferrero and originally published in Italian in 1893. This was the book—and not Lombroso's celebrated *L'uomo delinquente* (*Criminal Man*)—that in an early translation introduced American and British readers to work by the Italian criminal anthropologist who claimed to have discovered a new human subspecies: the born criminal. *La donna delinquente*'s significance also lies in its extraordinary impact on the study of female crime. This work, more than any other book in Western history, determined directions taken in that field of study, albeit in recent decades by providing a backdrop against which feminist criminologists have lobbed very different ideas. The translation presented here gives most readers their first full view of Lombroso's text. It also constitutes the first new English edition of *La donna delinquente* in over a century and the first new English edition of any work by Lombroso in close to one hundred years.

Cesare Lombroso (1835–1909) is widely recognized as one of the first people (some would say the very first person) to bring scientific methods to bear on the study of crime. A physician, psychiatrist, and prolific author, Lombroso is best known as the founder of criminal anthropology—the study of the body, mind, and habits of the "born" criminal. Lombroso's theory of the atavistic offender, a throwback to a primitive stage in human evolution, dominated criminological discussions in Europe, North and South America, and parts of Asia from the 1880s into the early twentieth century. His central idea of the born or genetic criminal continues to attract adherents, and the main legal implication of his work—that some offenders are not fully responsible for their acts—remains key in criminal jurisprudence. Today, Lombroso is becoming a basic reference point for historians of gender, race, law, and science. He is being recognized as one of the most fertile, if uncritical, thinkers in nineteenth-century Europe, and a man whose work marked a turning point in conceiving of the body as a sign of human worth.

La donna delinquente's significance to the Anglo-American world came partly from its rapid publication in English. In 1895, just two years after its original Italian publication, *La donna delinquente* appeared in English as *The Female Offender*. This was a full sixteen years before the release of an English translation of *Criminal Man*. Frequently reprinted in both New York and London, *The Female Offender* for many years formed one of the main bridges over which Lombroso's ideas passed from Italy to English-speaking countries.[1]

Although *The Female Offender* is today less well known than some of Lombroso's other writings, it actually had a greater long-term impact on the study of female crime than *Criminal Man* did on theories of male crime. For decades, there existed no other book on the causes of female crime and, indeed, very little other material in any form. *The Female Offender* continued to influence interpretations of female crime until the 1970s; it became the classic text in its field. In contrast, by 1911, when *Criminal Man* finally appeared in English, Lombroso's born criminal theory was already going out of vogue as an explanation of male crime. The dominance of *The Female Offender* led to the long-term emphasis on female crime as biological in nature. It led, as well, to a particularly heavy stress on sexual and psychological factors in explanations of female crime. Its influence persists into the present, moreover, due to the fact that Lombroso's pronouncements on female crime have become—rightly or wrongly—a much-discussed symbol of all that is wrong in methods and goals with criminology.

This new edition differs so radically from the original *The Female Offender* translation as to form an entirely different book. While Lombroso's original consisted of four major parts, *The Female Offender* translated only one part and bits of another. While Lombroso had titled his book *La donna delinquente, la prostituta e la donna normale, The Female Offender* omitted much of the material on prostitutes and all of the commentary on "normal" women—material crucial to Lombroso's argument because it established the general inferiority of women to men. It also omitted nearly all the material on the sexual characteristics of female criminals, such as lesbianism, virility, menstrual abnormalities, and anomalies of the breasts and genitals. In good Victorian fashion, moreover, it completely sanitized Lombroso's language and thought, for example by changing the phrase "a criminal lesbian" into "a woman" and dropping material on lasciviousness as a cause of crime. Reading *The Female Offender*, one would never guess that Lombroso had a keen interest in sexual pathology and contributed to the development of sexology as a field of study. This new edition includes all four parts of the original text and restores the sexual material excised and bowdlerized in *The Female Offender*. Following Lombroso's original, we have titled this new edition *Criminal Woman, the Prostitute, and the Normal Woman*.[2]

Goals of the New Edition

This new edition of *Criminal Woman*, and its forthcoming companion edition of *Criminal Man*,[3] has a twofold purpose: to provide, for the first time, adequate English translations of Lombroso's criminological work and to lay foundations for an emerging new generation of Lombroso scholarship.

Research on Lombroso's criminal anthropology has become very difficult due to the virtual inaccessibility of his texts in both the original Italian and in translation. Few of the Italian originals exist in the United States, and, in any case, due to their age it is almost impossible to borrow them through interlibrary loan offices. (To work on this translation, we had to begin by obtaining a microfilm copy of the original and Xeroxing from that.) Not only have Lombroso's criminological works never been adequately translated into English; even the previous translations are out of print. Scholars working in English have had no way to follow the unfolding of Lombroso's ideas. Research has tended to be misleading because it has been based on incomplete or garbled records. And criminology students have had no way to get a clear overview of Lombroso's work, despite its fundamental importance to the field.

Misunderstandings of Lombroso's work are so widespread as to constitute a distinct mythology. Some commentators have ridiculed Lombroso's work as a pseudoscience; others, misled by abbreviated editions, have mistakenly assumed that Lombroso was a political reactionary. In the early twentieth century, when the English prison physician and statistician Charles Goring set out to critique Lombroso's theory, he had only a few, inadequate English-language resources to work from and thus only a vague, inaccurate idea of the work he was determined to refute.[4] Later in the century, when the distinguished American evolutionist Stephen Jay Gould set out to critique Lombroso's thought, he failed to recognize the complexity of Lombroso's central ideas, implying in *The Mismeasure of Man* that Lombroso's born criminal theory derived primarily from the nineteenth-century concept of recapitulation.[5] Lombroso's daughter Gina Lombroso-Ferrero contributed to the confusion by including in her 1911 edition of *Criminal Man*—which became the standard reference text—emendations that cannot be distinguished from her father's text.[6] Even some of her bibliographical information is inaccurate. For much of the twentieth century, Lombroso existed only as a distant and unapproachable figure—extraordinarily famous, widely ridiculed, and largely misunderstood.

In recent years, as more has become known about the intellectual context in which Lombroso worked, it has become clear that he built on concepts widely held by nineteenth-century scientists and that in many ways he was a liberal and even progressive thinker. In addition, recent work on the history of science and the relation of science to society has erased the formerly easy distinction between "science" and "pseudoscience." Instead of dismissing criminal anthropology as a naive or aberrant science, scholars are beginning to locate it in the context of the production of scientific knowledge in the late nineteenth century. Thus the time is ripe for reissuing Lombroso's major works. To provide students and scholars with sound, complete, and accessible editions of Lombroso's key criminological texts is the first aim of our new editions.

Even with the inadequate resources presently available, Lombroso's ideas have been the focus of a number of recent studies. Nicole Rafter's *Creating Born Criminals* investigates Lombroso's influence on U. S. criminology and the U. S. eugenics movement, while Mary Gibson's *Born to Crime: Cesare Lombroso and the Origins of Biological Criminology* documents his influence in Italy. Richard Wetzell's *Inventing the Criminal* does the same for Germany.[7] Another sign of the reawakening interest in Lombroso lies in *Criminals and Their Scientists: Essays on the History of Criminology*, a collection centered on Lombroso and his impact.[8] Between 1975 and 2000, ten books on Lombroso were published in Italian[9] and another six in languages other than Italian and English.[10] Clearly, an international explosion of interest in Lombroso's thought is already underway. To provide the new generation of Lombroso scholars with adequate tools is the second main aim of our new editions. The new editions are likely to prove particularly relevant to biological theories of crime. Recent years have seen an upsurge of interest in such theories, in part due to work on the Human Genome Project and popular interest in DNA identification of offenders. The new editions will help scholars relate Lombroso's work to these developments and determine the degree to which he served as their forerunner.

While these new translations provide material for new research in criminology and the history of science, future Lombroso studies are likely to branch out in other directions as well. Lombroso was a multifaceted and exceptionally innovative thinker, and his work proves relevant to a wide range of fields. For example, in both his museum of criminal anthropology and in his book illustrations, Lombroso preserved examples of prisoner art and prison artifacts (graffiti, slang, tattoos, and wall drawings), work that qualifies him as one of the first cultural anthropologists. Better Lombroso resources also offer fertile ground for art historians and artists—as already demonstrated by exhibitions on the visual strategies of biological theories of crime[11] and a book on criminological museums.[12] Recognizing Lombroso's pioneering role in scientific applications of photography as well as the power of his visual rhetoric, *Criminal Woman* includes thirty-two reproductions of Lombroso's art work. (Another forty images will appear in the new edition of *Criminal Man*.) Lombroso's work will also likely figure in future histories of law and medicine. As a physician and psychiatrist who wrote extensively about legal medicine, moral insanity, epileptic criminality, and psychiatric jurisprudence, Lombroso helped accomplish the shift in authority from keepers who punished crimes to medical professionals who treated criminals. Other signs of Lombroso's broad relevance can be found in recent studies of women's history and anti-Semitism, a topic in which Lombroso, as a Jew, took special interest.[13] In retrospect, one can see that Lombroso worked along major intellectual fault lines in the contested areas where various trends in social thought collided. Tensions between, for example, feminism and antifeminism, racism and antiracism, and liberalism and conservatism characterize his life and work.

These new editions, then, aim at facilitating Lombroso scholarship in fields as diverse as anthropology; art history; criminology; and rhetoric; Italian and European history; the history of science, medicine, and psychiatry; law and legal history; studies of race and ethnicity; and gender studies.

Lombroso's Explanations of Female Criminality

Lombroso wrote *Criminal Woman* to reiterate and reconfirm his riveting theory of the born criminal, according to which lawbreakers constitute throwbacks to earlier evolutionary stages—atavisms whose primitive nature dooms them to violate the laws of civilizations in which they unwittingly find themselves. Having previously applied this theory to the criminal man,[14] Lombroso now tested it on female offenders.

The Female Born Criminal

Lombroso devotes over one-quarter of *Criminal Woman* to demonstrating that offenders are scarred by physical imperfections and abnormalities—the "stigmata of degeneration" that simultaneously signify and prove their primitive natures.[15] He proceeds by comparing the number and type of stigmata in three groups of women: criminals, prostitutes, and "normal," that is, law-abiding, women. In the chapter "The Skull of the Female Offender," for example, he reports that "prostitutes have the smallest cranial capacity of all," followed by criminal women, while "in average and above-average capacity, honest women and even lunatics surpass both criminals and prostitutes."[16] Similarly, "The lower jaw of female criminals, and still more of prostitutes, is heavier than in moral women."[17] Elsewhere he observes that "anomalous teeth, present in only 0.5 percent of normal female subjects, are to be found in 10.8 percent of criminals and in 5.1 percent of prostitutes."[18] Summarizing such data, Lombroso concludes that "almost all anomalies occur more frequently in prostitutes than in female criminals, and both classes have more degenerative characteristics than do normal women."[19] In other words, there is a female criminal type. It appears in only 18 percent of female criminals. (In comparison, 31 percent of male offenders fall into the born criminal category.) If we widen the lens to include prostitutes, however, as Lombroso insists we must, we find that "37.1 percent of prostitutes exhibit the complete type."[20] Female born criminals, Lombroso explains, "have a passion for evil for evil's sake . . . an automatic hatred, one that springs from no external cause such as an insult or offense but from a morbid irritation of the psychical centers which relieves itself in evil action."[21]

Indeed, the "criminal propensities" of female born criminals "are more intense and perverse even than those of their male counterparts."[22] Although "female born criminals are fewer in number than male born criminals, they are often much more savage." Like normal women, they are "by nature less sensitive to pain than a man," and like children, they are "deficient in the moral sense," leaving them "vengeful, jealous, and inclined to refined cruelty when they take revenge." All things considered, "women are big children; their evil tendencies are more numerous and more varied than men's, but usually these remain latent. When awakened and excited, however, these evil tendencies lead to proportionately worse results."[23] As a consequence, "The born female criminal is, so to speak, doubly exceptional, first as a woman and then as a criminal. This is because criminals are exceptions among civilized people, and women are exceptions among criminals. . . . As a double exception, then, the criminal woman is a true monster."[24]

The Nature of Female Crime

A second major purpose of *Criminal Woman* is to explain the nature of female crime. Lombroso shows little interest in the details of female offending (Are women likely to be burglars or murderers? Accomplices or initiators?), but instead wants to create a typology of female offenders and, above all, to explain why women have relatively low crime rates. Despite the primitive state of late-nineteenth-century crime statistics, it was widely known that women were arrested and convicted far less frequently than men. Lombroso was particularly concerned to explain this phenomenon.

Here Lombroso encountered an intractable problem. His born criminal theory pointed toward an obvious explanation: Women have lower crime rates because they are less atavistic than men. However, that argument contradicted another idea to which Lombroso was deeply committed—the inferiority of women to men. Thus Lombroso assigned himself the very difficult task of arguing that women were less criminal than men because of their inferiority to men. And he set out to demonstrate this scientifically. He did so by using a control group—perhaps the earliest example of this procedure in criminological history. Lombroso's control group consisted of the normal women to whom he devotes the entire first part of *Criminal Woman*. "Criminal women could not have been understood," Lombroso reminds us in his preface, "if we had not also had a profile of normal women." Compiling information on this control group called for enormous effort, Lombroso admits: "When we searched for such information, we found nothing (certainly very little that was definite)." Thus he painstakingly collected data on normal women from published studies and by corresponding with gynecologists and other experts. Without the facts they provided, it would have been "impossible to determine where the normal state ends and the pathological begins."[25] *Criminal Woman* offers a glimpse of one of the earliest efforts to define deviance scientifically and to identify the boundary between normality and abnormality.

Lombroso starts *Criminal Woman* at the bottom of the evolutionary ladder, using his first chapter to explain that in the most primitive forms of sexually differentiated life, females dominate: "As soon as differences between the two sexes become apparent, the female is superior to the male in size, strength, and number." Moreover, "as we go up the zoological scale, the female's superiority in size and strength recurs frequently."[26] However, "in the higher orders, males' struggle with one another—a struggle rooted in their stronger sexual desire and perhaps also in their larger numbers—has led to their development of greater size and force than females, and to their superior physique. . . . The male, then, is a more perfect and more variable female through the greater development of secondary sexual characteristics."[27] Females—retarded by their passive role in courtship, their reproductive apparatus, and their maternal functions—remain less evolved than males into the present.

The following chapters of part 1 comprise a multifaceted, systematic exposition of female inferiority, starting with the basics ("In human races the woman is nearly always inferior to the man in height and weight"),[28] moving on to the senses and intelligence ("Woman . . . feels less, just as she thinks less"),[29] and ending with the moral sense ("Lying is habitual and almost physiological in woman").[30] By the end of this opening section on the normal woman, Lombroso has established two broad kinds of comparison—the first between types of women and the second between women and men. He has shown that two general categories of women exist, one bad, primitive, and masculine in nature, the other law-abiding, civilized, and feminine. He has also demonstrated repeatedly that both types are inferior to men. While the original purpose of the control group was to establish yardsticks against which the criminal woman could be measured, it ultimately served to undergird Lombroso's subsequent pronouncements on the nature of female crime and to suggest that all women are to some degree deviant.[31]

Atavisms and Prostitutes

Here we arrive at the heart of Lombroso's argument. Female born criminals, he readily admits, are rarer than male born criminals, but this relative scarcity, too, is a sign of their inferiority: "Atavism . . . helps explain the comparative rarity of the criminal type in women." Like all females, criminal women "are less subject to transformation and deformation by the factors that cause progressive and retrogressive variations in the male." In other words, the male's relative abundance of degenerative traits or stigmata betokens superiority. Then too, Lombroso reminds us, among savages the most abnormal women had the least chance of survival, another factor tending to erase evidence of stigmata: "Primitive man not only spurned the deformed woman; he also ate her, preferring to keep at hand those more pleasing to his sexual whims. (In those days he was stronger and had a choice.)" Thus women's lower crime rates actually provide additional proof of their backwardness. Finally, Lombroso urges us to keep in mind that even female born criminals need to be attractive if they want men to invite them to serve as accomplices or if they want to succeed at such typical crimes as adultery and slander; and this factor inhibits the evolution of a telltale "repugnant face."[32] With this tortured logic, Lombroso accounts for the smaller number of stigmata in female offenders and hence the lower number of female criminals in general and born criminals in particular.

The *prostitute*—a term that sometimes narrowly denotes sex workers but at others refers to all women who experience sex outside of marriage—turns up frequently in Lombroso's discussions of the female born criminal, just as she does in his more general remarks on the female criminal. Yet it is difficult to pinpoint the prostitute's precise role in his theory due to Lombroso's characteristically rapid and confusing shifts in comparison groups. Occasionally, he declares that among women, not criminals but prostitutes constitute the real degenerates. On such occasions, he treats prostitutes almost as a distinct species, compiling separate tallies of their anomalies. But at other times, instead of comparing female criminals and prostitutes with one another, he groups them together, comparing them collectively with normal women. (Lombroso may have been inspired to include prostitutes in the population of female criminals by Richard Dugdale's *"The Jukes"* (1877), an American work he admired and which equated prostitutes with male criminals. In any case, in Lombroso's book as in Dugdale's, prostitutes swell the population under discussion, making the group of female deviants more significant numerically than it would have been otherwise.)[33] At still other times, Lombroso compares prostitutes with male criminals, at least obliquely, as when he states that "women's natural form of retrogression" is "prostitution, not crime. Primitive woman was a prostitute rather than a criminal."[34] In *Criminal Woman* the imprecise term *prostitutes* becomes a rhetorical device, invoked and applied to confirm a point or to help Lombroso escape from a tight logical corner. A clearer term would have had less explanatory power.

Like many other nineteenth-century scientists, Lombroso had a passion for classifying the phenomena of the natural world. He devotes most of the final part of *Criminal Woman* to his classification of female offenders, whom he divides into two main groups, criminals and prostitutes, and several minor categories (suicides, insane criminals, epileptic and morally insane offenders, and hysterical offenders). As in his typology of male offenders, the major categories are then subdivided, yielding chapters on the born criminal, the occasional criminal, and the criminal by passion, and also on the born prostitute and the occasional prostitute. The classificatory scheme proves both descriptive and etiological, with Lombroso using the groupings to profile the types and simultaneously explain their involvement with crime.

Tone and Strategy in *Criminal Woman*

On the surface, the tone of *Criminal Woman* appears dispassionate, clinical, and "scientific," and indeed this is the only tone conveyed by *The Female Offender*, the partial translation of 1895. The full text, however, discloses undercurrents of frustration, self-apology, and even apprehension. Lombroso seems worried about the persuasiveness of born criminal theory, the validity of his research methods, and the book's reception by critics. While he tries to anticipate objections and paste over problems, at times he evidently senses that certain problems remain unsolvable. Moreover, *Criminal Woman* occasionally has an exasperated and beleaguered air, especially in passages dealing with normal women. This tone confirms what Lombroso states in his preface: that the writing of this book was at best a "bitter pleasure."[35]

Born criminal theory, introduced in the 1876 edition of *L'uomo delinquente*, had attracted immediate attention in Europe and the United States, but it had also encountered stiff resistance. Clergymen and others who associated crime with sin objected that Lombroso's science negated free will and excused criminals as irresponsible beings, driven by defective biology rather than by choice. Prison wardens and others with direct experience of offenders doubted Lombroso's claim that criminals differed physically from law-abiding people. And scientists were put off by Lombroso's uncritical approach to evidence.[36] Lombroso's positivist or criminal anthropological school came under heavy attack at the Second International Congress of Criminal Anthropology, held in Paris in 1889, where the French anthropologist Léonce Manouvrier derided Lombroso's statistical naïveté and his failure to use control groups of "honest men."[37] Harsher still was the witticism of Lombroso's former admirer Moritz Benedikt, who pointed out that an enlarged median occipital fossetta (the skull anomaly that originally inspired Lombroso's theory) might just as well be used to hypothesize a predisposition to hemorrhoids instead of criminality.[38] Lombroso reacted "scientifically" to such criticisms, modifying his procedures and his theory. Nowhere does his interest in polishing his performance emerge more clearly than in *Criminal Woman*, where he sets out to test his theory on a completely new population and introduces a control group.[39] The substance and very structure of *Criminal Woman*, with its long introductory section on normal women, reflect Lombroso's willingness to take criticism to heart.

But these risks and innovations also meant that Lombroso had a great deal at stake in *Criminal Woman*; he might well have been apprehensive about the results. Moreover, self-criticism did not come easily to him, as we discover in a passage of *Criminal Woman* that acknowledges earlier errors but does so with such caveats, contradictions, and contortions that the final impression is one of responsibility evaded. The passage starts as follows: "When I began studying criminals some thirty years ago, I professed a firm faith in anthropometry, especially cranial anthropometry, as an ark of salvation from the metaphysical, a priori systems dear to all those engaged on the study of Man. I regarded anthropometry as the backbone—indeed, the entire framework—of the new human statue I was attempting to create. But as so often happens in human affairs, use degenerated into abuse."[40] Here Lombroso admits that his earlier studies relied too heavily on anthropometry (the measurement of body parts) in general and on cranial anthropometry (the measurement of the skull) in particular. However, he remains ambiguous about the identity of those whose "excessive confidence" led to abuse of anthropometrical methods and in the next paragraph hints that the responsible parties may have been anthropology professors. At the same time, he claims to have himself recognized some time ago the inadequacy of anthropometry for identification of born criminals. In fact, Lombroso continues, he himself now uses the superior method of "anatomico-pathological investigation" (a term he has not used earlier and does not use again). Had others followed his lead instead of foolishly persisting with anthropometry, they undoubtedly would now be more receptive to his work.[41]

After these twists and turns, Lombroso suddenly and astonishingly reverses direction to endorse anthropometry, extolling physical measurements as "the symbol, the flag of a school [criminal anthropology] in whose armory numbers furnish the most effective weapon."[42] And then he turns immediately to specific anthropometric studies, reporting their results as solid and significant data. What began as self-criticism becomes self-congratulation, and the fundamental issue—the validity of anthropometrical research—is dismissed as though it made not the slightest bit of difference. Lombroso here seems torn, even paralyzed, by conflicting impulses—ambition, scientific integrity, exasperation with critics, inertia, a sense of superiority, and simple annoyance at the need to acknowledge past mistakes.

Irritation and frustration surface again in *Criminal Woman*'s passages on women's nature. Lombroso's beliefs about female inferiority were fairly typical among men of his social class and time.[43] (Guglielmo Ferrero, the assistant whom Lombroso credits with coauthorship of *Criminal Woman*, clung fiercely to disdain for women's abilities well into the twentieth century. Ferrero may well have been the extremist of the pair.[44]) However, as the "pivot" around which his wife and children revolved,[45] Lombroso may have felt apprehensive about the growing independence of his two daughters, Paola and Gina, who were both approaching the age of twenty at the time he embarked on *Criminal Woman*. Moreover, while he was working on the book, Anna Kuliscioff, a leading feminist, spent a great deal of time with Lombroso's family, dining with them almost nightly and slipping the girls a copy of J. S. Mill's *The Subjection of Women*.[46] (It was Kuliscioff who converted the family to socialism. She first interested the girls, and Lombroso followed in their wake.)[47] Lombroso's home life, together with the women's movement that Kuliscioff represented, may from time to time have led him to view women with annoyance and even trepidation. Criminal anthropology's biological "proofs" of female inferiority formed part of a reaction against transformations in women's status. "With the arrival of industrial society," writes Delfina Dolza, "the door opened for some women to the possibility of entering the education and professional system, and some [scientists] found it necessary to delimit, with universal norms, the boundaries that could not be trespassed."[48]

Arguments at the family dinner table over women's status and roles may also help explain why, from time to time in *Criminal Woman*, Lombroso apologizes for his harsh words about women. At the end of the chapter on female intelligence, for example—immediately after remarking that "it is amazing, then, that woman is not even less intelligent than she is"—Lombroso adds a line suggesting that prejudice may contribute to women's lowly condition: "Certainly greater participation in the collective life of society would raise women's intelligence."[49] Another apology appears in his preface, where Lombroso claims that his emphasis on woman's relatively low crime rates and pathetic qualities should offset "a thousandfold" his conclusions about her inferior intelligence: "If I must show that in mind and body woman is a male of arrested development, the fact that she is somewhat less criminal than he, and a little more pitiful, can compensate a thousandfold for her deficiency in the realm of intellect." Most fulsomely of all, Lombroso later in the preface declares: "Not one line of this work justifies the great tyranny that continues to victimize women, from the taboo which forbids them to eat meat or touch a coconut, to that which impedes them from studying, and worse, from practicing a profession once they are educated. These ridiculous and cruel constraints, still widely accepted, are used to maintain or (sadder still) increase women's inferiority, exploiting them to our advantage."[50] But these nods to injustices against women clash with the misogynist tone of the book as a whole.

Lombroso's anxieties about *Criminal Woman*, his research methods, and the ultimate fate of criminal anthropology emerge most fully in the book's preface. Even before publication, he informs readers, *Criminal Woman* has elicited hostile attention. Some critics have objected to the apparent illogic of his central thesis, according to which women are less criminal than men because they are too weak and stupid to be bad. Others charge that he has been "insufficiently chivalrous" toward women, and still others think it foolish to equate prostitutes with male born criminals. Lombroso uses the preface to reply to these critics, but his tangled defenses sometimes make matters worse.

Criminal Woman in Context

English-language readers have lacked not only good translations of Lombroso's works but also an understanding of their historical context. While major criminological textbooks routinely cite Lombroso as the "father of criminology," they rarely mention the major currents of social, political, and intellectual change in nineteenth-century Europe which helped to shape his theories. Even the life of Lombroso himself is little known because all of his full-length biographies are available only in Italian.[51] Both Lombroso's personal story and his place in Italian history help to explain the passion of his quest to turn the study of crime into a scientific endeavor. We will therefore turn to a series of nineteenth-century contexts within which Lombroso lived and worked: the unification of Italy; the growing prestige of science, specifically Darwinism; the revolt against Enlightenment legal theories; and the birth of sexology.

The Unification of Italy

Lombroso grew up in the ferment of the *risorgimento*, the movement to expel foreign and absolutist powers and unify the Italian peninsula under a parliamentary government. Born in 1835, Lombroso spent his youth in the northern Italian provinces of Lombardy and the Veneto. These constituted the culturally richest and most socially progressive states of the Italian peninsula, in contrast to the more rural and often impoverished areas to the south. The Austrian Empire ruled both Lombardy and the Veneto, however, a fact that inspired Lombroso, like many others of his generation, to support the risorgimento. Lombroso's Jewish background also explains his youthful liberalism. Although never religious, he trusted that the leaders of the risorgimento, with their belief in individual rights and a secular state, would remove the discriminatory restrictions on Jews that still characterized parts of the peninsula.

After studying at the universities of Padua, Vienna, and Pavia, Lombroso completed a medical degree in 1858, with an emphasis on psychiatry.[52] When the long-anticipated war of unification broke out the following year, he volunteered as a doctor in the revolutionary forces.[53] Sent to the southern province of Calabria in 1862 as part of the new state's campaign to suppress brigandage, he was shocked by the population's poverty, illiteracy, and malnutrition. Most people were landless peasants, tending the large estates of noble landlords in a system that reminded him of medieval feudalism. While in Calabria, Lombroso developed a sense of mission to improve the physical and psychological health of the lower classes. He also had the opportunity to examine the soldiers in his unit, thus establishing his lifelong technique of classifying individuals based on physical measurements and interviews. He would later transfer this clinical approach to mental patients and criminals.

After completing his military service, Lombroso spent the rest of his life in northern Italy, working as a university professor and medical officer in insane asylums and prisons. As a patriot, he continued to be preoccupied with the problems of the new state. In his view, these included the threat to unity and stability posed by people who did not or could not conform to the role of respectable citizen. Rapid population growth was causing mass migration to both northern and southern cities, swelling the ranks of the so-called dangerous classes. The prostitute, a woman seemingly no longer bound by family or morality, emerged as a central figure in the iconography of the dangerous classes. To middle-class observers, the increasing numbers of homeless and unemployed women on urban streets seemed all to be prostitutes. Blamed for the spread of venereal disease, actual prostitutes were placed under police supervision immediately after unification, and they were required to live in state-regulated brothels, so-called closed houses. It thus comes as little surprise that Lombroso found the prostitute more threatening and atavistic than even the criminal woman.

Lombroso's preoccupation with female crime also reflected his anxieties about the growth of the women's movement in Italy during the decades after unification. Although individual female emancipationists had struggled since unification to win equal rights for women, they did not establish formal organizations until the 1880s and 1890s. It is not coincidental that *Criminal Woman* was published during a period when members of the women's movement were vociferously demanding access to education, entrance to the professions, equality within the family, and the right to vote. Politically liberal and a friend of feminists like Kuliscioff, Lombroso did not inexorably oppose all changes in women's legal status and even took a position, radical for his day, in favor of divorce. But the prospect of a fundamental restructuring of gender roles deeply, and perhaps unconsciously, troubled him, as his allocation of the first major section of *Criminal Woman* to proofs of the inferiority of normal women shows. His ridicule of intellectual women and his insistence on maternity as the proper aspiration for all women scientifically affirmed traditional stereotypes and directly challenged the vision of female emancipationists.

The Growing Prestige of Science

A second context for Lombroso's theories was the growing prestige of science, and specifically Darwinism, in the second half of the nineteenth century. In Italy, science became especially important as a weapon against the traditional hegemony of Catholic thought. The wars of unification directly challenged the church when revolutionary armies conquered the lands ruled by the pope in central Italy and finally Rome in 1871. Withdrawing into the Vatican, Pope Pius IX condemned the new Italian state and forbade Catholics to participate in its political institutions. Supporters of unification, mostly members of the middle classes, therefore had to find a new philosophical basis for national identity. Science offered the fledgling state a discourse compatible with its aspirations to liberalism and secularism and signaled its transition from feudalism to modernity. Lombroso, with his year of medical school in Vienna, readily conceptualized his own research as part of a wider European endeavor to spread the methods of science to new fields.

To emphasize the importance of applying science to the study of crime, Lombroso and his followers labeled themselves the positivist school. As a general term originally coined by Auguste Comte, *positivism* held that inductive reasoning based on empirical evidence was superior to the deductive method of philosophers. Enthusiasm for positivism swept Italy in the last half of the nineteenth century, spreading from the sciences to social theory and even to humanistic research in history and literature. As the "lay faith" of academia,[54] positivism promised to apply a modern empirical approach to solving Italy's social problems. It proved, moreover, compatible with socialism, a political movement that sought to analyze economic inequality based on material facts. Lombroso, like many of his followers, joined the Italian Socialist Party after its establishment in 1892 because the liberal government's inability to improve the lot of the poor left him disillusioned. Thus he never lost the humanitarian impulse that had inspired his work during his military service in Calabria.

Lombroso had already read *The Origin of Species* before its translation into Italian in 1864.[55] He became an immediate proponent of Darwin's theory of evolution in opposition not only to the spiritualism of the Catholic Church but also to the rival evolutionary theory of polygenism, which held that the white, yellow, and black "races" constituted different species.[56] Noting the similarities between the brains of monkeys and humans, Lombroso instead endorsed the Darwinian mechanisms of the struggle for existence and natural selection as responsible for the emergence of the black race and, from it, the yellow, and finally the white.[57] His conviction of the nonhuman animal origins of human life helps to explain why Lombroso included patently ridiculous chapters in *Criminal Woman* on theft, infanticide, and sexual licentiousness among mammals, birds, and even insects.

Despite Lombroso's defense of monogenism, or the common ancestry of all human beings, he nevertheless posited a racial hierarchy stretching from African blacks at the bottom of the evolutionary ladder to European whites at the top. He believed the superiority of whites to be legible from their bodies, which exhibited "the most perfect symmetry."[58] Black Africans, on the other hand, seemed clearly to bear the imprint of their animal origins in what he characterized as misshapen bodies and inferior intellect. In his appropriation of Darwin to delineate and rank racial groups, Lombroso typified late-nineteenth-century thinkers.[59] His "scientific" racism was innovative, however, in its equation of criminals with what he referred to as savages, members of nonwhite races. Throwbacks on the evolutionary scale, European criminals exhibited physical and psychological features that he believed were anomalies for the white race but normal for lower, less civilized races. This constitutes the fundamental message of Lombroso's first criminological book, *Criminal Man*.

In *Criminal Woman*, Lombroso again uses Darwinist terms, this time to naturalize gender differences. Among lower races, he writes, women resemble men in their strength, intelligence, and sexual promiscuity. Through sexual selection, however, males—whether animal or human—choose mates for feminine qualities like beauty, modesty, passivity, and domesticity. Evolution, therefore, increasingly differentiates the sexes, with men dominating the public sphere of politics and work and women relegated to motherhood in the home. Again, Lombroso was not unusual for his time in turning traditional gender stereotypes into supposedly scientific categories. But his work presented an enormous problem for the nascent Italian women's movement, which saw science as a potential ally in the struggle against the restrictive gender roles endorsed by religious and conservative thinkers. With the publication of *La donna delinquente*, however, supporters of women's rights were instead faced with a book purporting to present modern empirical proof of women's inferiority. Written by a well-respected intellectual of the left, *Criminal Woman* weakened the Italian women's movement in its quest for expanded legal and political rights for women.

Revolt against Enlightenment Legal Theories

The development of legal thought in Europe since the Enlightenment offers a third context for understanding Lombroso's intellectual efforts. By labeling his work *criminal anthropology*, or the study of criminal man, Lombroso consciously demarcated his approach from that of the eighteenth-century classical school, which dominated Italian legal thinking into the late nineteenth century. The principles of the classical school, originally laid out in the famous treatise by Cesare Beccaria entitled *Of Crimes and Punishments* (Dei delitti e delle pene), included equality before the law, presumption of innocence, and proportionality between crime and punishment.[60] Such principles would apply to all citizens because all were presumed born with the same inalienable rights and to exercise free will when committing crimes. As European nations reformed their criminal laws in the late eighteenth and nineteenth centuries, they adopted the classical approach of calculating punishment on the basis of the severity of the crime, with violent crimes considered more serious than those against property.

Criminal anthropology directly challenged classical thinking, arguing that individuals committed crime not out of free will but from biological or social determinism. Those who seemed to pose the greatest danger were the atavistic born criminals, who required removal from society no matter how small their crime. On the other hand, so-called occasional criminals, even if their crimes were serious, deserved alternatives to incarceration because outside environmental forces, rather than innate perversity, had tempted them to break the law. Lombroso thus shifted the focus of legal thinking from the crime to the criminal, a physical entity whose atavisms could be measured and counted. He sought to replace the old-fashioned philosophical approach of the classical school with a more fashionable positivist method based on scientific methods. And he sought to redefine dangerousness by stressing not the seriousness of the offense but the degree of criminality in the offender.

Although generally seen as the progenitor of positivist criminology, Lombroso was not the first to apply a biological approach to the problem of crime, and he generously acknowledged his debts. His precursors included phrenologists like Franz Joseph Gall and Gaspar Spurzheim, who in the early nineteenth century correlated sections of the skull with propensities for both good and evil. According to phrenology, which endured in popular culture even after its scientific decline, criminals could be identified by bumps or enlargements of areas associated with negative traits. Criminal anthropologists rejected the phrenological maps of the head and extended physical measurement to the criminal's entire body. But their emphasis on the shape of the skull and their assumption that external physical features reflected internal moral states can be traced back to the earlier movement.

The school of moral statistics also prefigured Lombroso, in this case his use of quantitative data to distinguish normality from deviancy.[61] Benefiting from the national crime statistics published by the French government beginning in 1825, Adolphe Quetelet and André-Michel Guerry began to study crime as an aggregate phenomenon with certain regular characteristics. Quetelet is best known for his statistical portrait of the "average man," from which he derived the demographic traits of the typical criminal: young, male, poor, and with little education. Showing that rates of crime varied little in France from year to year, he argued that only general social forces, rather than free will, could explain such statistical regularity. Guerry broke these regularities down by region, developing the technique of crime mapping later used by Italian criminal anthropologists. Both Quetelet and Guerry tentatively proposed that biological factors, whether phrenological or racial, complemented social forces in causing crime, again foreshadowing positivist theory.

Lombroso's initial explanatory concept of atavism drew on phrenology and moral statistics, but he later drew on two other theories as well to account for the born criminal. The first, moral insanity, appears only in the third edition of *Criminal Man* (1884), but early enough to show up in *Criminal Woman*. In response to criticisms of his concept of atavism, Lombroso expanded his list of physical and psychological conditions predisposing certain individuals to commit crimes. Moral insanity, a concept that extended back to the early nineteenth-century writings of the French psychiatrist Philippe Pinel, was the diagnosis applied to mental patients who retained their intellectual powers but could not restrain their emotional impulses. To his catalogue of hereditary conditions leading to born criminality, Lombroso also added degeneration, a concept adopted from the French physician Benedict Augustin Morel.[62] Unlike atavism (an inborn tendency to revert to a primitive state), degeneration was thought to result from outside influences such as tuberculosis, syphilis, and alcoholism. Social in origin, degeneration nevertheless caused a gradual and hereditary weakening of individuals and their offspring. In *Criminal Woman*, Lombroso does not carefully distinguish atavism from degeneration, often using the terms interchangeably to explain anomalies or criminal behavior.

Building on these earlier theories, Lombroso and his positivist colleagues constructed the first coherent criminological theory based on empirical data. Renouncing free will as an old-fashioned concept, they redefined crime as a disease for which its perpetrators held no moral responsibility. Society, however, had the right to defend itself against crime, either by incarcerating the incurable born criminal or reforming the occasional offender. Lombroso spent the last decades of his life campaigning to bring Italian law and institutions into line with positivist criminological theory. He sought to reform the Italian criminal code so that criminal anthropologists, rather than judges, would examine criminals and recommend sentences. Although punishment for born criminals would be harsh, he proposed alternatives to prison for most women, including those guilty of infanticide and abortion, on the theory that social pressures pushed them into crime. Few of his specific recommendations were adopted before his death in 1909, but Lombroso's theory of female crime had gained wide acceptance at both the academic and popular levels.

The Birth of Sexology

The final context providing an intellectual background for *Criminal Woman* is the birth of sexology. In contrast to his acknowledged role as a founder of criminology, Lombroso has never been listed as a pioneer in the study of human sexuality. The truncated nature of the translated *The Female Offender*, which excises most of *La donna delinquente*'s passages on sexuality, partially explains this omission for English-language readers. Yet Lombroso should be recognized as a transitional figure between Victorian prudery and the celebrations of sexual freedom characterizing sexology from its foundation in the early twentieth century on.

As a transitional figure, Lombroso shared many views with earlier nineteenth-century moralists. His contribution consisted of furnishing modern scientific underpinnings for traditional condemnations of nonmarital sexuality. Consistent with the bourgeois ideology of separate spheres for men and women, he points to the movement of sperm and the immobility of the egg to justify male public activity and female domestic passivity. Claiming that an unbridled and masculine sex drive characterizes "primitive" women, he champions monogamy as one of the treasures of civilization produced by evolution. And he concludes that white European women no longer desire sexual intercourse except for procreation, the defining act of womanhood.

Yet Lombroso resembled modern sexologists in his curiosity about a variety of sexual practices and his interest in cataloguing them. The original Italian version of *Criminal Woman*, unlike the English abridgment, devotes sections to adultery, frigidity, lesbianism, masturbation, and premarital sex. In a long section on the history of prostitution, Lombroso enumerates its many purposes in the past: to celebrate the gods, to entertain guests, and, in the case of Greek and Renaissance courtesans, to unite beauty and learning. Two chapters, cut by *The Female Offender*, offer an exhaustive analysis of the causes and characteristics of contemporary prostitution, both "born" and "occasional." Although Lombroso condemns sex outside marriage as a sign of arrested evolution for women, he draws his conclusions from a wealth of empirical data. This approach, while sometimes prurient, contrasts with many earlier writers' silence about sexuality.

Lombroso's approach to sexuality resembles that of another transitional thinker, the German psychiatrist Richard von Krafft-Ebing. Both men collected and catalogued information about "deviant" sexual practices, although Krafft-Ebing was more systematic in his famous work *Psychopathia sexualis*, first published in 1886. Both men championed an objective, positivist approach to sexuality while moralistically proclaiming monogamy as the norm. Both attributed deviations from this norm to degeneration and considered them dangerous to the future of the European race. Krafft-Ebing also shared Lombroso's interest in the legal implications of sexual "perversions," which he thought deserving of medical treatment rather than prosecution by the courts. Neither psychiatrist held individuals responsible for their deviant sexuality on the grounds that heredity had overridden free will.

Hobbled by contradictions and moralistic in tone, the writings of Lombroso and Krafft-Ebing merely constituted precursors to the work of Havelock Ellis, generally considered the founder of modern sexology. With the publication of *Sexual Inversion* in 1897, Ellis set the tone for later scientific studies that celebrated alternative sexual practices to monogamy and counseled toleration. For Ellis, homosexuality was neither a disease nor a sign of degeneration. Although congenital, it represented a healthy sexual variation consistent with a normal intellectual and emotional life. In later works, he demolished other Victorian taboos against, for example, masturbation, which had been thought to cause illness and even insanity. As Paul Robinson has written, Ellis "assumed the role of sexual enthusiast," emphasizing the normality rather than the deviancy of a wide array of sexual practices.[63]

Yet Ellis's analysis of female sexuality itself remains in many ways traditional and echoes the teachings of positivist criminology. Resemblances between the ideas of Ellis and Lombroso are not coincidental. Ellis admired Italian criminal anthropology and wrote a book, *The Criminal* (1890), to introduce Lombroso's theory to English-language readers. In the spirit of *Criminal Woman*, Ellis characterizes women as passive and modest and thus appropriate objects of aggressive male courtship. Evolution, with its goal of reproduction, requires such differentiated gender roles. Unlike Lombroso, Ellis recognizes that women have normal sexual needs possibly not satisfied by monogamy. But in his eyes, too, marriage is appropriate for most women because it encourages reproduction and protects children.

In sum, Lombroso's criminal anthropology, parts of which today seem odd and sometimes even comic, spoke to the anxieties of late-nineteenth-century Europe and was consistent with more general intellectual trends. A man of the risorgimento, Lombroso sought to help his nation solve major problems like disunity among geographical areas and social classes, disorder accompanying urbanization and industrialization, and violations of law by brigands, mafiosi, and common criminals. Like most men of his class, he was particularly troubled by the new mobility of prostitutes and other poor women, and by the new demands of bourgeois women for legal parity with men. To address these issues, he developed a new academic field within the wider European movement of positivism.

As a man of cosmopolitan learning and reputation, Lombroso proved instrumental in establishing a series of international congresses of criminal anthropology, which the Italian positivists initially dominated.[64] His theory of the born criminal did not, however, remain unchallenged, especially by French criminologists like Alessandre Lacassagne and Léonce Manouvrier, who considered social milieu more important than biology in determining criminal behavior.[65] Nevertheless, they continued to accept Lombroso's general framework, which defined the criminal rather than the crime as the appropriate object of research. They also left his theory of female crime untouched. The centrality of biology, and especially sexuality, to female behavior remained dogma among criminologists and even among progressive sexologists like Ellis. In the next section, we turn to the long life of *Criminal Woman*, prolonged through the repetition of its central tenets in major criminological texts until the birth of feminist criminology in the 1970s.

Criminal Woman's Influence

In what follows, we assess *Criminal Woman*'s impact by looking first at its influence on subsequent English-language work on women and crime and then at its more general influence on criminological thought. We make no attempt whatsoever to estimate the book's influence in such areas as scientific applications of photography; the evolution of the fields of anthropology, psychology, and sociology; the development of female stereotypes in European and American literature; jurisprudence, social control and sexuality; or gender, race, and social class relationships. Even the following comments on criminology are meant as suggestive, not comprehensive or definitive ones. The purpose of this new edition is not to answer questions, but to provide materials for others to use in answering standing questions and formulating new ones.

Influence on Subsequent Work on Women and Crime

No other study can rival *La donna delinquente* in its influence on subsequent thinking about women and crime. Yet the nature of that influence on American and English criminology has seesawed dramatically over time. In very early twentieth-century writings on women and crime, authors typically open by shooting furiously at Lombroso, ridiculing his work and disclaiming his influence, but going straight on to repeat his findings about women offenders as incontestable truths. This pattern appears, for example, in *Woman and Crime* (1912) by Hargrave L. Adam, a British writer on crime for popular audiences. Adam begins by rejecting criminal anthropology out of hand, speaking contemptuously of *The Female Offender* ("rubbish")[66] and of "the late Professor Lombroso and other so-called crime 'scientists.'"[67] But he goes on to parrot Lombroso, stating that there is a great deal of hidden female crime; that the female offender "far outstrips the worst male criminal known to the records"; and that "women of that kind are altogether abnormal and . . . not, in fact, women in the ordinary acceptation of the word."[68] Thus despite his mockery, Adam produces a book substantively close to *The Female Offender*.

This inability to escape Lombroso's influence resurfaces in a very different type of early-twentieth-century study, Hans Gross's *Criminal Psychology* (1911). One of the first titles in a prestigious American criminal justice series,[69] *Criminal Psychology* is designed to guide judges and investigators in the scientific study of crime and criminals. Its author, an eminent Austrian professor of criminal law, includes a long subsection entitled "Woman" in a more general section on ways in which the testimony of women and children differs from that of adult men. Dissociating himself from the most notorious aspect of Lombroso's work, Gross refers to "the scientific interpretation of [physical] phenomena which . . . went shipwreck in the form of Lombroso's 'criminal stigmata,' inasmuch as an overhasty theory has been built on barren, inexperienced, and unstudied material."[70] He also rejects the "unfounded, adventurous, and arbitrary assertions of the Lombrosists" on "the question of heredity."[71] However, much of Gross's specific advice takes its justification from references to *La donna delinquente*. Thus we learn that one cannot expect too much in the way of truth from women in a courtroom: "According to Lombroso, women lie because of their weakness, and because of menstruation and pregnancy. . . . Indeed, they are themselves no more than children, Lombroso concludes."[72] Here Gross parts company only with Lombroso's belief that deception has become a physiological characteristic in women. Later, explaining the nature of female crime, Gross reports that "nobody finds greater joy in revenge than a woman. Indeed I might say that revenge and the pursuit of revenge are specifically feminine. . . . Lombroso has done most to show this." In addition, "Lombroso has already indicated how fundamental women's inclination to cruelty is."[73] Throughout, Gross cites Lombroso as an authority on the nature of women in general and female offenders in particular.

After several decades, Lombroso's influence on the study of female crime waned, briefly. The 1916 English-language edition of Willem Bonger's *Criminality and Economic Conditions* ignores Lombroso, even in its section entitled "The

Criminality of Women." It strongly rejects biological explanations, holding that "the smaller criminality of woman is not to be sought in innate qualities, but rather in social environments."[74] *A Study of Women Delinquents in New York State* (1920) by Mabel Ruth Fernald and colleagues explicitly rejects Lombroso's methods ("puerile" and "worse than futile")[75] and arrives at opposite conclusions: "Any search for a well-defined type of individual, appearing as *the delinquent woman*, will probably be fruitless. Apparently the concept of such a type can not be saved even by expanding it beyond Lombroso's anthropological criminal type and pruning off certain of the absurdities incorporated in his idea."[76] Even more significantly, William Healy's *The Individual Delinquent* (1915), one of the most respected American criminological studies of the early twentieth century, rejects biological determinism in favor of a multifactor, psychological approach which Healy applies to female and male offenders alike. Although Healy occasionally evaluates girls in terms of their sexual attractiveness, he uses what he calls mental traits to account for law-breaking in both sexes.

Bonger, Fernald, and Healy channeled criminology away from criminal anthropology, and studies of male criminality thereafter pursued psychological and sociological explanations. Why studies of female criminality instead reversed direction, returning to biological causation, remains an unsettled issue in criminological history. But regress they did, yielding, in 1934, Sheldon and Eleanor Glueck's *Five Hundred Delinquent Women*. This study of prisoners at the Massachusetts Reformatory for Women returned to Lombroso's practice of judging female deviance more stringently than male deviance and according to primarily sexual criteria. The authors conclude that in women, extramarital sexuality is often a sign of biological inferiority and bad heredity, part of a syndrome that includes feeblemindedness or weak intelligence. For such "defective delinquents," even though the majority was convicted of nothing worse than prostitution, the Gluecks recommend up-to-life sentences. In their view, this is the best way to prevent biologically inferior women from reproducing their bad heredity.[77]

The Gluecks, while barely mentioning Lombroso, reiterate nearly all of his major ideas and carry his hereditarian implications to a eugenical conclusion. *Five Hundred Delinquent Women*—published by Knopf under the auspices of Harvard Law School, introduced by Roscoe Pound, one of the country's leading legal theorists, and written by two highly regarded criminologists—strongly reinforced Lombrosian explanations of female offending. Moreover, it did so at a time when nearly all investigators of male criminality (including the Gluecks themselves) downplayed biological factors in favor of sociological explanations.[78]

Otto Pollak's *The Criminality of Women* (1950) perpetuated this gender division in explanations of criminal behavior. The only significant mid-twentieth-century study of female crime in English, *The Criminality of Women* was nonetheless to a large extent *The Female Offender* warmed over. To be sure, Pollak places more emphasis on the masked quality of female crime, arguing that women commit much more crime than they receive statistical credit for; he pays more attention to social factors than Lombroso does in *The Female Offender*; and he does not try to show that all women are inferior to all men in nearly every respect. Nonetheless, Pollak lifts many of his key ideas right out of *The Female Offender*, including the view that much more female crime exists than statistics indicate. Pollak turns repeatedly to Lombroso for evidence (including evidence that "women are particularly addicted" to crimes "which are most easily concealed" and that "deceitfulness [is] the outstanding characteristic of female offenders").[79] He adopts Lombroso's analytic approach ("In the investigation of the causational aspects the purely statistic method will be abandoned and reliance will be largely placed on nonstatistical analysis").[80] And he uncritically recites findings that Lombroso had reported fifty years earlier ("Lombroso found that among eighty women who were arrested for resistance against public officials, 71 were menstruating at the time of the offense").[81] Pollak was a sociologist, but as British criminologist Frances Heidensohn points out, he "used none of the existing repertoire of sociological explanations of crime. There are no references at all to Chicago school authors, to Tannenbaum or to Merton. . . . Instead Pollak put forward a view of women as inherently deceitful and vengeful. . . . Although Pollak stressed cultural variables his explanations are rooted in biological 'facts' and are profoundly ahistorical and unsociological."[82] Had a study attempted to take male criminality down this explanatory path in the 1950s, it would have been dismissed out of hand; yet Pollak's *Criminality of Women* was reprinted and cited uncritically for the next two decades.

Lombrosian ideas reverberate in the women-and-crime literature through the 1960s. Gisela Konopka's *The Adolescent Girl in Conflict* (1966), for instance, while it does not draw directly on Lombroso and actually takes protofeminist stands, echoes *The Female Offender* by presenting ahistorical generalizations about gender roles as social-scientific truths; by reducing girls' delinquent behavior to psychological deviance; and by treating prostitution as "a personal problem [that] lies in the area of emotional disturbance."[83]

Lombrosian views on female crime remained plausible partly because few social scientists paid attention to women's criminal behavior. At best, each decade produced but one new volume on the topic, which meant that those who did do research in this area lacked social and intellectual support to break with the Lombrosian tradition. Moreover, the few researchers who did contradict Lombroso's pronouncements on women and crime were routinely dismissed by mainstream criminologists, who in this period tended to glorify male offenders as oppressed rebels and scorn female offenders as insipid and irrelevant. In addition, as sociologist Carol Smart notes, the teachings of Lombroso and his followers were compatible with the "ideological stance . . . of professional pathologists and agents of social control"; as a result, "female criminality . . . remained predominantly within the sphere . . . of medical and psychological professions,"[84] where most social scientists were content to leave it. Lombroso's ideas about female crime remained influential through the 1960s, far outliving their scientific credibility, because so few people were willing to challenge them.

But the fundamental reason behind the continuing influence of Lombroso's work lay with the way it built on age-old myths about women's nature. The equation of woman with nature, man with society; the tendency to dismiss the "natural" as unproblematic and beyond the reach of social analysis; and the ancient conflation of female deviance and sexuality—these deeply ingrained ideas were not born with Lombroso, nor did they die with him. The myths were so ubiquitous and their truths so seemingly obvious that criminologists, while questioning many other aspects of Lombroso's work, left them intact. They did not undergo serious questioning until the renaissance of the women's movement in the 1970s. With the arrival of the first generation of feminist criminologists, *The Female Offender* returned to center stage, becoming the symbol of everything that feminists objected to in criminology. These critics, like Lombroso himself, had an agenda, but it emphatically did not include advancing a theory of male superiority. The new scholars wanted to study women's crime in its own right and to free it from the fetters of biological myth which had constrained it for so long.

The new agenda was set first and with particular clarity by Frances Heidensohn in a 1968 article in the *British Journal of Sociology*. Pointing out that the "deviance of women is one of the areas of human behaviour most notably ignored in sociological literature," Heidensohn called for a two-pronged strategy, "a crash programme of research" on female crime and a sociological analysis of the factors that had led sociology to neglect it.[85] This second recommendation led Heidensohn directly back to Lombroso and *The Female Offender*, the basic arguments of which she laid embarrassingly bare.

Working independently in the United States and without knowledge of Heidensohn's article, Dorie Klein, a graduate student at the University of Berkeley, reached very similar conclusions. In her now-famous 1973 article, Klein, too, began with the observation that "female criminality has often ended up as a footnote to works on men that purport to be works on criminality in general,"[86] and she too called for analysis of not only female crime but also of sociologists' and criminologists' neglect of women lawbreakers. Like Heidensohn, Klein cogently critiqued Lombroso's work. Together, they laid a foundation for the new feminist criminology.[87]

The next step was the creation of courses on women and crime, an enterprise for which textbooks proved crucial. Carol Smart's *Women, Crime, and Criminology*, which appeared in 1976 and included a half-dozen closely reasoned pages on *The Female Offender*, provided material for graduate programs in both Great Britain and North America. Clarice Feinman's frequently reissued *Women in the Criminal Justice System* (1980), with a shorter but again incisive analysis of Lombroso's book, became the key text for undergraduate classes.

Lombrosianism resurfaced in the 1960s and 1970s in Katharina Dalton's efforts to correlate premenstrual tension with women's criminal behavior.[88] Dalton's criminological work sank under the weight of its own methodological problems, however, and exercised much less influence than it would have in earlier decades because it could now be put in perspective as part of a biological tradition. The rich outpouring of feminist criticism ushered in a new period of women-and-crime research, this one unencumbered by the Lombrosian tradition and dedicated to empirical, sociological investigation. Most researchers of the 1980s and 1990s included both sexes in their offender samples and began with the assumption that crime has similar causes for males and females. It remains to be seen, however, whether criminology will continue on this new trajectory or will instead, as part of the broader return to biogenic explanations, again adopt Lombrosian assumptions.

Lombroso bequeathed four interrelated but in some respects contradictory concepts to subsequent understandings of female criminality. The first concerned the nature of female crime, which according to Lombroso is fundamentally biological in origin. Lombroso was not original in equating female deviance with sexuality, but he powerfully reinforced the association by confirming it "scientifically." The effects reverberated through the criminal justice system: female crime such as shoplifting was explained in terms of sublimated sexuality, and in many jurisdictions girls arrested for delinquency were automatically given vaginal exams to determine their virginity. Related to Lombroso's emphasis on the biological nature of female criminality is the notion that female criminals are less evolved than both male criminals and law-abiding women, an idea that throughout the twentieth century reinforced infantilizing disciplinary modalities for women offenders, treating them as errant children.

The idea that criminal women are more masculine than law-abiding women constitutes a second major part of Lombroso's legacy. This concept reemerged with considerable fanfare in the 1970s when Freda Adler published *Sisters in Crime* (1975), a work arguing that women's crime rates are on the rise because women (especially women of color) are becoming more like men. Closely related to the masculinity thesis is the criminological tendency to conceptualize female criminality as what Heidensohn calls "a beauty contest,"[89] with the prize of greatest "reformability" awarded to the most feminine offender. This practice, which extends from Lombroso's photographs into the present day, reached an apogee in the Gluecks' recommendation that "defective" women be imprisoned until they can no longer reproduce.

A third influential facet of Lombroso's legacy is the idea that normal women, as well as criminal women, are inherently deviant, walking bundles of pathology, which can at any moment unravel into criminality. This pathologization of ordinary womanhood authorized physicians and other "normalizers" to intervene more frequently and deeply into women's lives than into those of men. Additionally, it made female sexuality automatically suspect.

Fourth and finally, Lombroso's work on the female offender helped establish "normality" itself as a standard for conceptualizing law-abiding behavior.[90] This standard was applied to male behavior as well, but there remained alternative ways of thinking about male deviance (heroic rebellion, for example, or the sowing of wild oats). Female deviance, on the other hand, almost always ran the risk of being labeled abnormal and hence pathological. This also put law-abiding women in peril, for any woman who challenged the status quo could be deemed abnormal.

A Guide to This Translation

No translation can fully communicate its source's meanings. All communications suffer from some degree of "noise" or distortion brought on by differences in the situations of the writer and the reader, a noise that naturally increases with translation. The act of translation involves figuring out how to communicate the original meaning while minimizing the chances for distortion and misunderstanding. Our key translation decisions followed from an assessment of differences between Lombroso's goals and ours. In writing *La donna delinquente*, Lombroso wished to advance his theory of criminal anthropology by applying it to an entirely new group, criminal women. In translating *La donna delinquente*, we wanted to give English-speaking scholars and students access to the book's text—not just to the bits and pieces translated by *The Female Offender* but to all four of its parts. While we were interested in Lombroso's methods of proof and types of evidence, we did not consider it crucial to present every one of his hundreds of examples. Moreover, our emphases on students and accessibility meant that our translation had to be a good deal shorter than the 640-page original, and affordable to boot. It followed that we had to boil down the original while preserving its meanings, procedures, and key examples.

Fidelity to the Original Text

Boiling *La donna delinquente* down to manageable size while including all four of its parts involved cutting sections, pages, paragraphs, and—within single sentences—words that seemed unnecessary. Our cuts involved nothing substantive, however. Indeed, we have restored a great deal of material excised, without notice, from the 1895 English edition, and we have made the full (albeit abbreviated) text available to English-speaking readers for the first time. However, we did eliminate two sorts of material—repetitions and examples. Repetitions appear to have left Lombroso untroubled, and indeed, he often presents material over and over again, approaching it from new angles or combining it in new ways with other topics. We eliminated major overlaps.

We also eliminated many of the examples Lombroso presents in support of his positions. To Lombroso as a scientist, a wealth of examples was important because it signified a wealth of scientific evidence. The sheer quantity of evidence mattered less to us, however. From today's point of view, moreover, the "science" of Lombroso's examples often proves dubious or even ludicrous. (Some of his contemporaries shared this opinion.) Our policy for each of Lombroso's new points was to translate one or two of the more vivid or clarifying examples but to omit the rest.

Our cuts created two translation effects. First, they minimize Lombroso's long-windedness. In this respect, our translation somewhat distorts the original. Second, by cutting some of the book's outlandish examples, our translation may, ironically, make the text seem more rational and scientifically sound than it in fact was. In this respect, too, our cuts may slightly skew Lombroso's original. However, without them, the book would have remained inaccessible to most contemporary readers.

Lombroso wrote in formal, scholarly Italian, using medical and scientific terms that are today obsolete. To twenty-first-century Italians, Lombroso's language seems old-fashioned, difficult, and at times even incomprehensible. However, its datedness in part results from the passage of time. To educated contemporaries, Lombroso's language would have seemed appropriately learned, and among nonscientists, his obscure terminology might have increased his credibility. Because one of our goals was to make Lombroso's work accessible, we translated obscure words into more familiar terms. We also tried to relax his prose style a bit, making it slightly more colloquial. Our rule of thumb was to write for our audience, not his. On the other hand, we did not aim at fully colloquial English. We attempted to make his prose comprehensible to modern readers while preserving some of its formality.

The Embarrassment Factor

In working on this translation, we occasionally flinched at reproducing Lombroso's gaffs and missteps—his sloppy use of numbers, uncritical examples, unsophisticated generalizations, internal contractions in the text, and overall incoherence. Our temptation here was akin to what translation theorists call ennoblement—the temptation, confronted most often by poetry translators, to make translated material more flowery or elevated than the original. But if our temptation was similar to that of ennoblers, it was certainly not the same; few translators can have had to cope as we did with outright foolishness on the part of the source author.

Lombroso's work is historically valuable despite its scientific and logical naïveté. In fact, it is valuable partly *because* it so clearly reveals scientific and scientistic vulnerabilities, making them available for study. For better or worse, moreover, one outstanding quality of Lombroso's work is its magnificent tangle of brilliance and nonsense, the way it combines what a recent biographer calls Lombroso's "encyclopedic ambition, his characteristically extreme mental adventuresomeness, and his titanic failures."[91] Our key concern was to produce a full (if abbreviated) and accurate translation, a concern that led to our explicit resolve to include the warts. We still flinched, but having recognized the temptation to hide Lombroso's faults, we were better able to resist it.

As we worked, we kept in mind a passage from an essay by criminologist Hans Kurella, written in 1911, two years after Lombroso's death, to commemorate his work:

> Lombroso was a philologist, philosopher, mystic, anatomist, anthropologist, neurologist, psychiatrist, sociologist, statistician, and social and political scientist. He was always original, always assembling piles of observations, everywhere paradoxical, bold in hypotheses, surprising in his ability

> to bring together otherwise disparate fields, and a collector of facts of the highest order. His not inconsiderable analytical capacities were completely outshone by his passion for synthesis; his titanic efforts toward inductive research were again and again crisscrossed and often paralyzed by his gifted eye for analogies.[92]

Kurella recognizes Lombroso's tendency to wreck his own creations, and he perceptively analyzes Lombroso's intellectual fallibility, but at the same time he is able to acknowledge the older scholar's creativity and achievement. Kurella's fair but tolerant assessment provided an example we tried to follow.

Lombroso's Attitudes toward Women

Lombroso's extremely negative opinions of women generally posed another major translation issue, at least potentially. *La donna delinquente* constitutes perhaps the most extended proof of women's inferiority ever attempted.[93] We thought this hostility might make it difficult for us, as translators and as feminists, to relate to the book's content. But in practice, this problem did not materialize. It proved easy to maintain our respect for the integrity of Lombroso's text while remaining dispassionate about his arguments. We were thoroughly familiar with Lombroso's opinions of women before we undertook the translation. We considered him an important thinker and recognized that many intellectuals of his day had shared his views on women. This is one reason why those views hold historical value. Another lies in the book's influence on other peoples' ideas about women.

In translating *La donna delinquente*, we viewed ourselves not only as conduits through which Lombroso's meanings could flow but also as collaborators in or coproducers of his meanings. We had no more interest in condemning him than in adulating him. Our aim was to open doors through which his text (in renewed form) and, metaphorically, he himself might pass into the present day.

Reading Criminal Woman

The text has two kinds of footnotes: Lombroso's and ours. Lombroso's footnotes are indicated with small letters and appear as page notes. We include all the notes appearing in the parts of *La donna delinquente* that we translate, aside from cross-references to other parts of this book or to *L'uomo delinquente*. Lombroso's citations indicate his familiarity with a vast range of international scholarship and show that researchers all over Europe were working on similar topics. We have not attempted to translate Lombroso's citations, partly because most of the works to which they refer were never translated, partly because leaving them the way he wrote them gives readers a clear sense of his documentational decisions and procedures. (Similarly, we simply reproduce without translating the citations that Lombroso occasionally inserts directly into his text.[94]) However, in the few cases in which Lombroso uses footnotes to make substantive comments, we do translate his notes.

Our own notes, which include glosses of difficult parts of the text, explanations of terms, and identifications of people to whom Lombroso refers, are indicated with numbers and appear at the end of the book. In them, we speak of "the author" and not of "the authors" because (as we explain in more detail in the first appendix) Guglielmo Ferrero's contribution to *La donna delinquente* was probably closer to that of a graduate assistant than a true coauthor. This edition also includes a glossary of Lombroso's key terms.

We do not use ellipses marks to indicate cut passages or words. We trimmed in so many places that to use ellipses marks would have meant to produce a book full of distracting dots. In any case, few readers will want to compare this text with the Italian original, and so for the majority, ellipses marks would have had little meaning. However, our appendix offers a sample chapter as it appeared in the original and in the 1895 (*The Female Offender*) translation. This example illustrates how we condensed the original, and it enables readers to evaluate our procedures.

Author's Preface

Among the many new studies of criminal anthropology, those on the criminal woman and the prostitute, more than any others, reconfirm the advantage of blind observation of facts. This objectivity is the secret of our triumph over our adversaries, who fight against us by reasoning deductively from universal principles.[1]

Our work has elicited criticism because from the very start, its results flew in the face of received wisdom. Moreover, some of our single and partial observations, taken out of context, appeared to contradict one another, so that lovers of logic had to wait for definite conclusions. But, faithful to the maxim that has sustained us throughout life, we blindly followed the facts, even when they appeared self-contradictory—even when they seemed to lead us down the wrong path. And fortunately we stayed the course, because at the end, the most contradictory facts fit together like pebbles in a mosaic, making a full and living picture. If the method of gathering them was at first uncertain and uninspired, as though we were groping in darkness, at the end the goal appeared bright and lucid. We tasted the bitter pleasure of the hunter who, after chasing his prey uphill and down, experiences the joy of success doubly due to his earlier fears of failure and the labor of his conquest.

In preparing this study we often experienced a kind of ricochet, which like the waves of the sea dragged us far from our original goal, even while they smoothed out the continuous contradictions that faced us. For example, in the lowest zoological series, the female is superior to the male in size and organic complication, almost the mistress of the species; but then she becomes a humble slave, diminished in power, variability, and so on. In the human race she appears equal or superior to the male before puberty—equal in strength and stature, even in intelligence; but gradually she falls behind, leaving proof of that precocity that is standard among the inferior races. Woman's relative scarcity of degenerative stigmata, which at first seems to be evidence of superiority, pertains nonetheless to her lesser variability, an inferior characteristic. At the lower levels of evolution, as for example in monsters, the sexes are equal in degenerative stigmata, but this is a condition that, curiously enough, human sexual selection removes.[2]

We have discovered that women are less sensitive than men, which explains their greater vitality, but contradicts both popular wisdom and clear evidence that women react more strongly to pain. This apparent contradiction resolves itself when we take into account women's greater excitability and lesser inhibition.[3]

The lesser frequency of the criminal type among female criminals appears to contradict the fundamental principle of our theory of the born criminal.[4] But it actually confirms the theory because it is linked to women's lesser frequency of degeneration and of cortical epileptic irritation, a condition that lies at the root of criminality.

A very unusual contradiction is presented by the coexistence of cruelty and compassion in women. It can be resolved by recognizing the influence of maternity, which often leavens cruelty with sweetness. Maternity, together with women's lesser intelligence, strength, and variability, explains why women are not only less moral but also less criminal than men.[5] Women's lesser criminality, their atavism, and men's rapacious sexual desire help us understand why women are less likely to be born criminals than born prostitutes. Logic alone could not lead one to this conclusion.

We want to make this point at the very start because some people of weak talent—incapable not only of initiating their own research but also of following that of others—are unaware that nature is never logical.[6] They try to discredit our new theory of criminal anthropology in the eyes of the public.

As for those who accuse us of wasting time in the study of honest as well as dishonest women, we remind them that criminal women could not have been understood if we had not also had a profile of normal women. When we searched for such information, we found nothing (certainly very little that was definite). This is because most anthropologists (with a few exceptions, such as Pagliani, Sergi, and Tarnowsky) waste reams of paper on sterile measurements of civilized and savage tribes but tell us nothing about the various stages in the development of women generally.[7] Thus it was impossible to determine where the normal state ends and the pathological begins.

In books on women, some people do not stick to facts but instead perpetuate the medieval tradition of chivalry toward the gentle sex. Such people charge that my work is insufficiently chivalrous. Yet I was true to my idea of the born criminal type and refused to be afraid of apparent contradictions which unprofessional critics use to attack my work. How could I pretend to agree with a conventional wisdom which is unscientific and falls apart when one probes it?

Although I argue that the female equivalent of the male born criminal is the prostitute and that she shares the same atavistic origin, I certainly need to state, very clearly, that she is less perverse and less harmful to society. While every crime involves calamity, prostitution can be a moral safety valve. In any case, it would not exist without male vice, for which it is a useful, if shameful, outlet. One might say that the more women degrade themselves and the more they sin, the more they are helping society.[8]

Thus, if I must show that in mind and body, woman is a male of arrested development, the fact that she is somewhat less criminal than he, and a little more pitiful, can compensate a thousandfold for her deficiency in the realm of intellect.[9] Just as musical harmony and beauty conquer all social classes, the respect that all people have for women's intensity of feeling and maternal sentiment more than makes up for women's deficiency of intellect. A scientist will have a hundred admirers who quickly disappear; but women are saints who have a million admirers, forever.

Not one line of this work justifies the great tyranny that continues to victimize women, from the taboo which forbids them to eat meat or touch a coconut, to that which impedes them from studying, and worse, from practicing a profession once they are educated.[10] These ridiculous and cruel constraints, still widely accepted, are used to maintain or (sadder still) increase women's inferiority, exploiting them to our advantage. The same happens when we shower a docile victim with hypocritical elegies and, while pretending that she is an ornament, ready her for new sacrifices.

How valuable women can be is demonstrated by the honored Signora Caccia, Signora Dr. Tarnowsky, Signorina Helen Zimmern, Signora C. Royer, Signora Rossi, and Signora Dr. Kuliscioff who, having understood my ideas better, earlier, and more extensively than many of our thinkers, provided documents, information, and advice at the most difficult times.[11] And you demonstrate it most of all, my darling Gina,[12] the last and only thread that ties me to life, my steadiest collaborator and inspiration, more stimulating than any of my books.[13]

I cannot conclude without an honest statement. In collaborative works, the first author is usually the one with the more famous name in the scholarly world.

But in this case, the opposite happens: The most laborious and vigorous parts, on psychology and history, are the work of the younger collaborator,[14] whereas I alone am responsible for the material on psychiatry and anthropology, and for the organization of the work.

Turin, 1 September 1892

C. Lombroso

Part I

The Normal Woman

1

The Female in the Animal World

At the present time, the moral sciences are interwoven or, rather, fused with the natural sciences. Thus it is impossible to undertake the study of the criminal woman without first analyzing the normal woman and also the female's place in the hierarchy of animal life.[1]

In the earliest organisms, reproduction occurred without sex. It took place through splitting (the division of one large cell into two); budding (the growth and detachment of one part of a cell); polisporagamia (in a multicelled organism, the growth and detachment of a group of cells); and monosporogamia (in a cellular organism, the growth and detachment of a single cell, which then develops through division). In all these cases, reproduction is asexual. The fundamental phenomenon of reproduction, from the dawn of life, is always the detachment from an organism of a part, which continues to live and develop on its own.

From asexual reproduction, we pass through a series of transitional forms (hermaphroditism, alternating reproduction) to sexual reproduction, which occurs through an external influence, fertilization by the male. In sexual reproduction, the fundamental phenomenon—the growth of those parts of the organism that make the new being—is accomplished almost entirely at the expense of the female.

The Relationship of Size, Strength, and Physique in the Two Sexes

Among the lower animals, according to Milne Edwards, individuals of the two sexes often can be distinguished only by the characteristics of their reproductive apparatus. Many creatures were long thought to exist in the feminine form only.

In many mollusks, the male could be distinguished from the female only at the moment of reproduction.[a]

But as soon as differences between the two sexes become apparent, the female is superior to the male in size, strength, and number. "I believe," the honorable Professor Emery wrote when we asked him about this matter, "that the superiority of the female sex is necessary for reproduction at this primitive evolutionary stage. The female's usual superiority can already be seen in cases of parthenogenesis among crustaceans and even among certain insects (*Rhodites rosae*) in which the male sex hardly exists or has a minimal function; it can also be seen in cases of alternating reproduction."

In worms of the genus *Bonellia*, the female is a massive creature, while the male is very small, lower in organization, and parasitical on the female. In a rotifer, *Hydatina senta*, the male has no abdominal organs and no organs of sex or motion, while the female has all these. Another example of female superiority is provided by the *Anilocra* and other crustaceans that are parasitical on fish: as long as they are young, they produce sperm and have male sex organs; when they reach maturity, the testicles and penis atrophy, and, developing ovaries and vulvas, they become female. In many parasitical crustaceans—so writes Emery—the female is large while the male is very small and almost parasitical on the female.

As we go up the zoological scale, the female's superiority in size and strength recurs frequently. In many species of spiders the female is larger and more robust than the male. An exception occurs in *Argyroneta aquatica*, says Brehm, in which the male is actually more robust and measures 14 mm to the female's 11 mm (*Vita degli animali*, VI, p. 627, Torino, 1871). In almost all the other species, however, the difference is in favor of the female, which in *Dolomede* is a centimeter and a half longer than the male (Id., id., p. 635).

The female spider of *Tegenaria domestica* is 16 to 18 mm long, the male but 10 mm. In couplings one can see how the female's strength causes fear in the male and dampens his ardor. When the male, writes Brehm, wants to mate, it approaches the female slowly and prudently, to see if she will welcome his caresses or will view him as a tasty morsel. If the female seems favorably inclined, the male approaches hurriedly, touching the bottom of her stomach with the two ends of his palp in alternation, and afterward flees quickly in order to avoid becoming her victim (Id., id., p. 611). De Geer saw a male spider which, in the middle of

a. Milne Edwards, *Leçons sur la physiologie et l'anatomie comparée de l'homme et des animaux*, Vol. VIII, p. 330. [We reproduce the substance of Lombroso's footnotes, even when we know they include inaccuracies, in order to show his approach to documentation. We do the same with the notes he inserts in the text. However, we do translate the footnotes in which he comments on his own text.—Eds.]

his preparatory caresses, was seized by the female, pulled closer in her web, and devoured (Darwin, *L'origine dell'uomo*, ecc., p. 245).[2]

Among birds, at the point on the evolutionary scale when the sexual struggle begins, so does the male's predominance in strength and size over the female. But even in the lower zoological orders, in one of the contradictions that we find frequently in this line of study, males are almost always superior in anatomical structure, variability, and motility. This is true even in species in which males are otherwise inferior (ants), which proves that males are more active in the sexual function. With the start of sexual competition in the higher species, males add physical power to their other forms of superiority.

Male birds are nearly always better provided with secondary sexual characteristics: rich plumage, song, and in many species heavier armor, not to mention the arsenal of tufts, wattles, tails, and crests which serve the male not only for adornment but often also to make his appearance more frightening. Thus the male of the New Zealand *Neomorpha* has a stronger beak (Darwin, p. 330); the male of the Indian partridge has spurs that the female lacks; and the same is true of the capercaillie. The male of the spurred goose has longer spurs than the female and uses them in defense of its young.

The predominance of the male cannot be predicted among these lower zoological orders, but it becomes more extensive and definitive among mammals. "In the mammals," says Darwin, "the males are always stronger and bigger than the females whenever there is a difference of size between the two sexes, which is almost always the case." Among carnivores the differences are particularly notable: the lion is stronger and bigger. It also holds for physique: the male lion has a mightier mane, muscles, paws, and canines than the female; in the roar it has another powerful weapon for breeding fear which the female lacks.

Primates

Among primates, sex differences become more accentuated and form perfect analogues with those of the human race. Male gorillas have a height of up to two meters, while the females never surpass one and a half. The female's skull is smaller and more rounded; less prognathous, lighter in weight, and lacking the bony crest, it forms a trapezoid, while the male skull is pyramidal. Moreover, the female's nose is smaller and pugged, with a shorter ridge. The body, the hands, the feet are slimmer in the female, the muscles less angular; the shoulders, arms, and legs are more delicate; the top of the humerus is less depressed, while the shinbone is smaller and less prismatic and the pelvic bones larger, flatter, and less hollow inside; and the ischium is more divergent in the woman. In addition, the female is feebler (Hartmann, *Scimmie antropomorfe*, Milan, 1881). Her canine teeth are blunter, shorter, and more compressed, with a triangular shape and less protuberance. Her molar has five cuspids, two external, two internal, and one posterior, which makes her similar to humans (Hartmann).

Synthesis

Thus among the inferior animals, female dominance in size and strength is typical. It manifests itself strongly in the zoological world and extends even to some species of birds. But little by little as one goes up the scale, the male begins to approach the female and then to become stronger, so that among the mammals without exception the male rules over the species.

Moreover, in the species in which the masculine is inferior in size and strength, it is nonetheless always superior in variability and physical perfection. One must also note—as Milne Edwards observes—that usually the specific differences which exist among individuals of the same type are smaller among females than among males. And according to Darwin, primitive strength and the hereditary tendency are greater in the female, while males are more variable, which explains the axiom of breeders and horticulturalists: *The male gives variation, the female the species* (Darwin, *L'origine des espices* [*sic*]).

Among insects, only the male has wings, the emblem and means of his greater motility. Due to the need to pursue, seize, and immobilize the female, males develop new organs—secondary sexual characteristics—which, according to Darwin, are more numerous throughout the animal world in the male than in the female, and which are extraordinarily variable, accounting for the great variability of the male. Females, on the other hand, must preserve the essential characteristics of the species, and so they are more fixed, and one notes a sameness in their major organs, a uniformity which Milne Edwards labels "the tendency to represent the average type of the species." This tendency reappears in the psychology of the normal and criminal woman.

These facts relate to the female's more important role in reproduction and to the struggle for possession of the female. We have already observed that the fundamental role in reproduction is exercised by the female, while the male plays only a minor part. Her greater importance is demonstrated by parthenogenesis and by the fact that in some *Hymenoptera* a single fertilization does the work of reproduction for the entire lifetime. Given the different functions of the male and of the female in reproduction, the female in primitive species must be larger, in order to nourish the part destined to form the new being. The male, whose destiny is to produce the fertilizing liquid, requires less organic energy and thus is of smaller size.

But in the higher orders, males' struggle with one another—a struggle rooted in their stronger sexual desire and perhaps also in their larger numbers—has led to their development of greater size and force than females, and to their superior physique. This fact illuminates Spencer's observation that in reproduction, antagonism produces growth and structural differentiation.[3] In sum, the male has in all creatures a potential for development superior to the female through the very fact of his relatively minor role in reproduction.

Since, according to Spencer (*Principes de biologie*, vol. II, p. 505 e 515), an opposition exists among reproduction, growth, and structure, in animals fecundity varies in inverse ratio to the development of size and structure. Similarly, there is an opposition between the evolution of the individual and the evolution of the species, so that the development and differentiation of the female is restricted by the great organic expenditure required for reproduction. Inversely, the boundaries of masculine development are broader. Thus we can understand how under the influence of the conditions of life the male, at first smaller, would, through a biological law, have been able to develop more than the female.

The male, then, is a more perfect and more variable female through the greater development of secondary sexual characteristics. This is also demonstrated by the fact, brought to light by Milne Edwards and Darwin, that throughout the animal kingdom, the adult female resembles the young male before he develops secondary sexual characteristics.

In terms of structure, male dominance is primitive,[4] but in terms of strength and size, it is recent, brought about by specific conditions which, if they are absent, will cause a return of the male to a primitive state in which he is subordinate to the female. Naturally—writes Emery—special conditions such as parasitism or a sedentary life induce regression, leading to predominance of the female, which when exaggerated in turn leads to the complete disappearance of the male.

2
Anatomy and Biology of Woman

Weight and Height

In human races the woman is nearly always inferior to the man in height and weight, an inferiority that increases with age and civilization. Even in embryo the male is quite a bit larger at the same point in time than the female. At puberty, on the other hand, females are equal to or have a slight advantage over males. This phenomenon is consistent with the precocity typical of inferior beings, that is, with the fact that the more superior the animal, the later its development. Studies by Pagliani, Quetelet, Bowditch, and Alex-Key prove that the growth of the female increases until the age of eleven or twelve years but suddenly dwindles at fourteen years, while in the male it continues until sixteen, as does his weight, vital capacity, and muscular force. If the value for weight, stature, and such at each age for males is 100, the values for the female would be those shown in table 1. The precocity or earlier development of the female is constant, aside from variations in the size of the lags, in all races, social classes, and climates.

As noted, the greatest growth spurts in females precede puberty. Thus, for example, girls who menstruate at twelve years have their strongest period of growth at eleven, while those who menstruate later find themselves at eleven years still waiting for their growth period (Pagliani, op. cit.).[5] In the adult state, the female seems to be always inferior to the male in height and weight as in vital force and thoracic circumference.

Anatomical Differences

In the adult woman, the richest patch of hair appears in a circle around the mound of Venus, while in the male it stretches like a band from the pubis to the navel.

Table I Physical Characteristics of Women by Age

		(male values = 100)		
age	for height	for weight	for vital capacity	for musc. force
3	—	90	—	—
4	99	97	—	50
5	99	97	—	75
6	98	98	—	70
7	96	90	83	74
8	97	91	95	69
9	92	47	92	62
10	100	99	89	68
11	101	101	92	63
12	102	101	89	65
13	102	106	89	67
14	103	105	93	68
15	101	104	90	67
16	97	95	85	62
17	96	90	74	59
18	96	90	72	57

When women grow old, their hair (unlike that of old men) grows longer everywhere, even on the face, thereby making them look virile.

The woman's trunk is proportionately longer than the man's and shaped like a pyramid, with its base on the hips and its apex rounded off by the chest. The vertebral column, according to Ploss (*Das Weib in der Natur und Völkerkunde*, 1887), is on the average 69.70 in the man, 66.69 in the female.[6] In the female, the cervical and lumbar parts predominate, while the dorsal and sacral parts are smaller. The thorax in the male has a length of 25–26, in the female 23–24. Riccardi found that the ratio of the trunk to height in women is 52 percent and in men 53 percent. Also according to Riccardi, in women, as in monkeys and children, the trunk is longer in relation to the lower limbs; but the same is not true of men (*Di alcune correlazioni di sviluppi*, ecc., Modena, 1891).

The woman's hip is located further back than the man's, with an ampler upper lip and rather horizontal position; its bones help create her more capacious pelvic opening and give special shape to the thighs of upper-class women. These bones also give to the walk of women its characteristic rolling motion.

The extremities, both upper and lower, are more graceful in women than men, with less pronounced protuberances. The foot is shorter and more delicate; and the neck of the femur is more right-angled toward the body in a manner that makes the trochanters project more. In addition, women's hands are usually smaller than men's, their arms shorter and more rounded.

Viscera, Fat, and Blood

The woman's heart, proportionate to her body size, seems a little smaller in volume than that of man; this is the effect of less work. According to Orth, the female's heart weighs 250 grams and the male's 300 grams. The heart's relationship to body weight is 1:162 in the female, 1:169 in the male.

In the male, the bone and muscular systems predominate; in the female, on the other hand, it is fat and connective tissue, which explains the greater rotundity of her form. In the Negro and Asiatic races, fat and connective tissue become even more developed through sexual selection and artificial means (immobility, special diet of beer and milk, and tight clothing). In these races, fat appears at a younger age than with us. Among some peoples (Hottentot, Kafirs, Bushmen) it even accumulates in the inner labia of the vagina, and in the buttocks in such a way as to form a support for a child. The latter occurs in part through sexual selection and in part through rather specific practices of maternity.[7]

The blood corpuscles, too, clearly reveal inferiority: Women have fewer red corpuscles than men. Hayem (*Leçons sur les modifications du sang*, Masson, Paris, 1882) gives an average of 4,900,000 red corpuscles for the female and 5,500,000 for the male. For white corpuscles, however, there is no sex difference.

Skull and Brain

Given woman's lesser height and lighter bones, it is not surprising that her skull and brain are notably smaller; and this is in fact demonstrated by all the statistics. According to Morselli the male skull in the Italian races weighs more than the female skull (602 to 516)[8] (*Archivio di antropologia*, vol. v, 1875).[b] Davis's data on the cranial capacity of men and women appear in table 2.

In cranial capacity as in weight, the inferior races present minor differences between the sexes, as becomes clear when we consult the figures of table 3 on the cranial capacity of women in relation to that of men when the latter is set at 1000 (Morselli, *Sul peso del cranio e della mandibola in rapporto col sesso: Arch. di antro.*, vol. v).

b. This is verified among savages and primitive races as well, although in small proportions (Caverna della Palmaria, m. skulls 582, f. 482; Peruvians m. 627, f. 488; Papuans, m. 671, f. 576); it is verified as well by primates (chimpanzee, m. 308, f. 175), etc. etc.

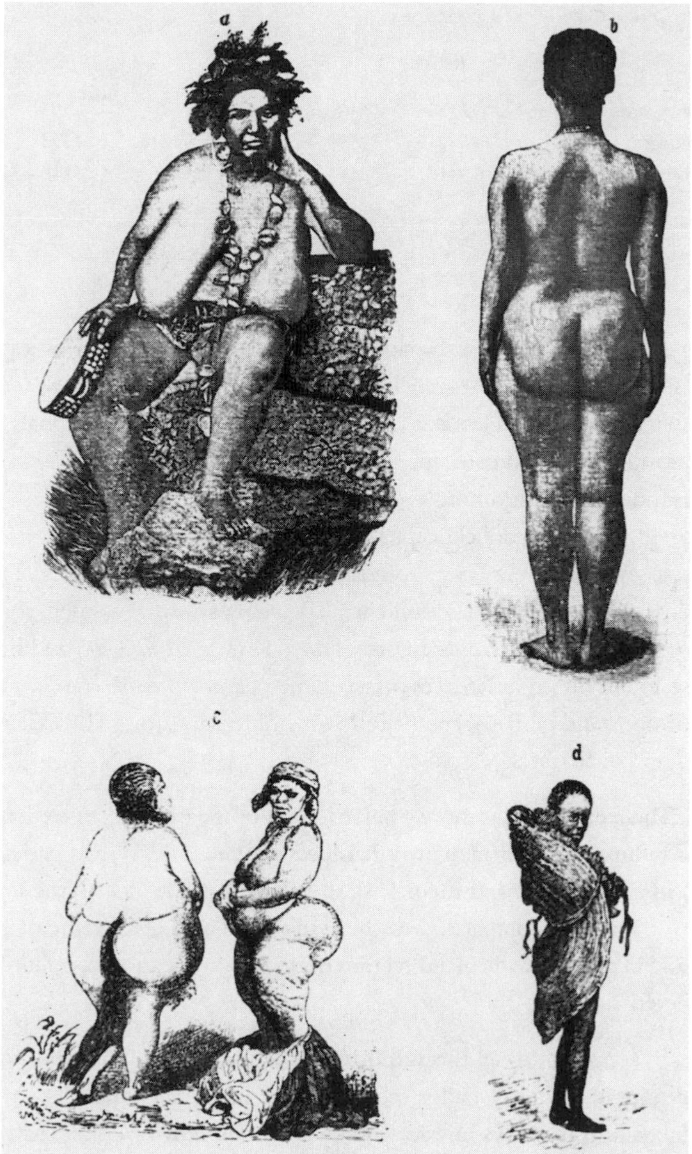

1 Obesity in an Abyssinian woman. The posterior cushion in African women. (a) Abyssinian ballerina or prostitute (example of African obesity) (Ploss); (b) Hottentot with posterior cushion (Ploss); (c) (1) Bongo woman (Schweinfurth); (2) Koranna woman with posterior cushion and overdevelopment of buttocks and thighs (Ploss); (d) Savage woman carrying baby on back, as do all primitive people (Ploss). *Source*: Lombroso, *La donna delinquente*, 1893. Photo courtesy General Research Division, the New York Public Library, Astor, Lenox, and Tilden Foundation.

Table 2 Cranial Capacity by Race and Sex

	male	female		male	female
in European races	1367	1206	in Asiatic races	1304	1194
in Oceanic races	1319	1219	in African races	1293	1211
in American races	1308	1187	in Australian races	1214	1111

Editors' note: *American* and *Australian* in this table refer to the aboriginal populations. Here Lombroso uses measurements of cranial capacity to create a hierarchy of not only gender but also of race.

Greater brachycephaly or broad-headedness among women is especially marked in the crania of Swiss, French, Negro, Capuans,[9] Chinese, and Papuans, as shown in table 4. Nonetheless this characteristic of greater brachycephaly among women cannot be called constant, since it is absent in the ancient and modern English, Indians, and Eskimos.

Table 5 gives data on dolichocephaly or long-headedness.

To these sexual differences we should add that of the lesser frequency of the median occipital fossetta, which is found in 3.4 percent of normal women, compared to between 4.5 and 5.6 percent of normal men. Krause (*Anatomie*) and Benedikt have also found minor differences between men's and women's crania.

More important, perhaps, are the following differences found by Ecker (*Arch. für Anthrop.*, V, 1872):

(*a*) The female skull is more similar to that of the infant than to that of the adult male in its frontal protuberances and more developed parietals

(*b*) In its dimensions, the female skull differs from the male in the smallness of the face in comparison to the skull (another characteristic of infants) and in the perpendicular direction of the brow (yet another infantile characteristic)

In general, according to all the authorities, and in all races, but more so in the civilized ones, the female skull is more childlike in capacity and shape than the masculine, and it is always inferior and always offers less variation than that of the male.

The brain of the woman weighs less than that of the man.[10] According to Manouvrier, the weight of the female brain relative to that of the male is about 89.0 to 100.[11] Average weights of the brain in individuals aged twenty to eighty years old appear in table 6. Topinard and Manouvrier in particular have noted that these variations, like those of the skull, could be solely effects of woman's proportionately inferior height and body weight (88.5 percent). But even taking this into ac-

Table 3 Female Cranial Capacity Compared to Male

	(males = 1000)			(males = 1000)	
Negro	984	(Davis)	Basque	855	(Davis)
Australian	967	(Davis)	Gypsy	875	(Koperinski)
Hindu	944	(Davis)	Lower Breton	873	(Koperinski)
Malaysian	923	(Tiedemann)	Chinese	870	(Davis)
Dutch	919	(Tiedemann)	English	860	(Davis)
Irish	912	(Davis)	German	897	(Welchker)
Neo-Caledonian	911	(Broca)		878	(Weisbach)
Italian	921	(Mantegazza)		838	(Huske)
Alvergnati [France]	904	(Broca)		864	(Tiedemann)
Slav	903	(Weisbach)	Parisians	858	(Broca)
Dutch	883	(Davis)	Anglo-Saxons	862	(Broca)
Guanche [Canary Islands]	869	(Davis)	Western Negro	874	(Broca)

Editors' note: Lombroso here gives numerical data without clearly identifying the unit of measurement or explaining the numbers' meaning. He is arguing that evolution leads naturally to increasing divergences between the sexes. Darker, more "primitive" women are closer to the male standard (= 1000). Modern white women develop specific "feminine" characteristics and are more markedly inferior to men.

Table 4 Brachycephaly by Race and Sex

	cephalic index			cephalic index	
	male	female		male	female
Swiss (His)	703	714	Guanche [Canary Islands] (Broca)	746	769
Negro (Huschke)	715	730	Western Negro (Broca)	728	714
(Davis)	736	740	Chinese (Davis)	774	766
Irish (Davis)	746	760	Tasmanian (Davis)	737	768
French (Sappey)	768	791	German (Krause)	793	807
Danish (Davis)	780	785	Kanaki (Davis)	800	805
Neo-Caledonian (Broca)	716	720			

Table 5 Dolichocephaly by Race and Sex

	cephalic index			cephalic index	
	male	female		male	female
Parisians (Broca)	794	777	Antique Romans (Davis)	770	757
Dutch (Davis)	802	785	Hindus (Davis)	768	753
Ancient Britons (Davis)	794	772	Basques (Broca)	868	702
Medieval skulls (Hölder)	773	771	Ancient Felsinei [Bologna] (Calori)	802	800
Lower-Bretons (Broca)	817	806	Greenlander (Davis)	725	704
English (Davis)	773	760	American Eskimos (Davis)	755	741

Table 6 Brain Weight by Sex

	man	woman
in Hannover (Krause, *Anatom.*)	1461	1341
in England (Sims, *Med. Chir. Trans.*, 1835)	1412	1292
in France (Sappey, *Traité d'anat. descr.*)	1358	1256
in Switzerland (Hoffman, *Anatomie*)	1350	1250
in Russia (Blosfeld, *Henke's Zeitsch. f. Staatsartzneilkunde* [*sic*])	1346	1195
in Austria (Meynert, *Vierteljahrssch. f. Psych*, 1867)	1296	1170
General average	1358	1235
Difference in general averages	123	

Table 7 Brain Weight by Body Weight and Sex

body weight	brain weight		body weight	brain weight	
(kilograms)	man	woman	(kilograms)	man	woman
20	—	4.47 percent	60	2.16 percent	1.99 percent
30	3.7 percent	3.37 percent	70	1.99 percent	—
40	2.98 percent	2.70 percent	80	1.59 percent	—
50	2.5 percent	2.29 percent			

count, the woman's brain weight remains somewhat less. We see this in Bischoff's work on the correspondence between the brain weights of members of the two sexes with equal body weight, as set forth in table 7. Clearly, the differences between men and women are here less pronounced. But women's actual inferiority does not vanish as a result.

Physiognomy

It is obvious that woman's physiognomy, from her lack of a beard through her greater rotundity and smaller size, especially in the lower jaw, is more childlike and more delicate than the male. Nonetheless, during the first and last ages of man, in the lower classes and above all in many savage races (Hottentots, Kafirs, Bushmen), the correspondence with the male is very strong; the woman's face becomes virile.

Degenerative Characteristics

The woman differs from the man not only in cranial shape, breast development, hair quantity, and all those things that Darwin has called secondary sex characteristics, but also in the quantity, type, and intensity of her degenerative characteristics. Women lack certain degenerative characteristics that are very marked in men, such as jug ears, enlarged frontal sinuses, severe cranial anomalies, and facial asymmetry; but on the other hand they exhibit a larger proportion of other characteristics such as adherent ears, early appearance of facial hair, and downiness. These traits appear frequently in normal women. Watching people on a public walkway, I noted that out of 560 women, 37 young women had moles and beards (7 percent); 34 had enormous mandibles (6.8 percent); and 9 were of a completely degenerative type (1.8 percent).

The female organ most subject to anomalies is the hymen, which can be full of holes, fringed, heart-shaped, ribbonlike, peaked, swollen, upswept like a chicken's rump, circular, or tailed, thanks to a sort of cord or elongated thread with a swollen end which descends from the outer lip of the hymen like a small Mierzejewsky polyp (Hoffmann, *Trattato di med. legale*, vol. 1, p. 20). This organ has no useful function in terms of the perpetuation of the race; in fact, it impedes reproduction and is, perhaps, a vestige of the monotreme sack. Lacking a reason for its existence and having lost its function, this organ varies for the same reason as the ear: Both are becoming vestigial.

Other anomalies, too, can be found in women's genitals, such as the Hottentot's apron created by hypertrophy of the inner labia and foreskin of the clitoris. This hypertrophy is more or less sizeable depending on the individual, but it is always very clear, and it appears toward the end of childhood due to the marked development of connective and fatty subcutaneous tissues found so frequently in inferior races. On the other hand, in women with the Hottentot apron, the outer labia remain hidden, and the mound of Venus sinks down to the point that it becomes imperceptible.

This anomaly of the labia can also be found in other races. Pliny has noted it in Negroes, Copts, and Moors. Among the Nere of the African coast, Vincent (*Contribution a l'ethnologie de la côte occidentale d'Afrique: Revue d'anthropologie*, 1874) found a large number of women with a five-to-eight-centimeter elongation of the inner labia that was in fact an apron of the hymen. Lemser observed the same thing in several women along the river Mellacorè and the river Nunè. Blanchard thought this anomaly might have an atavistic origin, since it is also found in gorillas and in *Troglodytes Aubryi* (Blanchard, *Sur la steatopigie des femmes Boschimanes*, 1883; Lombroso, *Sur le lipome des Portefaix*, 1884). Next Gratiolet and Alix (*Recherches sur l'anatomie des Troglodytes Aubryi*, 1886) demonstrated that in chimpanzees the outer labia are atrophied while the inner labia are highly developed. Hoffmann and Bischoff noted that in anthropoid monkeys the outer labia and mound of Venus are almost absent, while the clitoris is always highly developed and fluted on its inner surface. Moreover, the inner labia are highly developed,

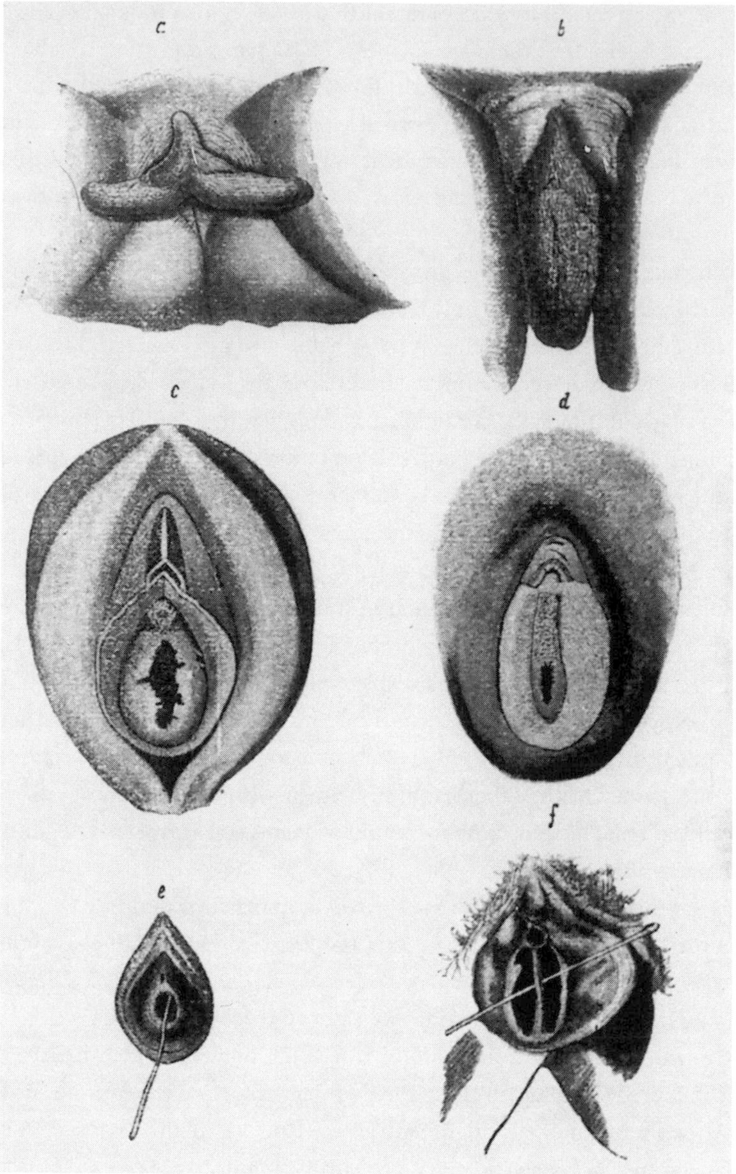

2 Anomalies of the vulva in Hottentots and Europeans. (a, b) Apron or overdevelopment of inner labia of Hottentots (Blanchard); (c) Fringed hymen in virgins (Hoffman); (d) Sieved hymen (Hoffman); (e) Pendulated or clappered hymen (Miriewsky); (f) Split hymen (Hoffman). *Source*: Lombroso, *La donna delinquente*, 1893. Photo courtesy General Research Division, the New York Public Library, Astor, Lenox, and Tilden Foundation.

especially in the chimpanzee, less so in the other three species of monkey. Most of these traits are shared by Bushmen women.

Anomalies of the female genitals can also be found among Europeans, although less distinctly. In a study by Carle, out of one hundred normal subjects, 38 percent had inner labia that were greatly developed. Another strange anomaly is the enormous buttocks of steatopygous women, but this is a product of their child-rearing customs.

Menstruation

Woman's most distinguishing function is menstruation. The age of first menstruation appears in table 8. Menstruation in Russia starts between fifteen and eighteen years (Tarnowsky); in Monaco between sixteen and seventeen (Haeker); in Paris between fourteen and fifteen (Brierre de Boismont). One does not find great differences between female students in institutions situated in cities and in the open country, other than that in the latter, menstruation is more prevalent in the springtime and in June and August.

According to Dubois and Pajot,

in warm climates	it appears between 11 and 14 years
in temperate climates	it appears between 13 and 16 years
in cold climates	it appears between 15 and 18 years

The influence of climate, however, can be counterbalanced by other factors. Thus, in the capital of Russia, the artificial temperature of heated apartments, frequent cohabitation with the other sex, and the popularity of erotic books lead to precocious onset of puberty. And there is also the influence of race: Thus in Mongolian races, although they live under frigid skies, women reach puberty at the same early age as do the Spanish and Italians.

Table 8 Age of Onset of Menstruation

	6,000 observations (Meyer)	(Kakuskine)		6,000 observations (Meyer)	(Kakuskine)
rich	15.51 years	13.0 years	urban	15.98 years	14.9 years
poor	16.50 years	—	rural	14.20 years	15.30 years

Source: *Funzioni sessuali delle donne di Tambow*, 1891.

Editors' note: Lombroso does not give information on the number of observations in the Kakuskine source.

Puberty occurs in females earlier than in males, even by two or three years, and from this point the two sexes begin to become markedly different. Menstruation in the female has greater importance than puberty in the male. For twenty or thirty years it circumscribes the sexual life of the woman. During this menstrual epoch, the woman is unsuited for physical and mental work, cantankerous, and inclined to tell lies.

Menopause occurs in Norway at forty-eight years, eleven months; in France, at forty-six years and eleven months; in northern Italy, at 44.9; in central Italy at 43.6; and in southern Italy at 47. Among the Italian well-to-do classes, menopause occurs at forty-one years; among laborers, at 46.1; and among peasants at 46.2.

The sexual appetite, already less marked in the woman, weakens with menopause and then diminishes and disappears. According to Tait—the greatest of gynecologists—there are women who during the climacteric fall into loathing and disgust for men and into a state similar to madness; but after menopause has passed, the sexual appetite can return with vigor, demonstrating that there is not always a strict relationship between the ovaries and the reproductive impulse.

Muscular Force

Among all peoples (Lotze, *Psychologie*, 1852), the female's strength is inferior to that of the male. According to Regnier, the man of twenty-five to thirty years is at the height of his powers and is able, squeezing a dynamometer forcibly in his hands, to create a force equal to fifty kilograms. Moreover, he maintains this strength until the age of fifty, after which it diminishes progressively. Regnier estimated the strength of the woman to be that of a male youth of fifteen to sixteen years, that is to say, two-thirds that of an ordinary man.

In women, there is only a slight difference between the strength of the two hands. Subsequent to Regnier, other studies showed that in women, ambidexterity and left-handedness are more frequent than in men. In a group of 280 normal women, I found 5.8 percent to be left-handed; Gallia, in 100 cases, found 12 percent—more confirmation of woman's atavistic nature.

In inferior races females even more closely resemble the male. There are some women in every country (even as near as Albania) who work the land, build huts, and carry weights while the men make war and hunt. It has been observed, moreover, that in many races the women even make war, as in regions of the White Nile, among the indigenous populations of the Antilles discovered by Columbus, in the Dahomey, and in medieval Scotland.

White Hair and Baldness

White hair and baldness demonstrate delayed aging and, indirectly, lesser sensitivity in women compared to men. White hair and baldness are found less frequently among women than men of the middle class, as is shown by data gathered in my laboratory by Dr. Ottolenghi.[c12] These appear in tables 9 and 10. Thus baldness and white hair appear somewhat later and less frequently in the woman, which might relate to her lesser mental activity.

Table 9 White Hair by Age and Sex

	men	women		men	women
from 20 to 29 years	29.87	8.11	from 40 to 49 years	82.35	84.00
from 30 to 39 years	60.97	31.00	from 50 to 59 years	96.51	90.00
from 35 to 39 years	77.15	57.00	from 60 to 69 years	100.00	100.00

Editors' note: The figures under men and women seem to be cumulative percentages. Lombroso does not explain why he gives data twice on people in their thirties. The 30 to 39 years entry may have been an error for 30 to 34 years, as in the next table.

Table 10 Baldness by Age and Sex

	men	women		men	women
from 20 to 29 years	10.09	7	from 40 to 49 years	25	26
from 30 to 34 years	19	13	from 50 to 59 years	40	37
from 35 to 39 years	21	18	from 60 to 69 years	41	45

Editors' note: The figures under men and women may be cumulative percentages.

Summary

Overall the woman is more childlike than the man: in height, weight, scarcity of facial hair, the greater length of the trunk in relation to the lower limbs, the greater wealth of connective and fatty tissue, the lower number and weight of the corpuscles, the lesser weight and volume of the skull and brain, and the lower number of and lesser variation in degenerative characteristics, except in the hymen and inner labia. This infantilism then extends to woman's weaker strength, more frequent left-handedness, and lesser frequency of white-headedness and baldness.

c. *Sulla calcizie e canizie* (*Arch. di psich.*, 1890).

3

Senses and Psyche of Woman

Senses

Woman's sensitivity is notably different from man's, as the anatomy of her organs itself suggests. Her eye is smaller and more on the surface of the head; her nose and ear are shorter. As for her ears, according to the observations of Autenrieth (Reil, *Archi.*, t, IX, p. 322), the auditory channel is narrower than that of man[d] when the length is equal; as a result it receives fewer sound waves than that of the man, and once received, they reverberate less.

Until now, everyone thought that woman must be more sensitive than man.[13] Lotze and Ploss claim that woman is more vulnerable to nervousness because she is more sensitive; and even Möbius, who denies this greater disposition to nerves, says that she is more inclined to extreme sensitivity. Yet scholars have also observed that she has fewer needs, eats and drinks less, and withstands aging, pain, and privations better than man, which should have made us suspect that woman's sensitivity is actually less developed than that of man. My laboratory experiments have in fact demonstrated this to be true.

Studying touch in one hundred normal women compared to one hundred men, I found:

	women	*men*
delicate touch (1 to 1.5)	16 percent	31.5 percent
medium touch (1.5 to 3)	56 percent	62.5 percent
dull touch (3.0 and over)	25 percent	6.0 percent[14]

Clearly, refinement of touch predominates in men.

d. On the skeleton, nose, and ear, also see Ottolenghi and Gradenigo, in *Archivio di psichiatria*, vol. XI, XII e XIII.

Sexual Sensitivity

Whatever others may say, woman's sexual sensitivity is also weaker than man's, as Tait has found (Congresso delle Società francesi di chirurgia, 1891). Thus Dante says,

> One knows
> How briefly love's fire lasts in women
> If it is not reignited by the eye or sense of touch.[15]

"Genital sufferings," writes Mantegazza,[16] "are almost always more severe in men, manifesting themselves in painful tension of the testicles and spermatic vesicles or in spasmodic and prolonged lechery. These pains can be accompanied by disquiet, agitation, and, in grave cases, a delirium which takes hydrophobic form. In woman, on the other hand, genital need rarely produces such pains" (Mantegazza, *Fisiologia del piacere*, parte II, cap. XII).

"The normal woman," Sergi writes to me,[17]

> loves to be courted and adored by man but gives in like a victim to his sexual wishes. I know of several ladies who become frigid and fastidious when their husbands approach, even though they love them greatly; some insist that girls who hope for pleasure in marriage find trouble instead. Everyone knows that women need a lot of stimulus before they succumb to sexual pleasure; without such measures, the woman will remain cold, neither giving nor receiving satisfaction. It is well known that many inferior races have adopted measures that seem like torments to excite their women; the men submit to painful operations to have these measures at their disposal. This gives us empirical confirmation of the lesser sensitivity of women, even women of the humblest grade.
>
> Without doubt, among us Europeans, girls are happier if they marry young men, but they rarely make a fuss about marrying one that is older. Sometimes they hardly hesitate to abandon a young man whom they loved for someone older and wealthier. Often, even if they have suffered from a reversal in love, they will give themselves easily to another who marries them immediately; or, with supreme indifference, they will give in to a man whom they had scorned, so long as he persists and presents a practical side—the possibility of matrimony.
>
> As a rule, the woman needs to have a sexual sensitivity equal to that of man in order for her to exhibit passion. It is true that once excited and loving, they are tenacious, but that depends on a psychological motive, not on the intensity of feeling; and it is also true that if a new lover appeals to their greater

practicality, they abandon the former lover cruelly and pitilessly. (*Arch. di psich.*, vol. XIII, fasc. I, 1892)

Another proof of woman's lesser physiological activity is offered by prostitution, a phenomenon that proves that men have greater sexual needs. Male prostitution is only slightly comparable, and it is found only among the degenerate classes.

Sexual sensitivity declines during menopause, when women develop a repulsion and loathing for sexual intercourse very similar to that found in female animals after pregnancy or at the end of the rutting period. When menopause ends, according to Tait, sexual desire can return to woman, but of course less intensely. The female's greater frigidity and passivity during coitus is common among all animals, the result of the nature of ovules and sperm. Ovules—as Tillet and Darwin have noted—are heavier and less mobile than sperm; those of plants have to be transported by the wind. And in the first animals capable of motion, it was always the male who went out looking for the female.

Woman's lesser sexual sensitivity is further demonstrated by:

- the rarity in her of sexual psychopathologies, and the relative lack of variation when they do occur;
- platonic love, which, although it is fundamentally impossible, is more accepted by women than men;
- the great length of time that women keep themselves chaste;
- the requirement of chastity, which has become general among many peoples but only for women;
- the ease with which women adapt to polygamy (and note how easily the Mormons find female followers);
- and women's scrupulous observation of monogamy, which men observe more in name than in fact.

Opposing views on the sensitivity of women depend on the paradox that love is the most important thing in their life. But that trait flows not from eroticism but their need to satisfy the maternal instinct and be protected, without which women's existence is incomplete. Rachel's words to Jacob—"Give me a son, otherwise I die"—contain a physiological truth. A famous obstetrician (Giordano) told me that: *Man loves woman for her vulva, while woman loves man as a husband and father*. One might summarize my view by saying that woman has less eroticism but greater sexuality than man.

Seeing, therefore, that woman is naturally and organically monogamous and frigid, one can understand how the laws of adultery in all populations have come down hard on her but not the man, who oftentimes is exempted. And it explains, if it does not justify, the eternal injustice with which law and custom treat women relative to men who have committed adultery. Behavior that amounts to not even a misdemeanor among men is, for women, the gravest of crimes.

This also explains why prostitution, which used to be legal and tolerated (since it provided an outlet to male ardor and therefore prevented crimes), gradually became a sign of infamy.[18] It further explains why prostitution exists, so to speak, totally for the benefit of men, while for women there is no equivalent: They have no natural need.

Sensitivity to Pain in General/Algometry

Women's lesser sexual sensitivity meshes well with her generally weaker sensitivity. Information on general sensitivity and sensitivity to pain appears in table 11. The difference between the two sexes with respect to general sensitivity are thus slight during youth, but for pain they grow more significant. Woman's greater dullness of touch is further confirmed by our observation—one that contradicts all previous wisdom on the subject—of two normal women who presented complete insensitivity to pain without any explanatory illness.

These data take on a greater importance in light of several practical observations which I collected from the leading surgeons of Europe. Everyone told me that although today differences in sensitivity are less detectable due to the use of anaesthetics, women withstand the pain of operations much better than men,

Table 11 Sensitivity by Sex

	number of observations	general sensitivity	sensitivity to pain
women of the common people	49	90.20	53.16
men of the common people	17	94.00	69.23
lads	4	95.76	78.76
lasses	13	91.07	70.15
men over 21 years	13	93.46	66.30
women over 21 years	36	89.86	48.41

Editors' note: Lombroso and other criminal anthropologists used a special machine, an algometer, to measure sensitivity. They termed the point at which a subject first felt the electric current "general sensitivity" and that at which the subject first felt pain "sensitivity to pain." Although Lombroso does not indicate his unit of measurement, it is clear that the higher the number, the greater the sensitivity.

everything else being equal. "Billroth said," Carle told me, "that when one had to attempt a new type of operation, it was best to make the first try on a woman, because she is less sensitive, and thus more resistant to pain. The woman," he added, "is, like savages, an inferior being, and therefore more resistant to injury."

Sergi writes, "One proof of woman's tolerance for pain is the great calm she shows in helping the sick,[e] an activity in which men are less skillful. Everyone knows that the sight of suffering makes us men suffer pangs of sympathy; and we cannot help sufferers if we, too, have spasms of pain or experience other side effects that make us absolutely incapable, such as depression accompanied by heart trouble and muscular flaccidity, loss of appetite, and digestive problems. If on the other hand one's emotional sensitivity is slight, slight will also be one's sympathetic sufferings in dealing with the sick, and so it will be easier to be useful. I have seen men who helped sick people in their own families waste away rapidly, while I have seen women, even mothers, assist the sick calmly, maintaining good cheer and a healthy appetite. This greater resistance and greater tolerance for others' pain is not a voluntary effort or heroic strength of woman, but rather the result of a relative insensitivity that enables her to tolerate suffering without becoming depressed" (*Arch. di psich.*, XIII).

Woman's resistance to pain is explained and at the same time substantiated by her greater longevity. This trait, too, is noted in proverbs: "Like cats, women have seven lives"; "Women are like cats: they don't ever die" (Sicily); "Like animals, women have seven souls." Of course there are those who say that woman has not less sensitivity, but rather greater resistance to pain. However, it is obvious that one resists pain better the less one feels it.

Also note that woman—as even advocates of the view that she is more sensitive admit—is subject to a total amount of pain immensely greater than that of man. "Woman," writes Mantegazza, "has greater resistance to physical pain and suffers less than we do from sexual deprivation and from cuts at self-respect; but these poor privileges are nothing compared to the great pains that fall her lot in the area of the feelings. If it were possible to make statistics of such a thing, one would see that she suffers one hundred times more than man. Woman's huge measure of pain is made even greater by sufferings associated with her sexual life. Remember the periodic humiliation of menstruation, which is often a true misery; remember as well the spasms of first intercourse and those of childbirth, and you will see why some call her the *pariah* of the human family" (Mantegazza, *Fisiol. del dolore*, parte I, cap. IX).

e. A German proverb says, "Unfortunate is the sick man who is not helped by a woman."

It might seem strange that there would be this constant and universal opinion in favor of the greater sensitivity of women; but the reason for this misunderstanding among many authors and the public is due to a confusion of the external signs of pain with pain itself. Women react to pain more expansively than men; as Sergi acutely observes, they are not more sensitive but in fact more irritable than men.[f]

"I believe," Sergi writes to me,

> that in woman irritability predominates over sensitivity. This irritability is the foundation of true sensitivity; it can either become actual sensitivity or remain in its primitive and incipient stage. It is the direct and the most powerful cause of movement, and therefore of external signs of pain and pleasure. Some women remain arrested at the stage of mere irritability; others achieve partial sensitivity; but all of them are quick to manifest signs of feeling. The most visible signs may seem to derive from greater sensitivity when in fact they derive from the earlier and lower level of irritability.
>
> Women, like children, are more irritable and less sensitive than men, but unlike children, they usually remain insensitive. If we judge women by external signs, we deem them more sensitive than men. Their greater irritability is linked to other characteristics and conforms to their general nature, which is at a stage between that of the boy and the adult man. In this respect, too, women exhibit an arrested development compared to men. In certain morbid states such as hysteria, this irritability reaches its maximum.[19]

Even Mantegazza, while resolutely maintaining that women are more sensitive, has admitted that the demonstrativeness of their grief is not always due to sensitivity. "In women generally," he writes, "paralytic tendencies or strong reactions predominate, and weeping is also common. It seems that one of the most salient characteristics of the female's nerve cells is rapid discharge of tension, as you also see in expressions of pain. In woman the cerebral hemispheres are weaker and have therefore a smaller moderating influence on reflex actions, leading almost always to more expressive and richer gestures. Another circumstance that contributes to the greater range of expressions of pain in women is upbringing. In her one expects not courage but rather grace, and gradually she learns just how much power can flow from her tears. She thus learns to weep well, weep often, and weep deliberately."

This, too, is noted in proverbs:[20]

f. *Archivio di psichiatria*, vol. XIII, fasc. I.

- Women keep tears in their pockets.
- Woman laughs when she can and cries when she wants to.
- Women have two sorts of tears: one for sadness and the other for deceit.
- Women cry the way dogs piss.

Moral Sensitivity

In addition, moral sensitivity is weaker in women than men. "People say," Sergi writes me, "that woman suffers more than man but resigns herself more easily to pain through habit; and sometimes they praise her as a heroine for sacrificing her life. However, heroic resignation calls for great willpower, and that is seldom one of woman's outstanding qualities. We must conclude, therefore, that it is due to her organic nature that woman has less emotional intensity, and thus more tolerance and resignation than man. Biologically there is no other explanation; it would be sheer fantasy to suppose that women dampen their emotions through willpower. They can dampen only demonstrations of emotion, and without doubt woman dampens those rarely (in any case less often than men)" (*Arch. di psich.*, vol. XIII, fasc. I).

Woman, therefore, feels less, just as she thinks less. This confirms the great maxim of Aristotle: *Nihil est in intellectu quod prius non fuerit in sensu*.[21] Her dullness to pain is Darwinian, not ordained by God. This is proved by the way she so easily falls back into pregnancy in spite of the pains of childbirth and despite her disinterest in the pleasures of lovemaking. Man would never do the same.[22]

4
Cruelty, Compassion, and Maternity

Cruelty

It is sad but true: among brutes, savages, and primitive people, the female is more cruel than compassionate, although she is not as cruel as the male.

Spencer writes of the savage woman: "In countries where it is the custom to torture enemies, women surpass men in cruelty. We have read of the atrocities committed by the two Dayake queens, of whom Rayah Brook has given us an account, and of the barbaric acts attributed by Winwood Reade to a queen of Africa. Women are as savage as men; if they do less harm, that is due to their powerlessness" (*Principes de sociologie*, II, p. 361).

Revenge

Woman reveals herself in revenge, a feeling that, as we will see in the section on The Moral Sense, is more developed in her than in man. She pours torments on her victim drop by drop and at great length, sometimes while joking. Moreover, due to her more impulsive nature, woman's vengeful reactions follow stimuli more rapidly than do those of men and thus stand less chance of being reined in by willpower.[23] This makes it dangerous for men to grant women wide powers and the liberty to tell men what to do. Weak creatures are safe from women unless they offend her; if they do offend her and she is able to do whatever she wants, then they will discover themselves in the hands of an inexorable executioner.

Cruelty toward Other Women

Schopenhauer notes women's instinctive and implacable hostility toward one another, the rapidity with which they seize on friendship and then break it. Even

Italian women frequently say that too many skirts in one spot builds up too much heat. It is enough to observe how, when two women who do not know one another meet even briefly, they look one another over from head to foot; in that glance there is almost an instinctive declaration of war. This is one aspect of women's psychology. An explanation for this hostility is not difficult to find when one considers the struggles for beauty, grace, elegance, and affability in which women engage, not only through vanity but also for survival, because for most women the single greatest business of life remains matrimony. This competitiveness is one factor that excites her cruelty; others include impulsiveness, vindictiveness, and contempt for weak creatures placed under her care.

Epidemic Cruelty

During revolutions, women become terribly enraged once they are set in motion. Many of the reported examples of female cruelty concern collective cruelty.[24] Worse than the cold deliberation of a woman is group fury, which multiplies itself, dragging everyone in. In 1789, women's role was one of ferocious revolt (Lombroso e Laschi, *Delitto politico*, p. 229). Women participated in the Paris Commune of 1870 with the greatest of violence. They were the most bloodthirsty heroes in the assassination of priests (which a woman initiated) and in the executions of hostages, surpassing in cruelty men themselves, whom they rebuked for knowing too little about killing. When it came time to shoot a prisoner, one woman gave the command to fire and then finished him off herself at point blank range. Another, after the massacre, lamented that she had failed to tear out one hostage's tongue. As described by Maxime du Camp, "They had but one ambition: to best men by exaggerating their vices. They were cruel: when sent in pursuit of defaulters, they were implacable; when serving as nurses, they gave liquor to the wounded to kill them" (Id., id., pp. 230–231).[25]

Zola, in *Germinal*, starts the strike scene with men; the women come later, distinguishing themselves through obscene ferocity, ripping the penis off the enemy's corpse, and turning it into a flag.[26] In 1799, the women of Naples, impelled by epidemic passion, even sank into cannibalism: they ate the flesh of the republicans, as did the women of Palermo in the 1866 insurrection.

In the intense heat of passion, all the moral restraints that evolution has built up slowly over time dissolve in a flash, like a fine veil in the flame, with even civilized men becoming killers and cannibals. Women, in these extraordinary, transient, atavistic reversions, become the cruelest of the cruel. They tear out the tongue of the corpse, disfigure its manhood, prolong their victims' agony, and demonstrate their thirst for inflicting pain.

Impotent Cruelty

In England under the Restoration, masses of women assisted in the hideous tortures of the Puritans (Taine, *Litt. angl.*, 111). These were acts of impotent cruelty, a type that gives pleasure without any expenditure of energy. Like all human activities in which a power outside the individual produces pleasure, so, too, ferocious or cruel activities can cause delight, the delight of blood intoxication. Today the long habits of civilization distance us from the joys of slaughter and torture—although they do not entirely eliminate the thrills of bullfights and gallows, before which modern man experiences a shadow of the pleasure that his ancestors tasted while wallowing in blood and slaughter. Ours is but a pallid shadow of that pleasure, to be sure, but on the other hand, it requires no expenditure of energy.

Compassion

To this series of facts one can oppose another, totally contradictory series, showing women to be more compassionate than men. Female compassion occurs in the animal world as well.

Compassion of Woman among Civilized Peoples

With Christianity begins the heroic period of womanly pity. Christianity certainly did not create woman's compassion, as some claim, since compassion was a slow, evolutionary formation; but Christianity unleashed it, put it in motion, brought it to life.

"Women," writes Legouvé,[27] "inserted themselves into Christianity like a moving battalion dedicated to charity. Under the apostles they maintained a position of solicitude and vigilance—a maternal position. At the time of the martyrs, women remained modest, even though equal in courage to men" (*Histoire morale des femmes*, p. 289).

Private charity in Paris, be it religious or lay, was almost always the domain of women. Usually it was a man who conceived of a great charitable institution, designed it, proposed it, and victoriously brought it into being; but then came the women who, acting as his hands, delicately and tirelessly ministered to the world's ills. The chief heads of the Christian church—Saint Frances of Assisi, St. Francis of Sales, Louis of Soubyran—organized women's great charitable associations.

In America, women's intervention in polling places has mitigated the violence of electoral customs. Judge Kingmann of Laramie City, in the territory of Wyoming, writes in the December 1872 issue of Chicago's *Women's Journal*: "In the four years since women obtained the right to vote and be elected to public office, they have indeed voted and participated, especially as jurors; and it cannot be denied that their participation has had a beneficent influence. Elections are carried out with great calm and order, and our courts are now able to punish crimes which previously went unpunished. For example, it used to be that there was almost no one who did not carry a revolver and use it with the slightest provocation. No male jury had ever convicted someone of pulling a gun. But with two or three women on them, juries now convict according to the judges' instructions."

Compassion and the Sense of Justice

Spencer has already noted how women's strong sympathy for the weak and their deficient sense of abstract justice makes them compassionate rather than fair. As a matter of fact, it seems that woman undermines the struggle for existence by softening the harshness of battle and deflecting men from violence, even though violence may be the shortest road to victory.[28]

Harsh sentences, even for the most despicable criminals, cause a woman to feel pity. She forgets the crime and sees only the future pain to which the criminal must submit. Compassion for the person in prison or sentenced to hard labor overcomes her horror of homicide. In the struggle between power and guilt, woman plays the role of mediator. Even the wolf—according to a German saying—seeks shelter near a woman, for she will let him live out of affection. Clemency petitions for those sentenced to die are almost always signed by women.

Cruelty, Maternity, and Compassion

How can these contradictory series of facts about woman's cruelty and her compassion be reconciled?

Cruelty, Weakness, and Dullness of Feeling

If one goes back over reports of female cruelty, one can detect a common element, whether they be about epidemics or individuals, the demoniacal atrocities of certain queens and criminals, or the smaller vulgarities of spitefulness and daily persecutions. That common element is woman's tendency to inflict the largest possible amount of pain—not to obliterate her enemy but to martyr him slowly and paralyze him with suffering.

Woman's cruelty and her reactions to life's trials stem from her weakness. Because she is unable to destroy her enemies, woman torments them, pricking them with needles of pain and immobilizing them with misery. Cruelty, like cunning, is a product of woman's adaptation to the conditions of life. And thus she acquired and developed her ability to torment. In sum, cruelty is a type of defensive as well as offensive reaction in woman.

Woman's cruelty is the daughter not only of weakness but also of insensitivity to pain, since one inflicts pain more easily the less one feels it personally. This explains why woman, on the rare occasions when she succeeds in committing a crime, clings more tenaciously to evil than man.

Maternity

The two contradictory and yet often simultaneous phenomena of cruelty and compassion are linked by an intermediary factor: maternity.

From the first appearance of sexual differentiation through the most elevated creature in the animal scale, the female is superior to the male in the great altruistic activity of maternity. There are a few exceptions in which the male helps raise the offspring, but his role is minor, as in the case of many birds (Richet) and the ostrich (Darwin). But most often (and this includes many mammals) the father abandons the offspring or is even hostile to them, as happens among turkeys and guinea pigs. The same law pertains in the human world; parental feeling is only a belated phenomenon of civilization, as the very ancient institution of matriarchy demonstrates.[29]

Sexuality and maternity are incompatible. The females of certain bird species refuse to mate after the second brood (Brehm). Female ruminants flee their mates after they are impregnated, and the same occurs with female dogs (Joveau de Courmelles, *Les facultés mentales des animaux*, Paris, 1891). In women as well, according to Icard, sexual desire fades almost entirely during pregnancy (Icard, *La femme pendant la période menstruelle*, Paris, 1890). But the reverse is also true: The sexual excitement of the mating period makes loving mothers turn wicked. When cows and cats are in heat, they scratch offspring whom they ordinarily caress.

Although there exists this antagonism between strong sexuality and maternity, maternity nonetheless seems to have a sexual basis, at least in humans, since nursing women often experience sexual arousal. There are even cases in which women become pregnant in order to experience the sensual pleasure of nursing (Icard, op. cit., p. 17). This pleasure may originate in the great responsiveness between the uterus and breast.

Maternity is therefore the characteristic function of the female and of the woman. From it derives nearly all of her organic and psychic variability. It is an eminently altruistic function.

Compassion

Compassion originated in maternal love. Weakness in all its forms is the chief inspiration for compassion. Children, the poor, the aged, the sick, derelicts, prisoners, those condemned to die, animals incapable of defending themselves—all are weak creatures who beg for compassion, and women pity them. Since the origins of human life, woman has played a particularly important role in protecting the weak: that of mothering. Man, on the other hand—tossed into the midst of the struggle for existence—has had the role of destroying the weak and favoring the strong.[30] For woman, each sight of weakness revives those tender sentiments aroused by her infant; this makes compassion a descendant of the maternal impulse. And in fact, if one observes woman in her acts of compassion and charity, one catches glimpses of the attitude, the gestures, the profile of the mother.

In women, compassion is linked to a spirit of abnegation, a desire for sacrifice. The origin of this feeling is difficult to explain. Woman abandons herself not only in charity but also in love. The love of the woman for man is a form of self-sacrificing devotion.

A slave at man's mercy in almost every race on earth, woman is weak and incapable of rebellion. She must have searched for ways to mollify and sweeten the brutish male with her devotion, gentleness, and fine manners; she would have tried to flood the man with tenderness in the hope that a small part of it might flow back to her.

Little by little perhaps these strategies became fixed, transmitted hereditarily and reinforced through continual exercise, to the point that woman used them even when she knew she would receive no recompense. It seems certain that at the bottom of all her self-abnegation lay, more or less clearly, her desire to trade it for tenderness and love. Thus in the pleasure a compassionate woman takes in doing good there are very likely even a few faint genital sensations.

In woman the spirit of abnegation and sacrifice can therefore be born out of both maternity and her weakness relative to man. Their origin and ultimate foundation lie in her desire for a little tenderness in return.

Morbid Compassion/Hysterical Altruism

In some women generosity is a by-product of hysterical excitement. In these cases an excitement of the psychic centers of the cortex, provoked by hysteria, expresses itself in a spirit of abnegation and sacrifice. Epilepsy sometimes produces the same effect in men; but more often in them epileptic excitation of the cortex gives rise to genius or criminality. Hysteria, the twin of epilepsy, sometimes gives birth to crime in woman, but never to genius. One might say that altruism in women is the equivalent of genius in men.[31]

Synthesis

To one who asks whether woman is compassionate or cruel, we would answer that in her compassion and cruelty coexist. Her weakness makes her cruel and compassionate at the same time. It makes her cruel because cruelty is the only offensive and defensive weapon that a weak being can use against one that is stronger. Other factors to consider here are woman's lesser sensibility, greater impulsivity, and lesser degree of control over wicked impulses. On the other hand, weakness makes woman compassionate because it forces her to use gentleness to win the affection of the stronger. Moreover, as Bain has observed, feelings of affection and tenderness cannot coexist with great physical or mental activity. In addition, weakness has kept woman away from weapons, from cannibalism, and from the alcoholic drinks that man reserves for himself through force.

But since weakness is a source of great impulsiveness, woman exists almost in a state of permanent instability. A single individual in a single day can easily pass from one extreme to another, reacting cruelly against that which seems threatening, compassionately toward that which seems weak.

As evolution progresses, such instability seems to abate and pity to overtake cruelty. The savage woman is more cruel than compassionate; vindictive, oppressed, and relatively strong, she has the motive and means, from time to time, to discharge her hatred in cruelty. The civilized woman, in contrast, becomes progressively compassionate. A host of factors contribute to this development, first among them the steady diminution of her strength. If the savage woman is less strong than man, the civilized woman is certainly less strong than the savage woman.[32] The savage woman is sometimes a warrior, and she often takes an indirect part in war, doing heavy agricultural work that otherwise would fall to men. Today progressive weakening has distanced woman completely from war and attenuated her cruelty because, although cruelty is the means of defense and offense of a weak being against the stronger, it requires a notable development of muscular strength, at least in its most ferocious manifestations.

Thus we see that in normal women cruelty is mainly moral (slander, spitefulness, derision, and so on, and so on) and that criminals are often stronger than normal women.[33] The longer the exercise of maternity, the greater the growth of family feelings. The increase in sedentary life has resulted in a slow accretion of piety which, although rare among savages, can lead among civilized groups to the establishment of great charitable institutions.

Add to that the fact that natural selection and sexual selection are intensifying.[34] While the wicked tendencies of men are not effectively repressed until the rise of well-organized governments, those of women are repressed much earlier by tyrannical men who, in most primitive societies, are free to kill women when it suits them. Naturally, in populations in which death is meted out for trifles, the most perverse women have been by and large eliminated.[35]

And sexual selection, as soon as primitive barbarism begins to diminish, gives preference not to the stronger women, but to the more charming and mild-mannered, honoring grace and the moral endowments that accompany it.[36] Thus women have worked to perfect in themselves courtesy and the other gentle arts; simultaneously, they have distanced themselves from the arts of strength and cruelty.

Today, the wicked man looks for a temperate woman and the depraved person seeks virtue. Evil men scout out wicked women to be not wives but only accomplices in crime. Because cruelty in women is becoming a disadvantage and compassion an attraction, women repress their wicked impulses and simulate compassion, as one sees all too frequently today in the hypocrites who behave charitably in order to seduce a man. On the other hand, the union of two born criminals produces not a normal couple but a band of brigands, and this is what families were probably like in ancient times.[37]

Cruelty, in sum, tends increasingly to become an exception and compassion to become a normal condition in women. Nevertheless, in every woman there remains a substratum of cruelty which erupts either when she has a wicked character or when she is assailed in her most intense feelings, those of the wife and mother. There is a proverb that says when someone touches her son, the mother becomes a tiger.

The psychological state of woman regarding cruelty and compassion is a contradiction that evolution will resolve in favor of grace and pity. This is to be expected, because in the realm of psychology, and especially that of the feelings, contradiction is the rule, not the exception. As Ardigò said, man is not a logical being. Humans are essentially contradictory, and only the rare superior person is true to himself and consistent in his acts and feelings.

5
Love

Love among Animal Species

According to Darwin, in nearly all species males have stronger sexual desire than females. Male mammals and some male birds pursue females, although often male birds do not so much chase the female as display their plumage, strike unusual poses, and produce unusual songs. Among the few fish that scientists have been able to study, and in alligators and batrachians, it seems that the males are more active than the females. In all classes of insects, the rule is for the male to follow the female's trail. Among spiders and crustaceans, males are usually more active and exploratory than females. Among insects and crustaceans, when organs of the sense of movement are present in one sex but not the other, or when (as is frequently the case) they are better developed in one sex than in the other, it is almost always the male who possesses those organs or in whom they are better developed. This shows that the male is more active in courtship. On the other hand, females—as Hunter observed—generally have a need to be courted and often try to flee from the male for a long period of time (Darwin, *Origine dell'uomo*, p. 197). As we showed previously, the explanation for this female behavior lies in the greater importance and more complicated function of the ovules compared to sperm.

In the lower animal orders, where the female is more powerful than the male, love is nonexistent. The female subordinates sexuality to maternity by getting rid of the male as soon as she has been impregnated. After mating, the female spider devours the male if he has not already fled. Only when the male becomes more powerful, forcing the female to submit to his domination and more ardent sexual demands, does love become linked to reproduction and maternity.

Love is found among birds, the first creatures on the animal scale to have durable relationships; and this love is stronger in males than females. When his mate is nesting, the male singing parakeet devotes himself to her, ignoring other females, zealously attentive, ardently affectionate. He brings her food, and when he enters the nest he sings his most joyful tunes (Brehm, op. cit., p. 102).[38] The male crossbill completely takes over his mate's work while she is hatching the eggs (Brehm, op. cit., p. 115). Among linnets, only the males become jealous (Brehm, op. cit., p. 103). The same is true of finches. In mating season, the male greenfinch will fly upward, singing continuously and touching his wing tips together, while the female remains calm (Brehm, op. cit., p. 193).[39]

In birds, sexuality and maternity are at odds, an antagonism that in the lower zoological orders is always resolved in favor of maternity. For example, a male canary will sometimes break the eggs because the female, preoccupied with nesting, ignores his sexual advances. This is explained by the male's stronger reproductive drive, which heightens the pleasure of intercourse and the intensity of his love for the female. The female's love is less intense because her reproductive sense is duller and because, even among birds, maternity is an important source of satisfaction.

Mammals

Love among mammals is much less rich and colorful than among birds. Mammals' unions last but briefly and are for the most part polygamous. Their unions seldom last past mating and the birth of children.

Sexual love is most developed among animals that live together for an extended period. Male and female guinea pigs cohabit and treat one another with much tenderness, licking and combing each other with their front paws. If one of them goes to sleep, the other stays awake to provide security; but if the first one sleeps too long, the other tries to wake it up with its tongue and paw (Brehm, II, p. 252).

Among rabbits, the male does not leave the female's side so long as she lives with him, and he covers her with caresses. The mother, very tender with her offspring, will every once and a while seek out the male to exchange short caresses (Brehm, II).

Polygamy is widespread among other mammals. Sometimes it is uninterrupted polygamy, as among horses and gorillas, while at others it is transitory, as among lions. Carnivores are all monogamous except the lion, which is sometimes found with one female but at others with two, three, or even five (Darwin, *Origine dell' uomo*, p. 193). In polygamous unions, females are bound to their mates by instinctual devotion. Among llamas (a polygamous animal), the female will rush to her mate when he is wounded or killed and will attack the hunter; but the male llama, if his mate is wounded, abandons her and thoughtlessly runs off with the herd.

Love among the Human Races

To a great extent, the phenomena we have observed in embryonic form among female animals are repeated in woman. Earlier, in discussing the senses, we demonstrated how in all types of sensitivity woman is inferior to man, most particularly in sexual sensitivity, and thus also in the intensity of love. Sergi confirmed this point for us, and Tennyson has marvelously summarized it in verse: "The passion of man is to that of woman as the heat of the sun is to that of the moon."

A. Dumas heard a high Catholic priest declare that after a month of marriage, 80 percent of new brides confess to being nauseated by sex and claim that had they known what it would be like, they would not have married.[40] Even prostitutes who give themselves to men at an early age find intercourse unpleasant. I have often been consulted by women who complain of being tortured by their husbands' sexual demands. One time, three sisters complained simultaneously.[41] Moreover, it is known that some women remain virgins even after marriage. One never sees anything like this in normal men.

The fact that women dislike sex might seem to be contradicted by the greater volume, number, and complexity of woman's primary and secondary sexual organs (breasts, ovaries, uterus, vagina, etc.) and by the notorious and proverbial fact that love is the most important thing in the female's life.[42] "Love," writes Madame DeStael [*sic*], "although only an episode in the life of man, is everything in the life of woman."[43] Moreover, as anyone can see, the great preoccupation of girls is men, the fiancé, the wedding. But one can reconcile the apparent contradiction by observing that in women, the needs of the individual are outweighed by those of the species and that it is maternity alone which pushes woman toward man. Female love is a function of and subordinate to maternity.

While woman's sexual organs are more complicated and numerous (vulva, uterus, ovaries, etc.), for the most part these are not so much genital as maternal organs, and insofar as the secondary sexual organs (breasts, hips, the Hottentot's "cushion" or overdeveloped bottom, etc.) are different from those of the male, they are involved not in mating but in the nourishment and development of the new being. Psychologically, too, sexual need in woman is subordinate to the needs of the species and maternal love.

Therefore, organically, woman is a mother more than a man's lover. If nonetheless she is sometimes very affectionate and devoted to her husband, it is for other, indirect causes rather than through sexual attraction. Woman looks to man not only out of maternal need but also for support. "It is part of her sexual instinct," write the de Goncourts, "to be dependent. She is happy when she belongs to a man. And through that sweetness of affection that is typically female, she is grateful to man as to a benefactor."[44]

Woman's affection for man is formed above all by instincts that develop through relationships of superiority and inferiority. A French navy official who loved a Tahitian girl complimented her on the beauty of her hands. "Do you like them?" she responded; "then cut them off and take them with you to France." G. Sand wrote that love is voluntary slavery to which women aspire by their nature.[45] Woman may try to please in the sexual act and may give herself to a man toward whom she feels affectionate; but she enjoys not so much sex as man's demonstration that he is her protector.

Many secondary considerations help us understand why woman chooses a sexual partner less for personal reasons than for the needs of the species. A man's choice involves more factors, for he cares about the beauty of his partner's face, the color and quality of her skin, the fullness of her flesh, the gentleness of her voice, her grace of manner, and so on, and so on, while woman cares only for the general shape of the person (so long as it is not faulty) and a few psychological traits. Thus the word *beautiful* has different meanings for the two sexes, and its meaning is less specific for women. A man's attractiveness and intelligence are matters of indifference to most women.

Woman does not appreciate beauty because her sexual sensitivity is weak. Man, with his finer sexual sensibility, enjoys woman through a number of senses (sight, odor, and, above all, touch). Beauty must satisfy all the senses that participate in the sexual act, and that satisfaction is a bit harder to come by for men. Women have fewer criteria. They do like strength in a man, but that is because what women seek is support. "Women who marry strong men," writes Spenser (*Introduzione alla sociologia*, Milano, 1886), "have a greater probability of bearing children. For that reason, women are more likely to attach themselves to strong and brutal men than to weak ones, even though the latter treat them better."

Synthesis

Female love is, essentially, nothing more than a secondary aspect of maternity. All those feelings of affection that bind woman to man are born not of the sexual impulse, but from instincts of subjection and devotion acquired through adaptation.

6
The Moral Sense

Lying

To demonstrate that lying is habitual and almost physiological in woman would be superfluous, since it is confirmed even by popular sayings. The proverbs we refer to are innumerable and turn up in all languages.

- "Tears of women, a fountain of malice" (Tuscany)
- "Women always tell the truth, but they don't tell all of it" (Tuscany)
- "The horse that sweats, the man who swears, the woman who cries: do not believe any of them" (Tuscany)
- "False as a woman" (Rome)

Women have something close to what might be called an instinct for lying. Caught at something unexpectedly, they start concocting a lie (though some do this better than others). Their first move, even when they are not guilty, is to dissimulate. This is so organic that they are unaware of it, and they are never able to be entirely sincere. Unconsciously, all are a little false.

That women lie habitually is confirmed by the common custom of refusing to accept, or to accept much of, women's testimony. This custom grew out of not only primitive man's disdain for woman's weakness but also his experience with her untruthfulness. Woman's incapacity for criminal responsibility was recognized in the laws of ancient Greece and Rome and in the codes of many Germanic peoples. Even today the Ottoman Code (article 355) provides that the deposition of a man should be worth that of two women. And in many languages the words *oath* [*giuramento*] and *testimony* [*testimonianza*] have the same root as *testicle* [*testicolo*].

A sequence of causes contributed to the development of women's ability to lie:

(1) Weakness. The oppressed and servile, having no power, need to use cunning and lies. Openness can be a virtue only of the strong.

(2) Menstruation. When menstruation became an object of disgust for man, woman had to hide it. Today, too, it is the first lie that one teaches girls; we train them to hide their real condition by simulating other illnesses. This means that women must lie for two or three days each month; perhaps we should call it an exercise in periodic dissimulation.

(3) Shame. "The drawback of shame," writes Stendhal, "is that it gets one used to lying."[46] And if *shame* [*pudore*] comes from *putere* [to stink], one can easily see how from earliest times it must have habituated women to lying.[47] Moreover, women are not allowed to reveal any feelings of love. While a man is permitted to tell a woman that he loves her, if a woman tries to let a man know that she is in love with him, she risks her reputation. Defecation and urination, too, having become for women objects of shame, acts which they had to hide, forced them daily into a state of lying.

(4) The sexual struggle. Woman must hide her defects, her age, her illnesses—everything that could harm her in men's eyes. She often needs to pretend to have wealth and comfort that she in fact lacks; often, too, she finds it necessary to hide certain superior qualities that men dislike in female companions, such as intelligence, generosity, and scorn for ludicrous social formalities. Rouge, hair dyes, toiletries: at base these are only lies in action, used by women as ammunition in the sexual battle.

(5) The desire to be interesting. Woman, like the child, is weak and thus has an instinctive need to be protected; in man's protection she finds her pride and joy. As a result, as Mantegazza and various proverbs note, she often feigns sadness. She cries or pretends to be sick to attract the attention and kindness of others; this is the source of the traditional misconception that women are more sensitive than men. One of the most common forms of malice in woman appears when she does not know how to extricate herself from an embarrassing situation: She pretends to faint. In hysterics, woman's natural need for protection becomes morbid, giving rise to strange and often inexcusable artifices.[48]

(6) Suggestibility. Women are extremely suggestible, overresponding to the ideas of others and even themselves. They easily accept the reality of things about which they are told or which they themselves invent. What is more, they experience things inexactly. Because they grasp the truth with less intensity than men, women are able to let go of it easily.

(7) The duties of maternity. Maternity obliges women to dissimulate be-

cause child raising depends on a series of clever or stupid lies designed to hide information about sex, to camouflage mothers' own ignorance of things, to guide children on the paths of morality through fear of God and the devil, and so on.

Woman is, in conclusion, a great child, and children are liars par excellence. It is all the easier for women to lie in that they have more reasons for lying than we do.

Vanity

With the advent of civilization, the vanity of men started to decline while that of women began to grow. The principal means through which women express vanity is clothing—a fact so well known that there is almost no need to demonstrate it.

In the animal world up through savages, vanity is exclusively or mainly an attribute of males; but with civilization it develops in women while at the same time transforming itself into ambition in men. Vanity is the instinctive tendency—acquired through heredity because it is advantageous and developed above all in social life—of showing off those qualities that are useful in the struggle for life and sexual partners.

The savage is vain about the trophies of the hunt and war and about simple ornaments. For him, small changes of face or person comprise aesthetic pleasure, constituting a sign of superiority. Savage woman was not yet (or was less) vain. So long as she was man's slave and not yet involved in the sexual competition for men, she had no need to put herself forward. She was like the peahen, which lacks fancy tail feathers and is sought out by the male. She had no need to turn cartwheels.

With evolution and social experience, vanity disappears from the man. Woman, as she evolves, acquires the trait of vanity, the sexual struggle now requiring that she put her attractions on display. This impulse is egotistical, as in savages, and involves the same defect of intelligence. Thus at festivals every woman hopes that every man will be interested only in her. Female vanity expresses itself specifically in clothing because modesty constrains women to cover the entire body, except for the hands and face (sometimes it calls for the face to be covered too). Clothing becomes even more important than corporeal beauty.

Vanity explains a sex difference noted by Lotze:[g] While men want to be known for their virtue—a trait recognized by all and considered superior by the entire group—women are happy to stand out for any reason at all, even the most point-

g. Lotze, *Microcosmus: Ideen zur Naturgeschichte und Geschichte der Menschheit*. Leipzig, 1869.

less. Whatever calls attention to their person, so long as it does them no harm, is instinctively desirable to women as a weapon in the sexual struggle. Woman's vanity is not an atavistic trait; rather, it is produced through evolution. It demonstrates that woman goes through the same stages of development as man, although at a slower rate.[49]

Synthesis

In sum, in women, as in children, the moral sense is inferior. Some would say that in a commercial period such as ours, honor, loyalty, and the like are losing their worth for men, and that false stock market tips fabricated by businessmen are as bad as anonymous rumors fabricated by ladies. We would respond that there is as much difference between one and the other as between a soldier who kills an enemy who threatens him and a soldier who kills an unarmed prisoner who happens to offend him. The dishonesty of a banker is a necessity occasioned by the commercial struggle—if he does not set a trap for his rival today, he will fall in it himself tomorrow. It is relatively normal behavior because it is adapted to the conditions, however transitory, of life. On the other hand, the vengeful fury directed by a lady against a rival who is better dressed at a celebration is immoral because it flows from her own excessive egoism and is aimed at someone who is merely exercising a right.

Here we find ourselves led back to the psychology of primitive man, who is happy if the smearings on his face attract the attention of his companions, and who is so vindictive that for him revenge constitutes a religious duty. We are also back to the psychology of the child who, when a favor is given to a companion but not to him, cries as if his rights had been violated.

That which differentiates woman from the child is maternity and compassion; thanks to these, she has no fondness for evil for evil's sake (unlike the child, who will torture animals, and so on). Instead—as we demonstrated in the section on cruelty—she develops a taste for evil only under exceptional circumstances, as for example when she is impelled by an outside force or has a perverse character.

But woman is always fundamentally immoral, and oftentimes her immorality is even a by-product of her compassion. We do not hesitate to deem immoral (even while we are touched by its signs of the dawning of civilization) the warnings savage women gave to European travelers to stay on guard against the plots of their husbands and brothers, because these were contrary to the interests of their social group. Similarly, we deem it immoral for criminal women to denounce their own accomplices, for by turning in their companions, they, too, demonstrate an inability to adapt to social life, albeit a life of crime.

Normal woman has many characteristics that bring her close to the level of the savage, the child, and therefore the criminal (anger, revenge, jealousy, and vanity) and others, diametrically opposed, which neutralize the former. Yet her positive traits hinder her from rising to the level of man, whose behavior balances rights and duties, egotism and altruism, and represents the peak of moral evolution.[50]

7
Intelligence

Female Intelligence in the Zoological World

In the lower orders, it is impossible to determine with exactitude which of the two sexes is more intelligent. However, one might suppose that in those crustacean and insect orders in which the male has superior powers of movement and sensation, his intelligence must be superior. Because he inhabits a more extensive and complex environment, his internal organization must also be more complex and extensive.

In the higher orders, among the few facts that reveal intellectual differences between the sexes, the first is favorable to the female. This concerns the *Hymenoptera*, in which only females are true members of the group, while the males are merely parasites. However, the former are not females in the true sense of the word, but rather constitute a third sex since their genital organs are atrophied.

Among birds one sometimes finds superiority in the male. In species of singing birds it is always the male that sings; and song is in many of them a true sign of intellect, an art that they practice and perfect.

In all those species in which a male assembles groups of females and leads them (seals, ruminants, monkeys), he undoubtedly has a superior intellect. Otherwise, his predominance would have no basis and would not last.

Intelligence in Women

Compared to male intelligence, female intelligence is deficient primarily in creative power.

Genius

This deficiency reveals itself immediately in the absence of female geniuses. There is no lack of names of illustrious women: in poetry, Sappho, Corinna, Telesilla, Browning, David John, Gauthier, Ackermann; in literature, Eliot, Sand, Stern, DeStael [*sic*]; in art, Bonheur, Lebrun, Maraino, Sirani; in science, Sommerville, Royer, Tarnowsky, Germain. Yet it is clear that we are far from the greatness of male geniuses such as Shakespeare, Balzac, Aristotle, Newton, Michelangelo. With respect to the frequency of geniuses in the two sexes, the man's superiority is widely recognized as immense.

Some, such as Sagnol,[h] attribute this inferiority to social conditions, especially to enforced ignorance in which woman is held and her lack of opportunity for intellectual labor. But women's ignorance is not in fact as general as some think. In the 1500s in Italy and in the first century of the Roman Empire, upper-class women received the same education as men; and in the French aristocracy of the last century, women were well educated and attended lectures by Lavoisier, Cuvier, and so on, and so on. Yet even under these favorable conditions no genius appeared. As for environmental difficulties, these did not impede Browning or Sommerville from emerging; and they are by no means as large as those that an impoverished male genius encounters. Yet from males of the lower classes geniuses emerge more often than from women, even women of the wealthy classes.

Moreover, as I have already demonstrated,[51] women of genius frequently have masculine appearances. Female genius can be explained as Darwin explained the coloration of certain female birds that resemble the males of their species: by a confusion of secondary sexual characteristics produced by a mismatch of paternal and maternal heredity. One need only look at pictures of women of genius of our day to realize that they seem to be men in disguise.

Lack of Originality/Monotony

While woman is barred from creating great things by her lack of genius, she is also less adapted than man to the minor productions at which average men succeed. This is due to her lack of originality, which is overdeveloped in the man of genius and found in more modest proportions in the average man. In fact, women have no particular talent for any art, science, or profession. They write, paint, embroider, sing; they move from dressmaking to millinery to being florists, good at everything and at nothing; but only rarely do they carry the stamp of true origi-

h. Sagnol, *L'égalité des sexes*. Paris, 1880.

3 European and American women of genius. *Source*: Lombroso, *La donna delinquente*, 1893. *Editors' note*: According to Lombroso, women of genius have masculine characteristics.

nality in any branch of work. This is the effect of a lesser differentiation in their brain functioning.

Automatic Types of Intelligence

Woman's lack of creative power is definitively demonstrated by the distinctly automatic nature of her most typical form of intelligence. This is her intuition, which is specifically adapted to discovering the feelings and thoughts of people. "Women," writes Spencer, "have another ability that is susceptible to cultivation and development: that of quickly perceiving the mental state of the people who surround them. Generally this particular gift consists of a true intuition which is not based on any specific logic" (op. cit.).[52] Intuition is psychological and a type of instinct; it also appears, though less strongly, in children and in animals such as the dog. It calls up from the well of hereditary unconsciousness images that are pleasing or repulsive according to their associations with the experiences of her ancestors.

Logical Sentiments

All this demonstrates that female intelligence is deficient in creative power. This phenomenon can be clarified by studying what Wundt calls the logical sentiments: those which accompany the processes of thinking and knowing, agreement and contradiction.[53]

The criterion for truth is different in women and men. Because women are more suggestible, they often believe things simply through their own suggestion or that of others, and thus they have little need to see and touch before believing. From this follows their quickness to believe in miracles and their openness to religious proselytizing.

In the American West, women were admitted to juries, but the law allowing this had to be abrogated since the jurors judged on the basis of feeling rather than evidence (A. Barine, *Revue des Deux Mondes*, giugno 1883).[54]

In girls' boarding schools intellectual tasks that are too demanding and abstract produce amenorrhea, hysteria, and nervousness (Dujardin-Beaumetz). "Women in general," writes Lafitte, "seem more struck by facts than by rules and more by specific ideas than by general concepts. A book by a woman, even by DeStael [*sic*] or Eliot,[55] will always be more beautiful in its details than its totality. The female intelligence is concrete, that of man abstract."[i]

i. Paul Lafitte, *Le paradoxe de l'égalité*. Paris, 1887.

This explains why women have acquired fame as travel writers and students of manners, topics for which the first requirement is to give specific and telling details; we see this in the works of Pfeiffer, DeStael [*sic*], Montaigue, Madame Adam, and so on, and so on. It is a sign of inferiority because abstraction is the highest grade of mental development. Animals, as Romanes observes, think in images.[56]

Diligence

Woman has more patience than man, as the types of work in which she engages demonstrates. Since the dawn of civilization weaving has been almost exclusively (except in Egypt) women's work; and it is well known how much patience weaving required before the invention of the automated loom. Work with pearls and diamonds, as well as the manufacture of certain musical and surgical instruments which require a great deal of patience and delicacy, is completely in the hands of women (A. Kuliscioff, *Il monopolio dell'uomo*, Milano, 1890).[57] Lace making and embroidery, highly painstaking forms of work, have become symbols of femininity. Only women are employed in the production of lace and in the French Gobelins tapestry factory.

That women are more patient explains their great numbers in modern industry, where we now have machines that require little from their operators in terms of muscular strength but rather continuous surveillance and patience. For the same reason women often do better than men in factory work; where work is piecework, the wife and daughters often carry home more earnings than the father and brothers (Kuliscioff, op. cit.). The professions in which woman does better than man are also those that require great patience, for example, elementary school teaching, for which women have been found preferable to men in Milan, England, and America.

Savage women manifest this same superiority in patience, sometimes even more clearly.

These observations might seem to contradict Darwin, who claims that men have more patience than women. But women's patience is an effect of her lesser sensibility and lower degree of cortical excitability, which lower her need for stimulation. Hers is not the type of patience that flows from great potency in the inhibitory centers, a power that enabled Darwin, for example, to spend years accumulating proofs for his miraculous discovery. In this respect man is superior. In fact, Vogt observed that his female students were attentive in class but highly incompetent at homework. Man has perseverance, woman has patience; and her patience is more that of the camel than of the man of genius.

Causes

It is indisputable that the inferior development of women's intelligence is partially caused by the physical inertia that men have imposed on her. But it would be an error to label this a man-made cause because the inferiority is also natural and because it reflects a general tendency among all animals on the evolutionary scale for males to participate more fully in the struggle for existence. It is mainly the male that fights to defend the species. Furthermore, he must fight other males to conquer the female, even more in the human than the animal world, because the variable of female choice has been almost eliminated. He is now free to select a woman as long as he has absolutely subdued his rivals. Among animals, on the other hand, it sometimes happens that while two males fight, the female flees with a third male who is weaker but more agreeable.

It is not so much work itself as the need to surpass rivals in the same activity that has developed the intelligence of man. This is demonstrated by the fact that among many savages, it is the woman who works (pitching tents, weaving, and so on) while the man fights wars and hunts. Yet that does not make the woman more intelligent.

And to the explanations for men's intellectual superiority one must add another natural cause—the way men continually change their types of activities and life circumstances. Rarely does the son enter the same profession and under the same conditions as the father. On the other hand, the woman must devote a precious part of her time to the duties of motherhood, which are always the same and therefore do not awaken and nurture the intelligence as does the constant mobility of men. In antiquity as at the present time, most of those who emigrate are men.

Underlying all these other causes is a biological one that serves as the foundation. The intelligence of the male, like his organic structure, has a primitive potentiality greater than that of the female thanks to his lesser role in the reproduction of the species. As I have demonstrated, intelligence varies inversely to fecundity in the entire animal kingdom; there is an antagonism between the reproductive and intellectual functions. Today, the work of reproduction has for the most part devolved onto the woman, and for this biological reason she has been left behind in intellectual development.

In fact, certain female bees, termites, and ants have acquired a superiority of intelligence over other females of the species by giving up sex. The queen, in contrast, is fecund and stupid. Moreover, as savages step by step become civilized, their females grow less fecund. Women of high intelligence, as Wirey noted, are often sterile.

It is amazing, then, that woman is not even less intelligent than she is. One can explain this only by agreeing with Darwin that a part of the male's acquired intelligence must be transmitted to women. Otherwise, the gap would be even greater.

Certainly greater participation in the collective life of society would raise woman's intelligence. In fact, such participation is already the case in the most evolved races, as in England and North America, where most literary and artistic journalism is now entrusted solely to women.

Part II

Female Criminology

8

Crime in the Animal World[a]

Crimes of Passion/Mad Frenzy

Among a species of ants, *Formica rufibarbis*, it often happens that female warrior ants go into a veritable frenzy, biting blindly into everything around them—larvae, companions, and the slave ants who try to calm them by holding them firmly until the fit passes. Leuret tells of an ant that, irritated by the resistance of an aphid, killed and devoured it. In the very hot months, female workers of the brown field ants, grown weary and hungry, sometimes grab another ant's leg and try to drag it out of the nest; in their irritation they sometimes crush the other ant's head with their mandibles and squeeze it to death. This would be a minor crime for an ant, analogous to the killing of a slave by a Roman matron, if it did not damage the species and fly in the face of usual practices. Thus it constitutes a crime in the jurisprudence of ants.

About 2 P.M. on 4 August 1833, a woman led a cow to Montmartre. Suddenly seized by a mad frenzy, the cow threw herself around, wounding and killing a great number of people and upsetting everything to the right and left until it was felled by a gunshot (Pierquin, vol. II, p. 505). Frequently, this kind of frenzy is caused by the animal's going into heat. Cornevin tells of a usually gentle mare which became unmanageable during the rutting period and almost broke his arm. Huzard Jr. mentions a mare that had uterine frenzies only occasionally; quiet at

a. Brehm, *La vita degli animali*. Torino, 1872–1875. Pierquin, *Traité de la folie des animaux et de ses rapports avec celle de l'homme et des legislations actuelles*. Paris, 1839. Houzeau, *Études sur les facultés mentales des animaux comparées à celles de l'homme*. Mons, 1872. Lacassagne, *De la criminalité chez les animaux. Revue scientifique*, 1882. Büchner, *Vie psichique des bêtes*. Paris, 1881. Romanes, *L'intelligence des animaux*. Paris, 1886.

other times, she sometimes became unmanageable for two or three days when in heat.

Banditry and Robbery

In his work on *Vita psichica delle bestie*, Büchner speaks of thievish bees that, to avoid working, assail well-stocked hives in mass, making an onslaught against the sentinel bees and other inhabitants and taking their provisions. After repeating this exploit, sometimes without success, they acquire a taste for pillage and violence. Then, as in countries plagued by brigandage, they recruit ever larger numbers.[1] They end up establishing new colonies of bandit bees.

Cannibalism

Ants will torment the dead bodies of their enemies and suck their blood (Lacassagne, *De la criminalité chez les animaux*; *Revue scientifique*, 1882). More often, cannibalism is linked to infanticide (see below).

Envy, Malevolence

A special type of criminality among females, particularly in the higher animals, is hatred for individuals of their own sex. Envious of her companions, the dove will hide food that she herself does not need under her wing. Among the anthropomorphic monkeys, particularly orangutans, females treat one another with an instinctive animosity, beating and sometimes even killing one another (Houzeau, II).

Sexual Aberrations

In herds where there are no bulls, cows will find a substitute bull among their own kind. Similarly, in large hen houses where males are rare, one chicken will often take on the cock's role (Scarcey). Such aberrations are particularly common among geese, ducks, and pheasants; as they grow old, these birds assume a number of masculine characteristics, including plumage (*Arch. psich.*, X, p. 561).

Alcoholism

Ants narcoticized with chloroform and paralyzed entirely except for their jaws will chew on whatever falls in front of them. Büchner observed that thievish bees can be produced artificially by means of a brew of honey and liquor. Such bees develop a taste for this drink, which has exactly the same pernicious influence that liquor has on humans. They get excited, drunk, and stop working. And if they get hungry? Like humans, they take up another vice, plundering and stealing. Among cows, a mixture of cannabis and opium causes homicidal madness.

Sex Crimes

According to Brehm, female adultery is not rare among birds and certainly occurs more frequently than among male birds, which content themselves with the female they have found, blinded to others by their ardor. Certain female pigeons simply abandon their mate when he is weak or wounded (Darwin). Carl Vogt tells how for several years a stork couple nested in a village near Soletta. One day people noted that when the male left to hunt, another, younger male came to court the female. He was first rejected, then tolerated, then welcomed, and in the end the two adulterers flew over the grassland where the husband was hunting frogs and killed him with their beaks (Figuier, *Les oiseaux*, 1877).

Crimes of Maternity

Some female cows, horses, and dogs are indifferent to the loss of their offspring, while others regularly abandon them (Lacassagne, id.). A hen abandoned several sickly and malformed chicks, going off with the healthy ones. Mares, especially those that have recently given birth for the first time, will obstinately refuse to nurse a newborn (*Archivio d'antropologia*, ecc., diretto da Mantegazza, XI, p. 439).

Infanticide is almost the rule in some species. Sexual jealousy drove a dove to kill her offspring with pecks of her beak (*Arch. psich.*, XIV, fasc. I). Infanticide can also be coupled with cannibalism. A predatory female goshawk had already raised several broods when she was shut up in a cage; although well nourished, she was unable to feed on freshly killed meat and thus devoured her own offspring (Brehm). The female crocodile, too, will sometimes devour her offspring, and the female mouse will eat her entire family if her nest is disturbed.

Infanticidal tendencies are frequently paired with a violent eroticism and manifested during the rutting period. An excessively fecund and nymphomaniacal Angora cat loved her little ones to a frenzy; but whenever she became pregnant, she took an aversion to them, hitting and biting them as they romped around her. Burdach and Marc compared the frequency of unmotivated infanticide among women who had recently given birth to the homicidal tendencies observed in nymphomaniacal cows and mares, not only during the rutting period but also much later. Sometimes female dogs, while raising a litter, will become thieves in order to steal food for their offspring. Among some species we find abduction of minors. Sterile mares and even mules kidnap colts, with the mules then abandoning the young ones to die of hunger. A female dog who loathed sexual relations with male dogs but could not bear the results of this voluntary sterility, stole little ones from others (Lacassagne, id.).

Summary

In general, as Lacassagne notes (op. cit.), females of the zoological world are less criminalistic than males.[2] In only a few species, such as ants and bees, do we find females with as well-developed criminal tendencies as males; but it is in precisely those species that the female also has strong intelligence, thus constituting almost a third sex.[3] It is only among pseudo-female *Hymenoptera* that one finds species organized for theft (*halictus*).[4] These are like born criminals. Formerly an honest and sociable species, through theft they developed new organs for taking things while at the same time losing the organs for work, such as organs for collecting pollen.

9

Crimes of Savage and Primitive Women[b]

Taboo

Among savage and primitive peoples, woman was governed by a series of prohibitions, some bizarre and apparently irrational, others based on male egotism, violation of which was considered a crime. Many of these prohibitions belonged to the *taboos* of the Oceanic peoples. In Tahiti, women were forbidden to touch men's weapons or fishing equipment; to enter spaces reserved for males; to touch the head of a husband or father, or objects that came into contact with those heads; and to eat with men (Radiguet, *Derniers sauvages*). Among the Hebrews, woman was prohibited from dressing like a man or touching male genitals.

One lengthy set of prohibitions pertained to menstruation. The Zend-Avesta considered a menstruation longer than nine days to be the work of a malign spirit; to get rid of the demon, they beat the women until bloody. Moreau of Sarthe asserts that Negroes, American indigenous people, and South Sea Islanders isolate their women in a hut for the entire menstrual period.

Adultery

An extremely serious crime for savage women was adultery. Yet in all savage populations, irregularities in the conduct of married women were considered violations not of chastity but property, like using a horse without the owner's permis-

b. Létourneau, *La sociologie d'après l'ethnographie*. Paris, 1884. Id., *L'évolution de la morale*. Paris, 1888. Giraud-Telon, *Les origines de la famille*. Hovelaque, *Les débuts de l'humanité*. Paris, 1881. Bertillon, *Les races sauvages*. Paris, 1882. Lubbock, *I tempi preistorici e le origini della civiltà*. Torino, 1875. Rudesindo Salvado, *Memorie storiche sull'Australia*. Roma, 1851. Ploss, *Das Weib in Natur, und Völkerkunde*. Leipzig, 1891. Richet, *L'homme et l'intelligence*. Paris, 1884. Icard, *La femme pendant la période menstruelle*. Paris, 1890. Dufour, *Hist. de la prostitution*, 1860. Lombroso, *Uomo delinquente*, vol. 1, IV ediz.

sion. The same man who would kill his wife for adultery might lend her to another man without difficulty. Tasmanians and the Australian peoples lent, rented, and even gave their wives to others while punishing these same women severely if they gave themselves without permission.

Moses declared that adultery should be punished with death. As for rape, it was punished with death only in cases when the girl was engaged. The girl died with the man who had violated her, at least if the crime had been committed in public, for otherwise she was suspected of not having cried out for help, or of having cried out too feebly.

The ancient Arabs and Bedouins viewed adultery as the most serious of all crimes; among them women who committed adultery were decapitated by their fathers or brothers. On the other hand, after Muhammad the punishment was reduced to one hundred lashes and life imprisonment.

Punishments set by law were (and still are) modified by usage over time. Thus one notes an extraordinary tolerance of adultery, particularly among aristocrats (such as the French and Milanese aristocrats of the eighteenth century).[5] By reviving the role of the ladies' man, they almost institutionalized adultery, just as some savage populations had done earlier. In contrast, even today, although the criminal law has become more lenient, in many cases adultery continues to be punished with death. Public approval of this severity can be seen in the frequency with which juries acquit wife killers.

Prostitution and Procuring

Prostitutes have often been regulated by special laws designed to control their movements—a sign that since ancient times people suspected them of imperfect adaptation to social life and affinity with criminals. Repressive rules flourished in particular after the victory of Christianity. A decree of the Council of Elvira denied communion and even last rites to mothers, relatives, or anyone else who had prostituted girls, and it also excommunicated everyone who had practiced procuration.

Medieval Bordeaux, which distinguished itself by the severity with which it policed morals, seems on several occasions to have drowned habitual prostitutes and pimps, using the practice known as *sinking the ship*. In this punishment, the population pronounced the sentence and carried out the execution. The malefactor, male or female, was shut inside an iron cage, which was then tossed into the sea and not drawn up again until asphyxiation was complete.

In eighteenth-century France, pimping was not tolerated. Procurers, male and female, were whipped and hunted down; they lost all rights, and their property was confiscated. "Sometimes," writes Muyart di Vouglans, "pimps were placed on a donkey, facing the tail, with a straw hat and signboard." Thus attired they were led through the city to be insulted by the mob, then whipped by the hangman, banished, or locked up.

Criminality of Punishments against Women

Sometimes we find examples of judicial savagery, which—like the severe punishments of the past for adultery—have more to do with bloodlust than love of justice. Many barbaric forms of repression were nothing but ferocious human orgies. We might almost call them crimes, although they may have helped to achieve a modicum of justice and honesty. Even today, the masses' pleasure in public executions impedes democratic countries' efforts to abolish these practices. The same holds true of lynching, a form of punishment in which even the dead body is mutilated.

Abortion and Infanticide

Abortion and infanticide were widespread among savage people, as they were among humanity in general. They were caused most often by the need to keep family size in line with resources. Other causes were women's desire to stay beautiful and jealousy. Forbidden to have sexual relations with their husbands while nursing, the Abiponi women of Paraguay would kill a baby rather than see their husbands with another woman (Ploss, *Das Weib*, ecc., Leipzig, 1891). Excessive work, too, induced women to rid themselves of the extra burden that a pregnancy would entail, as happened among the indigenous peoples of the two Americas under Spanish rule. Many Australians, when asked why they killed their children, answered that they wanted to avoid the trouble of raising them (Balestrini, *Aborto, infanticidio ed esposizione d'infante*, Torino, 1888).

According to Tuke, Maori women abort ten to twelve times. In many South American tribes, women let only two babies live, freeing themselves from the others through abortion. Indian women of Cadauba and Macsawa are particularly likely to seek abortions when the pregnancy occurs outside marriage (Smith and Ploss).

Witchcraft and Its Persecution

During the Middle Ages, witchcraft was women's most serious crime. No one doubts that witchcraft and witch-hunting were hysterico-epileptic phenomena. In fact, the main proof of demonic possession lay in the so-called signs of the devil's paw, spots where the suspect's skin could be pricked without her feeling pain or bleeding; evidently the investigators located those desensitized areas so common in hysterics.

There were many more female than male witches. Similarly, hysteria, which is best defined as an exaggeration of femininity, predominates among women. Another characteristic of witchcraft was speaking in foreign tongues. This phenomenon, too, is fairly common among hysterics. In reality, it is nothing more than the transmission of unconscious ideas into the sphere of consciousness.

Joan of Arc, who was burned as a witch, was said to have been able to predict the future. She boasted of having seen an angel and to have been led by him to victory. Most damning of all was the fact that she had never menstruated, as became clear when a midwife examined her.

Fear of witches was based in large part on confessions. Influenced by hallucinations that were mainly sexual in origin, these hysterics admitted to sex with the devil, to having been impregnated by him, and to attending his Sabbath celebrations. From such material the legends formed.

One of the most frequent tests to which these hysterics were forced to submit if they were young was that of their virginity. Investigators believed that if the devil took possession of a young girl, he would automatically violate her. Often the accused would deny being a witch. However, locked in a horrible prison, tortured, questioned incessantly by judges who tried to trick her with suggestions, the accused would finally confess to have attended the witches' Sabbath, describing it in minute detail.

Only with the arrival of scientific skepticism in the eighteenth century did witchcraft persecutions abate. But they did not end entirely until the appearance of Pinel at the start of the nineteenth century.[6]

Poisoning

Poisoning is one of woman's most frequent crimes. Caesar tells us that when a man died, the Gauls would burn all his wives along with him if there was even a suspicion that the death was not natural—an efficient procedure which must have originated in frequent poisonings. In China, the Mi-fu-Kau, a group of witches who knew how to make a man die, had a large clientele of married women (Kataher, *Bilden aus chinesischen Leben*, Leipzig, 1881). Poison is more likely to be sold by women than men in Arabia, where women are experts in lethal substances.

In Rome in the seventeenth century, four women—Maria Spinola, Giovanna De Grandis, Geronima Spana, and Laura Crispiolti—sold a poison (perhaps arsenic) known as Manna di S. Nicola. La Spana was beloved by the aristocracy, especially aristocratic women who had grown tired of their husbands, to whom she supplied the means to commit a great number of crimes (Salomone Marino, *L'acqua Tofana*, Palermo, 1882).

In general, savage women, like female animals, committed fewer crimes than men, although (as we have seen) they were more evil than good. The crimes for which they were punished were mainly conventional, acts that involved witchcraft and the violation of *taboos*. The women's crime that corresponds most closely to men's crime, as we will see, is that of prostitution.

10
The History of Prostitution

Modesty and Prostitution among Savages

Prostitution, like crime, has been a normal fact of life from the dawn of evolution.[7] It still is normal in the life of savages.

Modesty

Nudity is the rule among primitive people. In Australia, men and women go completely naked; when missionaries gave clothing to the indigenous inhabitants, they draped it over their shoulders (Rudesindo Salvado). In New Britain, men and women do not cover their genitals, while in New Hanover, girls and women wear no clothes, and one often sees a man holding his scrotum suspended in his left hand with his penis between the thumb and the forefinger.[8] In Tahiti, Cook saw an adult native have sexual intercourse publicly with an eleven-year-old girl who had received special instruction from the queen. Moreover, in Tahiti intercourse is discussed frequently by both women and men (*Primo Viaggio*, vol. v).

It is well known that the Greeks dressed scantily and that they willingly removed their clothes on any occasion (Taine, *Philosophie de l'art*). Our word *gymnastics* [*ginnastica*] derives from the Greek word for *nude* and from the Greek practice of disrobing for athletic games.

Secular Prostitution

At first, there was no such thing as marriage; prostitution was the general rule. The Caledonians shared their women, with children belonging to the entire clan. The Nair are completely promiscuous. Marriage, as Lubbock affirms, is unknown among Bushmen. Among the Adamani (and also some Californian tribes) women belong to all the men; and to resist any one of them would be a grave crime. Men and women sometimes form temporary couples, especially when the woman becomes pregnant, but these cease with nursing. Here we see the idea of marriage developing out of rape and prostitution, much as the criminal code developed out of crime.[9]

Sometimes marriage does exist among primitive peoples, but instead of preventing prostitution, it encourages it.[10] Among the Eskimos, if the husband consents, the wife can give herself to whomever she wants (Parry). In nearly all the indigenous tribes of North America, the woman is free before and after marriage to give herself to whomever she chooses. Sometimes temporary couples will renew their relationship at fixed periods, like animals in heat (Lombroso, *Uomo bianco e uomo di colore*, 1870).

Hospitable Prostitution

Primitive peoples view hospitable prostitution as a duty. In Ceylon, Greenland, the Canary Islands, and Tahiti, hosts offer their wives to guests, from whom refusal would be impolite. Years ago in Japan, Bousquet saw a father offer his daughter to a guest in the presence of the girl's husband.

Marco Polo, when he was a guest in Tibet, noticed that his host had slipped away, leaving him alone to enjoy the women freely. In Vietnam, a father will give his daughter to a guest, even a stranger, for a small amount of money without prejudicing her future (Létourneau).

Thus marriage in primitive times actually encouraged prostitution.

Polyandry

Man passed from sexual promiscuity to monogamy only by way of practices that we view as crimes, including polyandry, incest, and—even worse—rape and abduction. Among the Nair of Malibar (a noble Negro caste) a woman has from five to six husbands, although she can marry up to ten, cohabiting with each for ten days by turn. However—in a sign that polyandry is a transition out of complete promiscuity—she can extend the number of days only if she follows certain rules of caste and tribe (Spencer, *Sociologie*, II). Also, among the Singhalese, brothers are always husbands of the same woman. In such cases, we see promiscuity passing from the tribe to the family.[11] The wife is shared among members of the immediate family, not by the entire social group.[12]

Another advance in the transition from unrestrained sexuality to the regularity of marriage occurs when girls' sexual freedom is limited after marriage. Among the Chinook of America girls are libertines but married women are chaste. In Malaysia, while girls are highly licentious, adulterers are punished with death (Wallace).

Prostitution in Our History

In the ancient days of civilized people, we find the same phenomena that we find today among savages: prostitution in all its forms. Prostitution was especially widespread in early times, which clearly confirms that modesty and matrimony are a late product of evolution.

The East: Sacred Prostitution

According to Herodotus, Babylonian women were obligated to go at least once to the temple of Venus and abandon themselves to a stranger; they were forbidden to return home until a foreigner had thrown coins in their laps and invited them to have intercourse outside the holy place. This money became sacred (lib. 1, s.199).

The Phoenicians practiced both hospitable and sacred prostitution. According to Eusebio, they prostituted their virgin daughters to foreigners to demonstrate their hospitality. The temples of the goddess Astarte were consecrated to prostitution, and statues depicted Astarte with both male and female sexual organs to signify the changes of men into women and of women into men that were celebrated in the goddess's nocturnal festivals.

Among the Jews, before codification of the tables of the law, a father had the right to sell his daughter to a more powerful man who made her his concubine for a period of time established by contract. The daughter gained no personal advantage unless the contractor then engaged her to his own son. In short, the Jews trafficked in their own daughters until Moses prohibited this custom.[13]

Greece: Sacred Prostitution

To propitiate Venus, the Greeks gave the goddess a certain number of young girls. These prostitutes offered the goddess gifts, usually a phallus covered with gold and silver, ivory, or mother-of-pearl.

Sacred prostitution, which existed in all the temples of Athena, encouraged Solon to institute civil prostitution.[14] In Athens, civil prostitution generated money for the state. Solon wanted to procure for the government the same benefits that prostitution brought to the temples; at the same time, he wanted to provide sexual pleasure for young Athenian men and to protect honest women.[15]

Summary

At the beginning of evolution, modesty was unknown. The general rule was great freedom in sexual relations; and even where promiscuity was not complete, marriage served as not a brake on prostitution but rather an incentive for it. Later began a second period in which prostitution survived in attenuated form, as when girls had sexual freedom but married women were expected to be chaste. In the third period, prostitution disappeared as a normal social practice, surviving only as a morbid and retrograde phenomenon in a certain class of people.

Part III

Pathological Anatomy and Anthropometry of Criminal Woman and the Prostitute

11
The Skull of the Female Offender

When I began studying criminals some thirty years ago, I professed a firm faith in anthropometry, especially cranial anthropometry, as an ark of salvation from the metaphysical, a priori systems dear to all those engaged on the study of man. I regarded anthropometry as the backbone—indeed, the entire framework—of the new human statue I was attempting to create. But as so often happens in human affairs, use degenerated into abuse, demonstrating the vanity of my hopes and the damage that can be caused by excessive confidence.[1]

All the discrepancies between my work and that of the most authoritative modern anthropologists—who are, after all, nothing but anthropometrists—flow from the fact that the variations in measurement between the normal and the abnormal subject are so small as to defy all but the most minute research. I had already reached this conclusion as *Criminal Man* was reaching its second and third editions and became even more convinced of it when Zampa's observations[a] on the crania of four assassins in Ravenna disclosed an exact correspondence between their measurements and the averages of ten normal Ravennese. And while the anthropometrical system failed thus to reveal any salient differences whatsoever, anatomical-pathological investigation, applied to the same crania, detected no fewer than thirty-three anomalies.[2]

But unfortunately, scholarly attention had been diverted from the anatomico-pathological method to anthropometry, with the consequence that the former came to be rashly abandoned. And as a result, Topinard and Manouvrier, deficient as they were in anatomico-pathological knowledge, failed to detect the immense

a. *Archivio di psichiatria*, XII. Vedi *Sui nuovi progressi dell'antropologia criminale*, 1893.

anomalies existent in certain crania of assassins which they were examining. Because there were no salient anthropometrical differences between these skulls and the skull of Charlotte Corday,[3] they rejected the theory of anomaly altogether.

Measurement should not be totally abandoned, however. It should be retained as the frame, so to speak, of the picture; or, rather, as the symbol, the flag of a school in whose armory numbers furnish the most effective weapon. Such retention becomes all the more crucial when we realize that in the few cases in which measurement confirms anomalies, those anomalies become doubly significant.[4]

Studies of the female criminal were undertaken by Bergonzoli, Soffiantini, and me on twenty-six skulls and five skeletons of prostitutes owned by Signor Scarenzi. Varaglia and Silva[b] studied sixty female criminals who died in the prisons of Turin, while Mingazzini[c] and Ardù[d] investigated seventeen others who died in Rome. The overall distribution of offenses in the latter two studies was as follows: prostitution, four; infanticide, twenty; complicity in rape, two; theft, fourteen; arson, three; wounding, four; assassination, ten; homicide, fifteen; poisoning, four; abortion, one. As regards race, eleven were Sicilians, six Sardinians, thirty-one Neapolitans, seven natives of the Marches and Umbria, two Venetians, four Lombards, four natives of Emilia, three Tuscans, three Ligurians, and six Piedmontese.[5]

Cranial Capacity

Information on cranial capacity appears in table 12. Arithmetically speaking, the average cranial capacity of female criminals (1,322) is higher than that of prostitutes (1,244) and even a little higher than that of normal women (1,310–1,316).[6] But according to Mingazzini (a far better and more trustworthy observer), the average cranial capacity for criminal women is 1,265, an average very inferior to that of normal Italian women, for whom the figure found by Nicolini is 1,310, and by Mantegazza and Amadei, 1,322.[7] Very important also is the fact that Nicolini observed a capacity under 1,200 in 20 percent of these criminals and a capacity above 1,400 in only 5 percent, while among the normal women studied by Amadei and Morselli, only 14 percent fell below the former figure and 29 percent rose above the latter, a result which establishes the inferiority of criminals.[8]

b. Variglia e Silva, *Note anatomiche e antropologiche di 60 cranii e 42 encefali di donne criminali Italiane*, Torino, 1885.

c. G. Mingazzini, *Sopra 30 cranii ed encefali di delinquenti Italiane*. (*Rivista sperimentale di freniatria*, vol. XIV, I–II, nota I p. 14).

d. Ardù, *Note sul diametro biangolare della mandibola*. (*Archivio di psichiatria*, 1892).

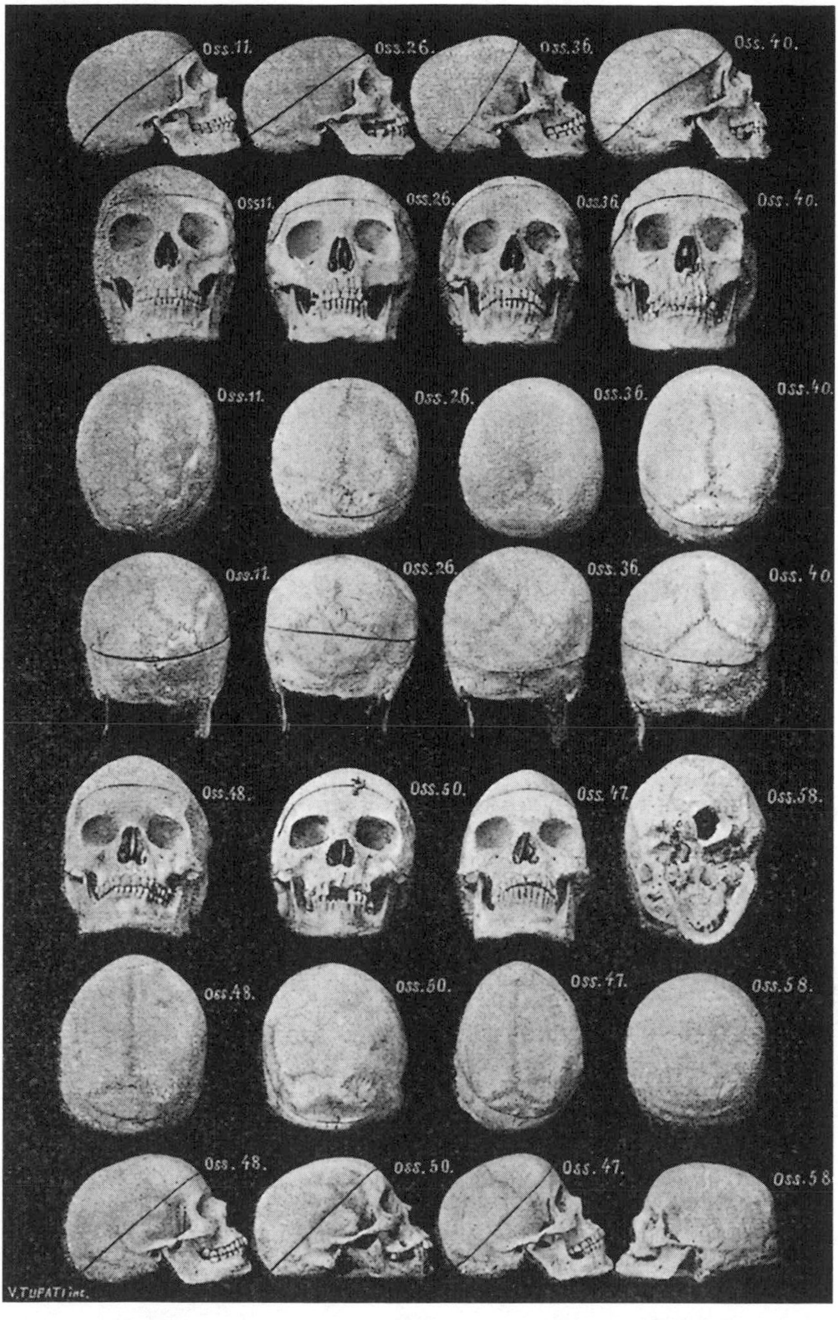

4 Skulls of Italian criminal women. *Source*: Lombroso, *La donna delinquente*, 1893. *Editors' note*: According to Lombroso, anomalies of the skull indicate criminality.

Table 12 Relative Cranial Capacities of Six Female Groups

Capacity	26 prostitutes	60 female criminals	normal females observed by Amadei	normal females observed by Morselli	female lunatics	female Papuans
1,000 to 1,100 cc	3.8	1.72	2.73	1.1	2.50	4.0
1,100 to 1,200 cc	15.3	19.1	6.45	9.2	7.47	12.0
1,200 to 1,300 cc	42.3	46.3	21.8	29.9	21.78	38.0
1,300 to 1,400 cc	23.0	22.5	30.9	30.1	37.12	24.0
1,400 to 1,500 cc	11.5	8.6	15.45	13.7	25.35	8.0
1,500 to 1,600 cc	3.8	1.72	10.90	12.6	4.64	2.0
1,600 to 1,700 cc	—	—	1.83	2.3	—	2.0
1,700 to 1,750 cc	—	—	0.91	1.1	1.07	—

Editors' note: The first two columns of this table seem to refer to the preceding paragraph of the text, in which Lombroso names his sources and describes the samples. However, the information on prostitutes seems to have been based only on twenty-six skulls, exclusive of the five skeletons referred to in the text. For the information on female criminals, it is unclear why Lombroso draws on sixty, not the seventy-seven cases mentioned earlier.

The columns give percentages, and each should total 100. The columns for prostitutes, female criminals, normal females observed by Morselli, and female lunatics do total 100, or close to it. However, the columns for normal females observed by Amadei and for female Papuans total 90.96 and 90.0, respectively, with no explanation for the discrepancies.

Orbital Capacity

The maximum orbital capacity among the sixty female criminals was 62, the minimum 44, and the median 52.76 cubic centimeters. The distribution according to crime type is shown in table 13. The high capacities predominate in the most serious forms of crime.

Area of the Occipital Foramen

The minimum area is 580 mm squared, the maximum is 850, and the average is 731.

Cephalo-Rachidian Index

The predominant figures are between 15.01 and 19; the minimum is 14.58, the maximum 21.69, and the average 17.72.

Cephalo-Orbital Index

The predominant figures are between 22 and 26; the minimum is 18.46, the maximum 30.90, and the average 24.64.

Table 13 Orbital Capacity by Crime Type

poisoning	57 cc	rape	53 cc	homicide	53 cc	theft	52 cc
assassination	54 cc	infanticide	52 cc	wounding	53 cc	arson	51 cc

Editors' note: Although Lombroso claimed a correlation between large orbital capacity and the seriousness of the criminal offense, the table does not clearly support this claim.

Facial Angle

The minimum angle is 69 degrees, the maximum 81 degrees, with a general average of 74.2 degrees. Among prostitutes, the maximum is 82 degrees, the minimum 72 degrees, and the average 74.6 degrees.

Horizontal Circumference

The predominating circumferences among criminals are between 470 and 490; among prostitutes, between 490 and 510; while among 52 percent of normal subjects, at least according to Morselli, the prevailing figures are between 501 and 530.[9]

Total Height of Face

Information on the facial height of criminal women appears in table 14. The minimum height is 60 mm, the maximum 99 mm. Most cases fall between 81–85 mm, and then between 76–80 mm, and 86–90 mm.

The distribution by crime type appears in table 15.

Table 14 Facial Height of Criminal Women

between 56–60	millimeters	1 = 1.66 percent
between 61–65	millimeters	1 = 1.66 percent
between 66–70	millimeters	3 = 5.00 percent
between 71–75	millimeters	3 = 5.00 percent
between 76–80	millimeters	13 = 21.66 percent
between 81–85	millimeters	26 = 43.33 percent
between 86–90	millimeters	11 = 18.33 percent
between 91–95	millimeters	1 = 1.66 percent
between 96–100	millimeters	1 = 1.66 percent

Editors' note: Lombroso uses the second column to indicate the distribution of his sixty cases: One case equals 1.66 percent of the total, three cases equal 5 percent of the total, and so on.

Table 15 Facial Height by Crime Type

wounding	83 millimeters	theft	80 millimeters
infanticide	83 millimeters	murder	80 millimeters
complicity in rape	81.5 millimeters	prostitution	78 millimeters
poisoning	81 millimeters	arson	75 millimeters

Editors' note: As Lombroso points out in his text, these data do not lead to obvious conclusions.

Weight of the Lower Jaw

A special and notably virile characteristic of the lower jaw among the twenty-six prostitutes is its greater weight relative to the cranium, as shown in table 16. The average of 65.9 is actually equal to the general average, but if we set aside two absolutely abnormal minima of 35.33,[10] we get an average of 70.5; and in any case, the weight relative to that of the cranium is 12.0, which is the same as in the male.

Table 16 Relative Weight of Jaws of Prostitutes

weight of jaw	weight of cranium
65.9 on an average	507
35 minimum (in syphilitics)	287
90 maximum	728

Editors' note: The unit of measurement is not specified here.

Conclusions

As I expected and had already found through research on the male criminal, these data lead to few conclusions. Most important is the information relating to cranial and orbital capacity, to the weight and diameter of the jaw, and to the cheekbones.

It is clear, indeed, that prostitutes have the smallest cranial capacity of all and that they and criminals predominate on all the lower levels of the scale up to 1200.[11] In the 1200–1300 range, normal women appear more frequently, and prostitutes and criminals are closer to the mentally afflicted than to the sane. In average and above-average capacity, honest women and even lunatics surpass both criminals and prostitutes.

In cranial capacity, honest women are five or six times higher than criminals, prostitutes, and lunatics. In this respect, prostitutes are also slightly superior to criminals; among the latter those with largest capacity are the poisoners. As a group, prostitutes are more remarkable than criminals for small as well as large cranial capacity, although when compared with honest women, they rank below lunatics—a peculiarity that they share with male criminals, especially thieves.

The maxima and minima among prostitutes more nearly resemble those of Papuan women than of normal females. Moreover, prostitutes are wider across the cheekbones than criminals in the proportion of thirty-six to sixteen in all the higher numbers, and are inferior to the same class in all the lesser figures.

The lower jaw of female criminals, and still more of prostitutes, is heavier than in moral women, and the cranio-mandibular index is nearly always as virile as it is heavy.

12
Pathological Anomalies

As we have already said, cranial anomalies yield far more striking differences between criminal and normal women than do cranial measurements. It is evident from table 17 that although anomalies are frequent in female criminals, especially murderers, they are rarer than among male criminals. For example, the median occipital fossetta is found in four times as many criminal men as criminal women, while irregularities in the occipital area are found three times as often, and oversized jaws twice as often. On the other hand, the female criminal exceeds the male in a few characteristics, such as her larger number of wormian bones and her more frequently anomalous palate. Nevertheless, a comparison of criminals' skulls with normal women's skulls reveals that female criminals are closer to males, both criminal and normal, than to normal women.[12]

In table 17, I indicate the average frequency of the main anomalies found in normal women, criminal women, and prostitutes. Anomalous teeth, present in only 0.5 percent of normal female subjects, are to be found in 10.8 percent of female criminals and in 5.1 percent of prostitutes.[13] The median occipital fossetta occurs in 3.4 percent of normal subjects, 5.4 percent of delinquents, and 17 percent of prostitutes, the latter figure exceeding that of male criminals (16). The narrow or receding forehead is found in 10 percent of normal women, 8 percent of criminal women,[14] and 16 percent of prostitutes. Prognathism distinguishes 10 percent of normals, 33.4 percent of criminals,[15] and 36 percent of prostitutes.

Proportion of Anomalies

The very much larger number of anomalies in prostitutes than in female criminals may be demonstrated by the fact that 51.5 percent of prostitutes have more

Table 17 Pathological Anomalies

	percentage of male criminals (out of 66)	percentage of normal women	percentage of criminal women (out of 55)	percentage of prostitutes (out of 47)
enormous pterygoid apophisis	12	—	12.6	6
largely developed parietal and temporal prominences	43	—	1.8	6
largely developed occipital and temporal prominences	—	—	3.6	—
cranial depressions	—	—	34.2	10
anomalous teeth	14	0.5	10.8	51
median occipital fossetta	16	3.4	5.4	17
very irregular occipital form	10	—	3.6	23
receding or narrow forehead	36	10	5.4	16
prominent (prognathous) jaw	34	10	32.4	36
anomalies of the palate		—	1.8	—
enormous nasal bones	—	—	10.8	3
virile type of face	—	—	1.8	3
wormian bones	59	20	64.8	26
prominent cheekbones	30	6.9	1.8	16

Editors' note: Lombroso does not specify the total number of normal women in this table. The original of this table gives data on about twice as many physical characteristics as here and breaks down the "criminal women" category with additional information on thieves, infanticides, and homicides. The original table also has a column on female criminals observed by Mingazzini out of seventeen. We have omitted data that do little or nothing to clarify the arguments made in the text and that in fact have an overall effect of obscuring Lombroso's main points.

There are three discrepancies between the text and table 17, as specified in notes 13, 14, and 15 to this chapter.

than five cranial anomalies, while the same is true of only 27 percent of female criminals (see table 18). Moreover, the mean among prostitutes is five anomalies per cranium, while among female criminals it is only four. But these figures sink into numerical insignificance when compared to those on male crania, where the average number of anomalies is three and four times higher (78 percent) than in the case of female delinquents and prostitutes. Many abnormal characteristics in

Table 18 Cranial Anomalies

	50 male criminals	female criminals	prostitutes
2 anomalies	0 percent	12.6 percent	6.5 percent
3 anomalies	8 percent	27 percent	16 percent
4 anomalies	0 percent	32.4 percent	26 percent
5 anomalies	2 percent	12.6 percent	1.6 percent
6 anomalies	4 percent	7.2 percent	9.5 percent
7 anomalies	78 percent	7.2 percent	26 percent
typical (5 and more anomalies)	84 percent	27.0 percent	51.5 percent
averages of the anomalies per cranium	11.4	4.0	5.5

Editors' note: Lombroso does not here specify the size of his female samples. The original of this table breaks down the data on female criminals by thieves, infanticides, and homicides, and it also gives data on the number of abnormalities found in a study by Roncoroni and Ardù of 19 male offenders' crania. We have omitted data that do little or nothing to clarify the points made in the text.

The penultimate row gives totals on the proportion of cases with five, six, or seven anomalies. These totals add up for column one (2 + 4 + 78 equals 84 percent) and for column two (12.6 + 7.2 + 7.2 equals 27 percent). Lombroso's addition breaks down in column three, however, because 1.6 + 9.5 + 26 equals 37.7 percent, not 51.5 percent. Thus the difference between female criminals and prostitutes is less dramatic than the inaccurate figure suggests.

the skulls of female criminals are almost normal characteristics in men.[16] These are virile traits.

Political Criminals (Female)

Not even the purest political crime—that which springs from passion—is exempt from this rule.[17] My rapid inspection of the skull of Charlotte Corday affirmed the presence of an extraordinary number of anomalies, an assessment confirmed not only by Topinard's very confused monograph but also by the photographs of the cranium, which Prince R. Bonaparte presented to me, and which are reproduced in figure 6.[18]

Corday's cranium is platycephalic,[19] a peculiarity rarer in woman than in man. Also noteworthy is her most remarkable jugular apophysis,[20] and the two strongly arched eyebrows that are concave below and confluent with the median line and beyond it. All the sutures are open, as in a young man of twenty-three to twenty-five years, but simpler. The cranial capacity is 1,360 cubic centimeters, while the average among French women is 1,337; the shape is slightly dolichocephalic (77.7); and in the horizontal direction the zygomatic arch is visible only on the left—a clear instance of asymmetry. The insertion of the sagit-

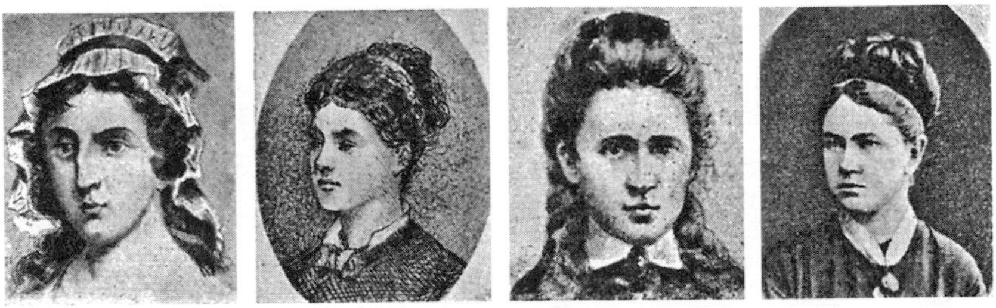

5 Revolutionaries and political criminals. *Source*: Lombroso, *Atlante*, 1897. *Editors' note*: The image at the top left is of Charlotte Corday, the political assassin whose skull Lombroso analyzed at length.

6 Cranium of Charlotte Corday (2 views). *Source*: Lombroso, *La donna delinquente*, 1893. *Editors' note*: From these photographs, Lombroso felt he was able to detect numerous anomalies in Corday's skull—proofs of her criminality.

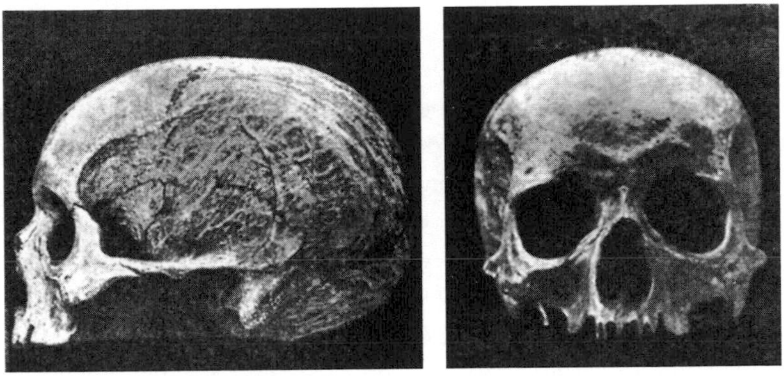

tal process in the frontal bone is also asymmetrical, and there is a median occipital fossetta.

Virility can be further demonstrated in Corday's skull through anthropometrical measurements. The orbital area is 133 mm squared, while the average among Parisian women is 126. The height of the orbit is 35 mm, while among Parisian women generally it is 33.

13

The Brains of Female Criminals and Prostitutes

The maximum brain weight of healthy women is greater than that of criminals, and their minimum brain weight is less.[21]

Anomalies in the brain convolutions of female criminals are quite rare, certainly rarer than in the case of male criminals. In the right hemisphere of a woman convicted of corrupting morals, Mingazzini found a cruciform furrow dividing the superior parietal lobule from the lower. In two other cases, he found that the left superior temporal convolution communicated with the incisura occipitalis; and in one case, this convolution continued uninterrupted to the free margin of the malleus. But while the external surfaces of the brain hemispheres are similar in female criminals and normal women, the signs of degeneration are nonetheless more frequent among the former.

In a study of morphological brain anomalies, Mingazzini found a total of nineteen anomalies among thirteen male criminals and a total of nineteen anomalies among seventeen female criminals, as shown in table 19. Thus the proportion of brain anomalies is 1.46 among males and 1.11 among females, or notably greater among the males.

On the other hand, some female criminals exhibit quite a few brain anomalies. Ferrier, for instance, relates the case of a lesbian woman whose right brain hemisphere was smaller than her left one. Moreover, in her brain the fissure of Rolando was interrupted by a deep annectant convolution following on the ascending frontal fold, which, in addition to being atrophied, was crossed in the middle by two sulci. Ferrier had seen this sort of malformation only twice before in his study of eight hundred normal brains.

In a female thief, Flesch found pachymeningitis and an interruption of the ascending frontal convolution on the left side. He also found a median lobe on the

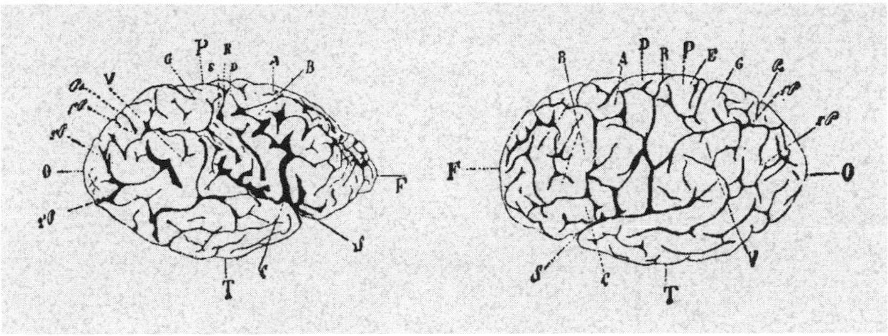

7 Anomalous brain of a child murderer (female) (2 views). *Source*: Lombroso, Atlante, 1897. *Editors' note*: Lombroso's lettering system indicates atrophy of the frontal lobe (F) and parietal lobe (P). "Second fold of the external fissure is doubled and shallow." Even in prison, Lombroso notes, this occasional criminal "proved to be resistant to discipline" (*Atlante*, xxiv–xxv).

cerebellum that was formed, as in many mammals, by two sulci that started in the median fissure, diverged in front, and crossed the horizontal convolutions of the median lobe for the entire length of the hemispheres.

More important still are the pathological anomalies. Out of thirty-eight female criminals, a postmortem examination revealed in eleven serious macroscopic lesions of the central system and its involucra, such as thickening of the spinal dura mater; abscess on the cerebellum; meningoencephalitis; cerebral apoplexy; syphilis; endocranial abscess; paralysis of all the extremities for the last month of life; meningitis of the base; and a soft, mother-of-pearl–colored tumor under the arachnoid.

Hotzen, in the *Archive of Psychiatry* (1889), relates the case of Maria Köster, who at the age of eighteen, having until then seemed quiet and industrious, killed her mother with sixty blows of a hatchet in order to obtain just a scanty sum. She became a domestic servant, then a typographer, then a needlewoman; and she presented asymmetry only of the face and one pupil. She had hysterical attacks after puberty (which in her case began late, at age nineteen); but more often still she feigned these attacks. After death she was found to have had consumption; in addition, there were traces of adherent dura mater and of hemorrhagic pachymeningitis, as well as a decided atrophy of the cerebral cortex. This was a case of congenital and hereditary atrophy of the cerebral cortex. It was characterized by underdeveloped frontal convolutions, small convolutions, incomplete enclosure of the cerebellum by the large hemispheres, and overly abundant segmentation of the cerebral cortex. Its furrows and folds were not the result of superior evo-

Table 19 Brain Anomalies in Male and Female Criminals

	men (n = 13)	women (n = 17)
absence of vertical anterior fissure on left side	—	1
total deepening of the first annectant convolution	1	—
partial deepening of the first annectant convolution	5	3
division of the first annectant convolution	—	1
superficiality of the gyrus cunei	1	2
anomalies of the frontal lobes	1	2
complete and central postcentralis	1	1
postcentralis separated from interparietalis	—	1
divided ascending parietalis	—	1
superior temporal convolution between the frontal and lateral lobes	1	0
superior temporal convolution attached to the incisura occipitalis	—	2
superior temporal convolution reaching to malleus	—	0
absence of superior medial temporal convolution	3	0
absence of occipital temporal convolution	1	—
absence of sulcus extremus	3	1
calcarine fissure connected to collateralis	—	1
calcarine fissure connected to sulcus extremus	—	1
calcarine fissure connected to sulcus occipitalis	1	0
total	19	19
number of anomalies per brain	1.46	1.11

lution, for no new cerebral substance was laid down in their area. In fact, they revealed atrophy of the cerebral matter.

Lambl, in *Westphal's Archiv. für Psychiatrie* (1888), gives the history of Marianna Kirtecen, who, with her mother's encouragement, gave forth oracles and was consulted by peasants and even persons of high rank, showing much ability in guessing at their maladies and prescribing strange remedies, for which she was extravagantly paid. She was, in short, a clever swindler, although only twelve years old. She was lame, squint-eyed, flat-skulled, and left-handed, her right arm being, indeed, almost paralyzed. Fluent in her speech, she gave very appropriate replies to questions, and she had a real curiosity—passion even—for seeing and treating the sick. When she died of consumption, the autopsy revealed a long-standing porencephalia in the left hemisphere of the brain. The gyrus fornicatus was flattened in the middle portion, while the convexities of the pia mater and arachnoid enclosed a large number of pacchionian granulations such as are found in the aged.

14
Anthropometry of Female Criminals

Authors and the Cases They Studied

In the list of those who have recently studied the characteristics of female criminals we must include: Marro,[e] who investigated 41 cases; Troisky,[f] 58 cases; Lombroso and Pasini,[g] 122 cases; Ziino,[h] 188 cases; Lombroso, 83 photographs; Varaglia and Silva,[i] 60 crania; Romberg,[j] 20 cases; and, recently, Salsotto,[k] 409 cases; Tarnowsky,[l] 100 female thieves; and Roncoroni,[m] 50 normal women.[22]

The characteristics of prostitutes, which cannot be studied separately from those of female criminals, have been investigated by Scarenzio and Soffiantini[n] in 14 crania; by Andronico[o] in 230 subjects; by Grimaldi[p] in 26; by De Albertis[q] in

e. Marro, *I caratteri dei delinquenti*. Bocca, 1889.

f. Troisky, *Cephalometria nei delinquenti in rapporto con alcuni sintomi di degenerazione fisica. Arch. Charkow*. Russia, 1884.

g. Lombroso e Pasini, *Archivio psichiatria*, 1883.

h. Ziino, *Fisiopatologia del delitto*, 1881.

i. Varaglia e Silva, *Note anatomiche e antropologiche su 60 cranii e 46 encefali di donne criminali italaine. Archivio psichiatria*, vol. VI.

j. Romberg, *101 cefalogrammi*. Berlino, 1889.

k. Salsotto, *La donna delinquente: Rivista di discipline carcerarie*, 1889.

l. Tarnowsky, *Étude anthropométrique sur les prostituées et les voleuses*. Parigi, 1887.

m. Roncoroni, *Ricerche su alcune sensibilità nei pazzi: Giornale della R. Accad. di med., 1891*; *I caratteri degenerativi su 50 donne e 50 uomini normali: l'olfatto, il gusto e l'udito in 35 normali. Arch. di psichiatria*, 1892.

n. Scarenzio e Soffiantini, *Archivio di psichiatria*, 1881, vol. VII, p. 29.

o. Andronico, *Prostitute e delinquenti. Arch. di psichiatria*, 1882, p. 143, vol. III.

p. Grimaldi, *Il pudore: Il manicomio*, vol. V, N. 1, 1889.

q. De Albertis, *Il tatuaggio su 300 prostitute genovesi. Archivio psich., scienze pen. ed antrop. crim.*, vol. IX, 1888.

28; by Tarnoswky in 150; and by Bergonzoli and Lombroso[r] in 26 crania; while Berg[s] recently researched the tattoo marks of 804. Gurrieri examined the sensitivity of 60 cases; Fornasari covered the anthropometry of a similar number;[t] and Riccardi[u] and Ardù[v] studied the weight, height, and so on of 176.

To these we added studies (*Giornale della R. Accademia di medicina* di Torino, N. 9 e 10, 1891; *Arch. di psich.* XIII, fasc. VI) of degenerative characteristics in 200 normal women, in 120 Piedmontese female thieves, and in 115 prostitutes of Turin. We further studied the criminal type in 300 other women (234 of whom were in the female lifers' penitentiary and 56 in the judicial prison of Turin). In addition, we collaborated with Tarnowsky in the study of 69 Russian female criminals and 100 Russian prostitutes, and with Ottolenghi.[w]

This comes to a total of 1,033 observations on female criminals, 176 observations on the skulls of female criminals, 685 on prostitutes, 225 on normal women in hospitals, and 30 others on the skulls of normal women.

Weight and Height

Weight appears to be often equal to or above average in thieves, murderers, and (especially) prostitutes, but rarely above average in women who commit infanticide. On the other hand, average height appears to be rarer in all female criminals and prostitutes than in moral women.

Prostitutes' greater weight is confirmed by the notorious obesity of those who grow old in their unfortunate trade and gradually become positive monsters of fatty tissue. Some attain the weight of 90, 98, and even 130 kilograms.[23]

Thigh and Leg

Measurements for the circumferences of the thigh and leg were taken of only fourteen normal women, it being difficult to find subjects who would submit to the experiment.[24] Between the circumference of the ankle and the calf, Fornasari found a difference in Bolognese prostitutes of from 70 to 150, and in normal women of from 100 to 140, the average for the first named being 120, and for the last named 100.[25] Normal women consequently have the least developed calves, on the average, while prostitutes show the maxima and minima of development.

r. Bergonzoli e Lombroso, *Su 26 cranii di prostitute*, 1893.

s. Berg, *Le tatouage chex les prostituées Danoises. Arch. psich.*, vol XI. e fasc. 3 and 4, 1891.

t. Gurrieri e Fornasari, *I sensi e le anomalie nelle donne normali e nelle prostitute*. Torino, 1893.

u. Riccardi, *Osservazioni intorno una serie di prostitute*, 1892. *Anomalo*, N. 8, 9.

v. Ardù, *Alcune anomalie nelle prostitute*. Torino, 1893.

w. Ottolenghi e Lombroso, *La donna delinquente e prostituta*. Torino, 1892.

Prostitutes' thighs, too, are bigger than normal women's in proportion to their calves.

Cranial Capacity and Circumference

Here, as far as measurements can be exact in the case of women with their large amount of hair, Marro found the capacity in forty-one criminals to be 1,477, lower than that of normal women (1,508).[26] Table 20 reports Marro's series of probable cranial capacities.

Moreover, Tarnowsky's work confirms the prevalence of small cranial capacities among prostitutes.[27]

According to Salsotto's data, the largest average cranial circumference is to be found among murderers (532), after whom come poisoners (517), then women who commit infanticide (501), and finally thieves (494). Ziino's results are almost identical. Tarnowsky discovered an average circumference of 535 in thieves, 531 in prostitutes, 537 in illiterate peasants, and 538 in fifty educated moral women, the result being a smaller cranial circumference in the female criminals. Several other researchers have reached the same conclusion. Thus the cranial circumference of prostitutes is less than that of criminals.

Hair

The hair of criminals and prostitutes is darker than that of honest women.[28] According to Tarnowsky, however, more blondes can be found among prostitutes than thieves since fair-haired specimens of the former class are most sought after. Marro, notwithstanding the meagerness of his data, also noted the predominance

Table 20 Relative Cranial Capacities of Criminal and Normal Women

	41 criminal women	25 normal women
1400–1450	28.8 percent	— percent
1450–1500	45.6 percent	44 percent
1500–1550	16.8 percent	44 percent
1500–1597	7.2 percent	12 percent

Editors' note: The precise percentages of the first column are odd, given that 28.8 percent of 41 women would be not a round number but rather 11.8 women; and so on. Moreover, the first column adds to 98.4 percent, not 100 percent. The second column's figures make more sense: 44 percent of 25 women is 11 women; and these figures do total 100.

Table 21 Hair Color

	criminal women	normal women
fair-haired	26 percent	12 percent
dark-haired	26 percent	20 percent
red-haired	48 percent	0 percent
chestnut-haired	41 percent	68 percent

Editors' note: While the second column adds up to 100 percent, the first inexplicably totals 141 percent.

of blond and red hair among women offenders against chastity, an observation that accords with my own. Marro's findings appear in Table 21.

Among criminal women we also find an unusual quantity of hair. In a group of thirty-three prostitutes, Riccardi found six with an exaggerated amount of hair, nine with a moderate quantity, and four with wavy hair. Fornasari found forty-eight out of sixty with very abundant hair.

Women famous for their quantity of hair include Heberzeni, Trossarello, and Madame la Motte. Of the last named, Samson, the executioner, observed, "The most remarkable thing about her was her abundance of hair."

Wrinkles

Taking into account only the deeper wrinkles, I concluded, after examining 158 normal working-class and peasant women and 70 criminal women, that among the latter wrinkles are not more common than among the former. Nevertheless, certain wrinkles, such as the fronto-vertical, the wrinkles on the cheekbones, crow's-feet, and labial wrinkles, are more frequent and more deeply marked in criminal women of mature age.

In this connection we may recall the proverbial wrinkles of witches and the case of the vile old woman, the so-called Vecchia dell'Aceto [Old Woman of the Vinegar] of Palermo, who poisoned a large number of people simply for love of money.[29] When already of mature age, she got the idea of murder on hearing of a man who used arsenated vinegar to remove vermin from the heads of children; she realized at once that with a similar liquid she could kill adults with impunity and at a small cost. Our image of this criminal (from a photograph kindly presented by Prof. Salinas, director of the Museum of Palermo), so full of virile angularities, and above all so deeply wrinkled, with her satanic leer, suffices of itself to prove that the woman in question was born to do evil, and that if she had failed to commit it on one occasion, she would have found others.

Prostitutes lack wrinkles.

White Hairs and Baldness

Grey hair (both precocious greyness and the grey hair of old age) is much more common among female than male criminals. Moreover, it is even more common among criminal than normal women. This is because the female criminal, who is almost always a criminaloid, reacts more emotionally than the male to an agitated life. Among normal women, on the other hand, grey hair appears later than in man because these women lead a more tranquil life.

Women do not go bald more frequently than men, in spite of coiffures, which more or less spoil the hair, and special physiological circumstances, such as pregnancy and childbirth, which tend to cause hair loss. Baldness is even less common among female criminals than among normal women.

Summary

While these accumulated findings do not amount to much, this result is only natural. For if external differences between male criminals and normal men are few, they must be fewer still between female criminals and normal women. We noted earlier that stability of type is much greater in the woman and differentiation much less, even when her skull is anomalous.

The following are our most important conclusions:

- Female criminals are shorter than normal women; and in proportion to

8 Old Woman of the Vinegar *Source*: Lombroso, *La donna delinquente*, 1893. *Editors' note*: Lombroso used this photograph of a statue of an elderly Sicilian poisoner to prove that she was a born criminal. Contemporaries criticized him for using evidence of dubious scientific value.

their stature, prostitutes and female murderers weigh more than honest women

- Prostitutes have bigger calves than honest women
- Female thieves and above all prostitutes are inferior to honest women in cranial capacity and cranial circumference
- Criminals have darker hair than normal women, and this also holds good to a certain extent for prostitutes. Several studies of prostitutes, however, have found that in these women rates of fair and red hair equal and sometimes exceed those of normal women
- Grey hair, which is rare in the normal woman, is more than twice as frequent in the criminal woman. On the other hand, in both young and mature criminal women, baldness is less common than in normal women. Wrinkles are markedly more frequent in criminals of ripe years. Little of all this can be positively affirmed for prostitutes, who are painted and made up when not (as is usual) very young; but so far as it is possible to judge, prostitutes are as little subject to precocious greyness and baldness as are congenital male criminals.

15

Facial and Cephalic Anomalies of Female Criminals and Prostitutes

The outstanding facial and cephalic anomalies of female criminals and prostitutes observed by us and others are itemized in table 22.[30] Most prevalent are the following anomalies:

Cranial Asymmetry

Present in 26 percent of criminals and 32 percent of prostitutes; especially prevalent among murderers (46 percent) and poisoners (50 percent).

Platycephaly

Present in 15 percent of poisoners and 2 percent of thieves. The average for criminals of all classes is 8 percent, while among prostitutes it falls to just 1.6 percent, about the same as that of normal women. However, platycephaly is not particularly characteristic of criminal women.

Receding Foreheads

Present in 11 percent of criminals and 12 percent of prostitutes, but only 8 percent of normal women.

Jutting Brows

Present in 15 percent of our criminal cases and 8 percent of normal women. Tarnowsky, working with her own sample, found that 6 percent of women who committed homicide had jutting brows, as did 12 percent of the thieves and 10 percent of the prostitutes, but just 4 percent of the honest women.

Table 22 Anomalies in Criminal Women and Prostitutes

	normal women			crimi											
							Lombroso and Pasini								
	normal women (Marro)	normal women (Lombroso)	normal skulls (Lombroso)	criminal women	criminal skulls (Lombroso)	criminal photos (Lombroso, Marro)	all criminal women	thieves	women who commit infanticide	murderers	poisoners	all criminal women	thieves	murderers	
number of cases	25	100	30	25	66	83	122	20	22	61	19	409	90	130	2
cranial assymetry			17		21		40	45	36	46.1		30	22	46	2
round-headedness	1											5	1.1	5.3	
flat-headedness	1	0	0.1	15								8.5	7.7	5.3	
pointed skull												13.5	1.04	22	
big-headedness												6	5.5	15	
small-headedness						6						1			
elevated skull		2													
extreme short-headedness												6			
cranial anomalies		4	18				40	45	36	46		70	37.3	93.6	3
receding forehead			10	5	6.8	2	4.2	10	4.5	1.6	16	7.5	5.5	5.3	
forehead bumps												5.5		3.8	1
big nasal cavities	4	8	19		29	15	5.8					6	6.6	10.7	
extreme orbital angle	16		6		7							3.5			
forehead anomalies	20	8	35	5	42.8	17	15	15	9	8.2	33	15.3	12.1	19.8	1
facial assymetry		6		45		13						5	4.4	8	
enormous lower jaw		12	6.3	10		36	9.8	15	4.5	9.8		0.25			
protruding cheek-bones		8	6.9			12	14.7	30		11.4					
jug ears	4	5				3						10.5	17	4.6	1
anomalous ears	16	35													
strabismus	4	3				6	3	10		3.3		7.5	5.5	8.8	
protruding teeth	4	4	10			8						1		3.2	
virile physiognomy		2				22	9.8	9	4.5	14.7		5	3.3	10	
ferocious physiognomy		1	1.5	5.6											
cretinous physiognomy		4													
Mongoloid physi-ognomy												5		9.6	
anomalous teeth		4					4.1					5		14	
nasal anomalies															
thin lips		2				14	15	15	9	18.3					
hairiness		7					13	10	36	10					
premature wrinkles		11													
tattoos												2.3			
overdeveloped occipital bone															
assymetrical facial projection															

Editors' note: All figures below the row labeled "number of cases" appear to be percentages, but neither the rows nor the columns should be expec to add up to 100 percent as the data are not cumulative. Lombroso does not explain why he sometimes uses a 0 to indicate no cases, while at ot times he uses a blank. Criminal women and prostitutes are best compared by looking at the columns headed "average," and these two groups can

	men									prostitutes					average		
	sotto																
	offenders against morality	swindlers	arsonists	women who commit infanticide	criminal women (Ziino)	criminal skulls (Varaglia and Silva)	thieves (Lombroso and Ottolenghi)	thieves (Tarnowsky)	thieves (Marro)	Grimaldi	De Albertis	Andronico	Tarnowsky	Lombroso and Ottolenghi	criminal women	prostitutes	normal women (Roncoroni)
	25	20	4	100	188	60	120	100	47	26	28	230	150	115			50
	12	15		20		12.6	8.44	23		23			40.9		26	32	
	20													4	4.5		
	16			13			2		5					1.61	6.5		
				17						26.9					13.5	26.9	
	15.7	5		12													
	4		75		7.9		1.14							3.22			
							4								4		
							18.4			20				24.11			
	67.7	20	75	62	11.7		33.98	23		73		35	41.3	33.11	35.5	45	
		10		8				27	7			15	12	10	11	12	8
											1		9.9				2
		10			15	23			5	3.8					10		4
					9				7	65							
		20			24	23		27	19	68.8	1	15	12	10	20	22	6
				4	9		10.9					1.74			7.7	1.8	
							27		15					26.2	15	26	14
							33							40.17	19.9	40	14
	4	5		10			11.35		12.5	7.7	2	15.2		12	9.2	9.9	6
							35.11	33		46			42	52			
		5		7					17.5		7	1.36		6	8.5	5	4
	4			7					12	23.7		3.4			7	13	
.7											4				11.8	4	
											5						
		5		4					4					10	13	7	
							38.7	24				16	40.92	41	16	28	8
																	6
							9.8										12
														9			2
											7						
								34						40.92			
								59						41.24			

ughly compared with normal women by looking at data in the first three columns and the very last column. However, the table is better designed as display of data-for-data's sake than as a comparative device.

The figures in the table do not always correspond to those in the text's discussion of this table.

Cranial Anomalies

Present in 35.5 percent of criminals and 45 percent of prostitutes.

Anomalies of the Forehead

Present in 20 percent of female criminals, 22 percent of prostitutes, and 6 percent of normal women.

Facial Asymmetry

Present in 7.7 percent of criminals and 1.8 percent of prostitutes.

Enormous Lower Jaw

Present in 15 percent of criminals, 26 percent of prostitutes, and 9 percent of normal women.[31]

Anomalous Ears

According to Gradenigo's comparative data on the ears of 245 criminal women and 14,000 normal women, anomalies are twice as frequent among criminals. The exception is Darwin's tubercule, which is present in 2.9 percent of criminal women and 3 percent of normal women.

Strabismus

Present in 8.5 percent of criminal women, 5 percent of prostitutes, and 4 percent of normal women. Looking at criminals only, we find that strabismus[32] is more common in thieves (16 percent)[33] than in poisoners (10 percent).

Virile Physiognomy

Present in 11.8 percent of criminals and 4 percent of prostitutes. Especially in profile, this virility gives a hard, cruel look to faces, which on a front view are sometimes beautiful. I found crooked noses in 25 percent of criminals and 8 percent of prostitutes.

Anomalous Teeth

Observed in 16 percent of criminals, 28 percent of prostitutes, and 8 percent of normal women.

16
Other Anomalies

Here we complete the list of characteristics of degeneration.

Moles

Although seldom studied, hair moles must be added to the signs of degeneration in women. They are a kind of indirect supplement to the beard and make females look masculine. We found this anomaly among 14 percent of normal women, 6 percent of criminals, and 41 percent of prostitutes. Zola mentions the moles of Nana and those of her worthy rival, the lascivious countess.[34]

Hairiness

Professor Riccardi found an exaggerated development of pubic hair in 21 percent of prostitutes, Gurrieri in 27 percent. Gurrieri further observed a lack of pubic hair in 18 percent and a scarcity of it in 10 percent. He further discovered that 1.8 percent had a veritable crest of hair from the navel to the pubes and that 16 percent had a virile distribution of hair.

Among 234 prostitutes, I found, as did Ardù, a virile quantity of hair in 15 percent of prostitutes, as compared to 5–6 percent of normal women and 5 percent of female criminals.

Cleft Palate

While I did not find this trait in the women I examined, it turned up in Tarnowsky's sample in 18 percent of the thieves, 14 percent of women who had committed homicide, 12 percent of the prostitutes, and 8 percent of the normal women. It must be characteristic of Russian women. In addition, Tarnowsky found asymmetrical eyebrows in the women she examined: 44 percent of the prostitutes, 40 percent of the women who had committed homicide, 20 percent of the thieves, and 4 percent of the normal women.

Breasts

Gurrieri found a lack of nipples on the breasts of 15 percent and an enlargement of the nipple in 20 percent.[35] Out of 130 cases, I myself found nipple atrophy in 12 percent. One swindler lacked nipples entirely.

Genitals

As for genitals, in 16 percent I found enlargement of the inner labia. Two of these cases were truly monstrous; six others were accompanied by enlargement of the clitoris and of the outer labia. Gurrieri found an exaggerated development of the clitoris in 13 percent, of the inner labia in 13 percent, and of the outer labia in 6.5 percent.

Riccardi examined thirty prostitutes and found:

Five with hypertrophy of the inner labia
Two with hypertrophy of the clitoris
One with hypospadias of the clitoris[36]

In sixty prostitutes, Gurrieri found eight examples of overdeveloped clitoris and eight examples of excessive development of the inner labia. Through lasciviousness, a famous adulterer and killer had enormously developed her clitoris and inner labia. Almost all the pseudohermaphrodites studied by De Creccio and Hoffmann had exaggerated sexual tendencies toward one sex or the other.

Nonetheless, I believe that vice does not correlate directly with organic abnormalities other than a profusion of pubic hair, at least not to the extent believed. Out of about 3,000 prostitutes, Parent-Duchatelet found only three with extraordinary development of the clitoris.[37] In one of these, the clitoris reached the length of a baby's penis (8 cm), but this deformity was associated with neither lesbian tendencies nor a masculine appearance, even though she lacked a uterus, menses, and breasts. She had thus, it seems, been reduced to her sad profession by misfortune, through small inclination of her own. The other two cases, in which there was no trace of hermaphroditism, were similarly apathetic. They had no beards, no clitoral anomalies,[38] and no lesbian tendencies.

Contrary to common belief, prostitution neither dilates the vagina nor deforms it. Only among new prostitutes who were recently virgins can one find distended vaginas. Parent-Duchatelet also found fifteen or twenty girls with exaggerated development of the inner labia, and a few with the vaginal membrane hardened into

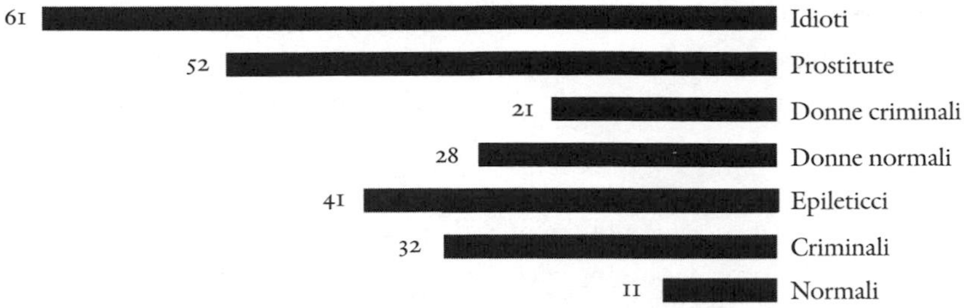

9 Bar graph of prehensile feet. *Source*: Lombroso, *La donna delinquente*, 1893. *Editors' note*: This graph compares the proportion of prehensile feet (an anomaly recalling monkeys) in normal men (11 percent), criminal men (32 percent), epileptics (41 percent), normal women (28 percent), prostitutes (52 percent), and "idiots" (61 percent). It purports to demonstrate that prostitutes are more atavistic than criminal women.

skin and with both inner and outer labia becoming a shapeless mass of fatty tissue, a tumor in fact, which recalled the apron of the Hottentot and even more her overdeveloped buttocks. Nevertheless, he concluded that there was less variation in these organs than in the corresponding male organs.[39]

To show the importance of these anomalies as atavisms, we call attention to the anomalies of the inner labia of the Hottentot, which constitute a new organ. One finds this same anomaly in 33 percent of normal European women, but in their case the cause is childbirth, while among prostitutes childbirth is the exception rather than the rule.

Prehensile Feet

A study by Ottolenghi and Carrara concluded that normal women are three times more likely than normal men to have prehensile feet (28 v. 11 percent). While criminal women are a little less likely than normal women to have this trait (24 percent), prostitutes have it nearly twice as often (42 percent).[40] In one of the sixty prostitutes studied by Gurrieri, the second and third toes of one foot had partially fused.

Larynx

The larynx of the prostitute presents several characteristic anomalies. Professor Masini, studying fifty prostitutes,[x] found fifteen with deep voices and vocal chords that were large in proportion to the size of the laryngeal opening. Twenty-

x. *Arch. di psych.*, XIV, fasc. I–II.

seven had even more masculine voices, with high bursts of sound followed by low, deep tones. In each case the larynx resembled that of a man, thus demonstrating (as did the face and cranium as well) the special virile nature of prostitutes.

Summary

Almost all anomalies occur more frequently in prostitutes than in female criminals, and both classes have more degenerative characteristics than do normal women. Prostitutes are almost free of the wrinkles and other anomalies that create ugliness, but they have more marks of degeneration. Murderers, poisoners, and arsonists have the most prominent cheekbones, and women who commit infanticide show the largest number of asymmetrical faces and exaggerated jaws. On the whole, however, murderers—both those who use violence and poisoners—form a more degenerate type than do those who commit infanticide.

17

Photographs of Criminals and Prostitutes

Anyone wishing to observe personally the anomalies we have described, can refer to our photographs of French and Russian offenders. We have used these examples from distant countries instead of photographs of Italians for two reasons: first, the outstanding cooperation provided by our Russian colleague Tarnowsky;[41] and second, Italy's legal impediments. Among the most ridiculous laws in Italy, whose bureaucracy is certainly not Europe's leader in these matters, is the absolute ban on measuring, studying, or photographing offenders sentenced to prison. In Russian prisons, in contrast, Tarnowsky was afforded every convenience, and after thoroughly studying the body and mind of female offenders, she forwarded their photographs to me.

Female Criminals

We will deal first with five murderers, of whom the first two show the pure type for their class.[42]

The first,[43] aged forty, killed her husband with repeated blows of a hatchet while he was skimming the milk, then threw his body into a recess under the stairs, and fled during the night with the family money and her own trinkets. Arrested a week later, she confessed her crime. This woman was remarkable for the asymmetry of her face. Her nose was hollowed out, her ears projected, and her brows were more fully developed than is usual in a woman. Moreover, her jaw was enormous, with a lemurian protuberance.

The second, aged sixty, was constantly mistreated by her husband until she and her son strangled him; afterward they hung him to give the impression of suicide. Here again we have asymmetry of the face, breadth of jaw, enormous frontal si-

10 Physiognomy of Russian criminals, photos 1–15. *Source*: Lombroso, *La donna delinquente*, 1893. *Editors' note*: In Lombroso's view, photographs of criminals can provide scientific evidence of their degeneracy.

11 Physiognomy of Russian criminals, photos 16–25. *Source*: Lombroso, *La donna delinquente*, 1893. *Editors' note*: Lombroso obtained his photographs of Russian offenders from Pauline Tarnowsky, one of Europe's leading criminal anthropologists.

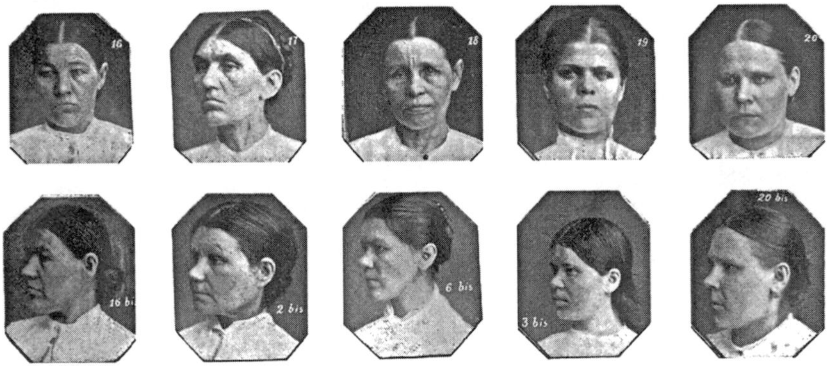

12 Physiognomy of French, German, and Italian criminal women, series 1. *Source*: Lombroso, *La donna delinquente*, 1893. *Editors' note*: According to Lombroso, the virile criminal type remains the same across national borders. This sequence of photographs (Figs. 12–15) from three different European countries was designed to make that point.

13 Physiognomy of French, German, and Italian criminal women, series 2. *Source*: Lombroso, *La donna delinquente*, 1893.

14 Physiognomy of French, German, and Italian criminal women, series 3. *Source*: Lombroso, *La donna delinquente*, 1893.

15 Physiognomy of French, German, and Italian criminal women, series 4. *Source*: Lombroso, *La donna delinquente*, 1893.

nuses, numerous wrinkles, a hollowed-out nose, very thin upper lip, and deep-set eyes, wide apart and wild in expression.

The third, aged twenty-one, was married against her will and mistreated by her husband until, after a nighttime fight, she killed him with a hatchet while he slept. In her we find only a demitype. Her ears stand out, she has big jaws and cheekbones, and her hair is very black. In addition, there are other anomalies which do not appear in the photograph, such as gigantic canine teeth and dwarf incisors.

The fourth, aged forty-four, strangled her husband by agreement with her lover and threw him in a ditch. She denied her crime. Hollowed-out nose, black hair, deep-set eyes, big jaw. Demitype.

The fifth, aged fifty, a peasant, killed her brother while he was eating supper in order to get an inheritance. She denied her guilt persistently, but was sentenced, with her hired accomplices, to twenty years of hard labor. She had black hair, grey eyes, diasthema of the teeth, a cleft palate, early and deep wrinkles, thin lips, and a crooked face. Demitype.

Now I will turn to poisoners. One of the most remarkable examples is that of a woman, aged thirty-six, who came from a wealthy family and had an epileptic mother and alcoholic father. After sixteen years of marriage, she poisoned her husband with arsenic. Nose hollowed out and club-shaped, large jaws and ears, squinty eyes, and weak reflex action of the left patella. She confessed nothing. Character resolute and devout. Full type.

Looking at photographs of these women, people may say that these faces are not after all too horrible, and I agree, insofar as they are infinitely less ugly than the male criminals portrayed in my *Atlas of Criminals*.[44] Among the females there is sometimes even a ray of beauty; but when this beauty exists, it is more virile than feminine.

It is interesting to note the physiognomic resemblance among extremely different criminals. Several women in the photographs look like members of the same family. Moreover, if we compare these with the French thieves presented by Macé,[y] it is obvious that race makes little difference; for the French women seem Russian, and the Russians French. All have the same repulsive, virile air, the same big, sensual lips, and so on. The French women, however, are infinitely more typical and ugly, and here I would observe that the more refined a nation is, the more its criminals deviate from the average.

Gabriella Bompard exhibits—as Brouardel, Ballet, and Motet correctly noted[z]

y. *Mon Musée Criminel*, Paris, 1890, p. 148.
z. *Archives d'anthropologie criminelle*, Lyons, 1891.

—all the characteristics of the born criminal, no matter how exceptional they may be in women generally.[45] Her stature was 1 meter 46,[46] her hips and breast rudimentary, and she consequently looked so masculine that, when dressed as a man, she was able to accompany Eyraud everywhere without being recognized. She had thick hair, abnormal and premature wrinkles, a livid pallor, a short, hollowed-out nose, and a heavy jaw. Above all, she had an asymmetrical and flattened face as in Mongolians.

Even more typically lascivious and homicidal, it seems to me, was Berland.[aa] Here we find overly close eyes; a receding forehead; a small head; ears too tightly attached to the head; numerous, deep and premature wrinkles; crooked lips; a flat, crooked nose curving outward; a receding chin; and a virile physiognomy. Another female criminal, Thomas by name, who was alcoholic and libidinous, had committed hundreds of abortions, falling into a dipsoepileptic stupor immediately after each crime. Her face was asymmetrical, her protruding ears were abnormally tight against her head, her nose was oblique and twisted, her lips were thin and crooked, and her wrinkles were extraordinarily plentiful.

These two photographs give a very good idea of the female criminal type. When the type is pure, it is less brutal than the pure male born criminal. Very often in women the criminal type is disguised by youth; the lack of wrinkles and plumpness of youth mask the size of the jaw and cheekbones, softening the virile and savage aspects of the features. When the hair is abundant and black and the eyes are bright, these criminals can even present a pleasant appearance. Moreover, sex appeal may affect our judgment, encouraging us to think erotically and making the offender seem more beautiful and free of degenerative traits than she really is.[47]

Prostitutes

With Tarnowsky's help, I studied one hundred prostitutes, all from the same city (Moscow) and therefore similar in background, and all eighteen to twenty-two years old. I cannot guarantee that none come from Germany or that none are Jews; but the majority certainly are Russians from Moscow. In contradistinction to female criminals, these prostitutes are relatively, if not generally, beautiful. While the criminal type appears among them, it can be found in only 10 percent of the cases. Another 15 percent show just a half-type; and the examples of both criminals and prostitutes exhibit characteristics of madness as well as criminality.

aa. I owe these portraits to the kindness of Prince Rolando Bonaparte, who has one of the best anthropological collections in Europe and had these made especially for me.

16 Gabriella Bompard. *Source*: Lombroso, *La donna delinquente*, 1893. *Editors' note*: Lombroso considered Bompard, a French prostitute convicted of premeditated murder, to be an example of the full born criminal type.

17 Berland (2 views). *Source*: Lombroso, *La donna delinquente*, 1893. *Editors' note*: Lombroso describes this criminal as lascivious, homicidal, and virile in appearance.

18 Thomas (2 views). *Source*: Lombroso, *La donna delinquente*, 1893. *Editors' note*: In this photo, Lombroso detected the wrinkles, protruding ears, twisted nose, and overall virility that he considered typical of female born criminals.

19 Physiognomy of Russian prostitutes. *Source*: Lombroso, *La donna delinquente*, 1893. *Editors' note*: In Lombroso's view, prostitutes are even more atavistic than female criminals.

The wild eyes, perturbed expression, and facial asymmetry of some remind one of women in insane asylums, especially the maniacs.

The scarcity of the criminal type and lack of ugliness may cause many to doubt our theory that prostitutes are not only equivalents of criminals but in fact have the same characteristics in exaggerated form. However, in addition to the fact that true female criminals are much less ugly than their male counterparts, in prostitutes we have women of great youth in whom the "beauty of the devil," with its abundance of soft, fresh flesh and absence of wrinkles, masks anomalies. Another thing to keep in mind is that prostitution calls for a relative lack of peculiarities such as large jaw and hardened stare which, if present, might cause disgust and repulsion; it also requires that such peculiarities be concealed through artifice. Certainly makeup—a virtual requirement of the prostitute's sad trade—minimizes many of the degenerative characteristics that female criminals exhibit openly.

Where delicacy of feature and a benevolent expression are useful, we find them—a truly Darwinian phenomenon.[48] But even the most beautiful female criminals have a virile nature, and in them the exaggerated jaw and cheekbones are never lacking. Similarly, these traits are never lacking in Italian coquettes; the family resemblance almost wipes out differences between Russian prostitutes and those who pass their lives in Italian cities, whether it be in gilt coaches or humble rags. When youth vanishes, those jaws, those cheekbones and sharp angles hidden by adipose tissues emerge and the face becomes virile, uglier than that of a man. Then the wrinkles deepen, becoming like scars, and the once pleasant face fully reveals the degenerative type into which it was born.

18

The Criminal Type in Women and Its Atavistic Origins

Frequency of the Type

The mere frequency of degenerative traits is insufficient to give us an exact idea of the criminal type among women; that type emerges clearly only when we study various characteristics in combination. We can refer to a complete type when we find four or more degenerative traits; a half-type when at least three such traits are present; and zero type when the offender exhibits only one or two physical anomalies or none whatsoever.

Of the female criminals examined, 52 were Piedmontese, in the prison of Turin; another 234, sentenced to the female penitentiary,[49] came from other Italian provinces, especially the south. Thus we ignored ethnic characteristics pertaining to prisoners' areas of origin.[50] We studied the criminal type in these offenders, in the 150 prostitutes we had previously examined, and in another 100 prostitutes from Moscow whose photographs were sent to us by Tarnowsky. Finally, to get comparative results, we applied our classification system to data supplied by Marro, Grimaldi, and Tarnowsky. The results appear in table 23.

A single glance at table 23 demonstrates the tremendous agreement among the results. The penitentiary prisoners resemble those we saw in the Turin prison; and our own results are close to the averages of the other observers, allowing for personal differences in the assessment of a single trait.[51]

These are the key results:

(1) The criminal type is a rarity in female compared to male criminals. In our homogeneous group (286 cases),[52] the proportion of those with the complete type is 14 percent, a figure that rises to 18 percent when one takes into consideration the other data in the table.[53] Even this is a small figure,

Table 23 The Degenerative Type

	number	zero type (0-2 anomalies)	0 anomalies	1 anomaly	2 anomalies	half-type (3 anomalies)	full type (4-8 anomalies)	4 anomalies	5 anomalies	6 anomalies	7 anomalies	8 anomalies
soldiers	71	89	37.2		51.8		11.8	11.8				
normal men	200	84	32		52		16	16				
normal women	600						1.89					
criminal men	353	64.8	8.2		56.6		35.2	32.6		2.3	0.3	
dangerous criminal men	346	59.1	11.9		47.2		40.9	33.9		6.7	0.3	
criminals (photographs)	228	61	16	17	28	16	24	14	7.5	1.3	1.3	
German criminal women (photos)	83	15					28					
Italian criminal women	122	16					26					
criminal women (Marro)	41	58.7	4.8	32	21	22	19	7.3	9.7		2.4	
criminal women (Tarnowsky)	150	55	3	18	34	21	24	10	10	4		
criminal women (penitentiary)	234	55.9				29	14.9					
female murderers	106	55.7				31.1	13.2					
female thieves	38	55.2				28.9	16					
women who commit infanticide	45	64.4				26.6	8.7					
female swindlers	18	61.1				27.8	11.1					
female procurers	16	50				31	18.7					
female poisoners	12	33				25	41.6					
female thieves (prison)	52	55.8				28.9	15.3					
average: 286 women (Lomb. and Ott.)		57				29.3	14					
criminal women (photos)	56	62.4	19.6	26.8	16	19.6	17.8	7.1	10.7			
prostitutes (Grimaldi)	26	38		23	15	27	31	26	7.6	7.6		
prostitutes (Tarnowski)	100	32.9		10	22.66	23.33	43	20	9.33	4	2.66	0.66
prostitutes (Lomb. and Ott.)	100	30				32	38					
average for criminal women	533	57.5				25.7	18.7					
average for prostitutes	226	33.6				27.5	37.1					
insane women (Ronco-roni)	40	59	2.5	12.5	45	17.5	22.5	15	7.5			

Editors' note: Column 1 lists the number of cases. The figures in the remaining columns represent percentages of these cases. The columns labeled "zero type" (normal men/women), "half-type" (criminaloid) and "full type" (born criminal) should add up to 100 percent, but in several cases they do not. The zero type and the full type are followed by columns indicating subcategories of each type based on numbers of anomalies. The row labeled "Average: 286 women" refers to the total number of women in the previous seven rows. These seven rows, however, add up to 287, not 286.

roughly half the average for the male born criminal (31 percent).[54] (The type shows up among only 2 percent of normal women.)[55] Moreover, all observers agree that the criminal type is rare among women; overall, 57.5 percent of the female criminals are of zero type. The half-type appears in very similar proportions in all the samples. It turns up in 22 percent of Marro's cases and 21 percent of Tarnowsky's, in 29 percent of our penitentiary cases, and 28.9 percent of our prison cases. Overall, an average of 25.2 percent[56] of female criminals can be classified as half-type.

(2) Prostitutes differ notably from female criminals in that a complete type appears much more frequently among them.[57] It appears in 31.0 percent of Grimaldi's prostitutes, 43.0 percent of Tarnowsky's cases, and 38.0 percent of our cases. Overall, an average of 37.1 percent of prostitutes exhibit the complete type. Earlier we reached similar conclusions from our study of specific features and the various types of born prostitutes compared with common female criminals.

(3) There are differences in the prevalence of the complete type among female criminals according to offense. We first classified our 286 prison and penitentiary cases solely by their number of anomalies, without knowing of their type of crime. Later, when we did classify by crime type, we found that of the thieves in the Turin prison and in the penitentiary, 15.3 percent and 16 percent, respectively, showed the complete type. Among murderers, the type appeared in 13.2 percent, and among those sentenced for procuring (a group that included aged prostitutes), it rose to 18.7 percent. The lesser frequency found among swindlers (11 percent) and among women who committed infanticide (8.7 percent) was predictable, for they are typically occasional criminals.[58]

The female criminal seems almost normal compared to the male criminal with his abundant abnormalities.

Atavistic and Social Reasons for the Scarcity of Type

The surprising rarity of anomalies in the female criminal does not contradict the incontestable fact that like other female animals, atavistically she is nearer to her primitive origin than the male and thus ought to be richer in abnormalities. As we have seen (this volume, 114–15), 78 percent of the crania of male criminals have anomalies, as compared to 27 percent for female criminals and 51 percent for prostitutes. We have also seen that only some of the deformities are increasing in women and that when they occur, it is due to prenatal damage.[59] But the opposite is true of those truly atavistic abnormalities that more strictly define the degenerative character or type, and as in cretinism, madness, and (much more important to us) epilepsy, they manifest themselves less markedly and less frequently in women. Moreover, anomalies are rare even in normal women, compared to normal men.[60] In addition, we have seen that aside from a few exceptions in the lower animals, this phenomenon of lesser female variability occurs up and down the zoological scale, thus proving that variations are smaller in females than in males. As Viazzi (*Anomalo*, 1893) has wisely noted, the female of the various species reveal the *general* character of the group to which they belong. Most naturalists agree[bb] that the type of a species is represented more straightforwardly by the female than the male, an observation that one can extend to the moral world as well.[61]

Helen Zimmern, in her *Philosophy of Fashion*, observes that women express their individuality better than men in the details of their clothing, while the main lines of fashion in every age are determined by man's active, creative element. Starting with the primitive Greek chiton—sleeveless, flowing, and belted (the origin of all later clothing for men and women alike)—male attire has changed from age to age and from country to country, while female attire has remained substantially the same (Viazzi).

Scholars have noted women's conservative tendency in matters of social justice, a tendency rooted in the immobility of the ovule relative to the sperm. Add to this the fact that the main burden of raising the family—an occupation sedentary by nature—falls on the female and that she is less exposed than the male to variations of time and space in her environment. For most vertebrates and even more for savages, the struggle for existence and for the children's survival devolves primarily on the male; this struggle is therefore a cause of incessant change and special adaptations in the functions and organs (Viazzi, op. cit.).

Now, once we admit that the primitive type of a species is more clearly represented in the female, we must proceed to argue that the typical forms of our race—which are better organized and fixed in woman by time, long heredity, and minimal ancestral variation—are less subject to transformation and deformation by the factors that cause progressive and retrogressive variations in the male (id.).

Another very potent factor contributing to the relative absence of anomalies among female criminals has been sexual selection. Primitive man not only spurned the deformed woman; he also ate her, preferring to keep at hand those more pleasing to his sexual whims. (In those days he was stronger and had a

bb. Morselli, *Lezioni di antropologia*, in corso di pubblicazione, p. 220.

choice.) An anecdote tells of an Australian savage who, when asked why there were no elderly women in his country, answered, "Because we ate them." When others showed shock at such treatment of his wives, he explained, "For every one that we lose, there are a thousand others." Those thus lost were certainly not the most attractive. Anomalies that persist are those that pose no obstacle to sexual selection because the male finds them either convenient or unobjectionable, as in the anomalous inner labia and strange buttocks of Hottentot women, which they use for carrying children. Anomalies are perpetuated only when they prevail among the women of a given tribe and become stable through that tenacity that characterizes all feminine traits.

Atavism, too, helps explain the comparative rarity of the criminal type in women.[62] Savage females, and still more civilized females, are less ferocious than males. It is the occasional offender whom we meet most frequently among women criminals; and as occasional offenders have no distinctive physiognomy, they provide no examples of the type. Even the true female born criminal does not stand out clearly because she tends to be an accomplice or to commit types of crime—adultery, slander, swindling—to which a repugnant face would be an obstacle.

Primitive woman was rarely a murderer; but she was always a prostitute, and so she remained until the end of the semibarbaric period. Atavism again explains why prostitutes have more regressive traits than do female criminals.

While all these observations help explain the relative scarcity of anomalies among female offenders, I think there is an additional cause. Women today, like the lower animals and uncivilized women, experience less activity than men in their cerebral cortex, especially in the psychical centers. Thus the irritation provoked by degeneration fixes itself there less firmly and tenaciously, and thus it leads only to motor and hysterical epilepsy and to sexual anomalies rather than to crime.[63] Because of the greater development of their cerebral cortex, men more often exhibit genius than women. This same sensitivity causes men to become delirious, intoxicated, or mad from drugs, while lower animals show little reaction to even the strongest narcotics.

Female criminality increases with the march of civilization. The female criminal is an occasional criminal, with few degenerative characteristics, little dullness, and so on; her numbers grow as opportunities for evildoing increase. The prostitute, on the other hand, has a greater atavistic resemblance to the primitive woman—the vagabond Venus—and thus she has greater dullness of touch and taste, greater fondness for tattooing, and so on.

In sum, the female criminal is less typical physiognomically than the male crimi-

20 Negro Venus. *Source*: Lombroso, *La donna delinquente*, 1893. *Editors' note*: Although there is no indication that this woman had broken the law, Lombroso uses her photograph to demonstrate the supposedly savage, masculine appearance of black women, traits he then uses to illustrate his theory that criminals are atavisms.

21 Patagonian girl. *Source*: Lombroso, *La donna delinquente*, 1893. *Editors' note*: In the case of this young South American Indian, too, Lombroso is trying to draw a connection between "savage races" and criminals.

nals because she is less essentially criminal; because in all forms of degeneration she deviates to a lesser degree; because, being organically conservative, she retains the characteristics of her type even when she deviates from it; and finally because beauty, being for her a supreme necessity, resists the assaults of degeneracy. But one cannot deny that when depravity in woman is profound, then the general law according to which the physical type correlates with crime wins out over every obstacle, at least among the most civilized races. This happens above all when she is a prostitute, for prostitution is closer than criminality to woman's primitive behavior.

Atavism

Atavism also shapes the criminal type in woman, affecting its substance as well as its frequency.[64] Its influence is found in the virility which forms the nucleus of the criminal type. What we look for above all in the female is femininity, and when we find its opposite we usually conclude that there must be some anomaly. To understand the significance and atavistic origin of virility, we have to keep in mind that it was one of the outstanding traits of savage woman. We can see this best by looking at portraits of American Indian and Negro Venuses taken from the work of Ploss (*Das Weib*, terza ediz., 1890). It is difficult to believe that these are really women, so huge are their jaws and cheekbones, so hard and thick are their features. The skulls and brains of savage women, too, often resemble those of men.

Because the criminal is above all a reversion to a primitive evolutionary type, the female criminal naturally presents the two most salient characteristics of primitive woman: precocity and similarity to the male. Her lesser differentiation from the male manifests itself in her stature, cranium, brain, and muscular strength, the latter of which is far greater in her than in the modern female. Examples of these masculine traits may still be found among Italian peasant women, especially on the islands.

Atavism may also be the cause of prostitutes' excessive obesity. "The stoutness of many prostitutes," observes Parent-Duchatelet, "strikes those familiar with their lives. Close observers claim that their obesity begins at about the age of 25 to 30 years. It is rarely noticeable in young girls or beginners." Parent-Duchatelet attributes this obesity to the great number of hot baths that prostitutes take throughout the year and, above all, to their inactivity and abundant nourishment. However, the lowest prostitutes, who are the fattest, do not take hot baths; and if their daytime lives are inactive, their nocturnal hours are filled with dances and orgies. While we admit that, as a rule, prostitutes grow fat only after reaching the age of twenty years, pictures show that they can be disposed to obesity from youth. Recalling the Hottentot, African, and Abyssinian women who when rich and idle grow extremely fat, we suggest that in the case of stoutness, too, atavism may be part of the explanation.

The posterior cushion of Hottentot women is an atavistic trait, produced by maternal and sexual functions. In fact, in Oceania and in Africa, people measure beauty in terms of weight, which they increase by various means, such as drinks of beer and milk until the hips of these immoral Venuses become monstrous.

In conclusion, I note that in prisons and insane asylums, one is more likely to find extraordinarily fat female lunatics than male lunatics. In Imola there is a twelve-year-old girl with hypertrophied breasts and buttocks (the former weighing about two kilograms each)[65] that are even larger than those of Hottentot women; she has to wear a special corset.

19
Tattoos

Criminals

Among male criminals the practice of tattooing is so common as to constitute a defining trait; but among female criminals the practice is almost nonexistent. Out of 1,175 sentenced women studied by me, Gamba, and Salsotto, only 13, or 2.15 percent,[66] were tattooed. Among female lunatics, however, the percentage is larger.

A murderer and thief who was twenty-four years old, violent and epileptic, a former model who became a prostitute and killed her lover (a painter) because she was jealous and he did not want to pay her, bore on her forearm in large letters starting with a *W* the name of the man she had killed. Underneath was the date on which he had abandoned her, while on her other forearm appeared the contradictory declaration, "I love Jean."

Prostitutes

Among prostitutes, especially those of the lowest class, the proportion of tattooing is higher. Segre found one tattooed prostitute among 300 in Milan, and De Albertis found 28 among 300 in Genoa, while I found 7 out of 1,561 in Turin—in all, 36 out of a total of 2,161, or 2.5 percent.[67] The key features of the practice almost have to be described through negatives. There are few religious symbols (only one out of thirty-three cases), although allusions to lovers are frequent (only two of these tattoos referred to parents, while twenty-four out of thirty-three referred to lovers). The inconstancy of their affections is revealed by the multiplicity of references to lovers—two tattoos alluded to two lovers and two others to three lovers. The marks consisted of:

In thirty-one cases—names and initials
In six cases—transfixed hearts
In three cases—men's heads
In two cases—mottoes
In three cases—their own names

Prof. Filippi studied a dissolute lesbian, fifteen years old, daughter of a pimp, who bore on her shoulders two pierced hearts under which was another heart and the initials of her mistress.[cc] Elderly lesbians of Paris often tattoo the name of their mistresses between their genitals and the navel, thus confirming their obscene habits.[68]

In Paris, as a rule prostitutes are tattooed only with the initials or names of their lovers, followed by the declaration "For life," flanked sometimes by two flowers or two hearts. These marks almost always appear on the shoulders or breast. Only twice was there an obscene allusion.

Parent-Duchatelet noticed that tattooing occurs most often among the most degraded prostitutes, who are accustomed to marking themselves with the names of lovers, always effacing the old with the new, so that in one case there had been fifteen names. Elderly prostitutes prefer to tattoo themselves with the names of women. De Albertis, too, observed that among prostitutes, those who tattoo themselves are the most depraved.

22 Tattoos of prostitutes—Peppenella. *Source*: Lombroso, *Atlante*, 1897. *Editors' note*: A prostitute ("Peppenella") had a tattoo made on her stomach by her lover ("Raffaele") in 1873. The numbers *6* and *16* in criminal jargon denote the openings of the anus and vagina (*Atlante*, xv).

cc. *Archivio di psichiatria*, XIII.

Very accurate research by Bergh in Denmark yielded similar results.[dd] Among the streetwalkers of Copenhagen, tattooing became fashionable when a young man, a former sailor with an aptitude for drawing and tattooing, began taking advantage of their well-known frivolity. Out of 801 women, Bergh found 80 who had been tattooed within the last five years, 49 (or more than half) of them by the sailor in question. Others had been tattooed by female friends while in the houses of correction or police stations, and some had been tattooed by pimps. Thirty-four were decorated with letters, ten with names, twenty-two with letters and images, eleven with names and images, and eight with images alone. Most of these tattoos were in red and black. Two bore the name of a female lover beside that of a male lover.

Five women had tattoos of the torso of a young man; four showed two clasped hands; nine had a heart, that banal symbol of love; three had a kind of ribbon; two showed a branch with leaves; and two had a leaf only. Eight had a bracelet, funeral cross, rosary, ring, star, ship with sails, or flag with cannon. Two women were tattooed in nine places, one in eleven, and another in fifteen. Most of these marks were on the upper part of the body; very few appeared on the legs or chest, and eight were on the finger joints.

In Copenhagen as in Paris and Genoa, tattooed prostitutes were the lowest of their class. However, none exhibited obscene designs. Generally their tattoos alluded to the love of men. There is a difference, however, in that in Copenhagen, prostitutes tattoo themselves only with male names, while in Paris, prostitutes often decorate themselves with the names of female lovers.[ee]

Conclusions: Atavism

On the whole, there is much less tattooing among criminal women than criminal men. In females of this class, the proportion is 2 in 1,000, while in young men, especially those in the military, the proportion rises to 32 or 40 percent, with a minimum of 14 percent. In prostitutes, the average is higher than among criminal women, 2.5 percent, a figure that has trebled lately through the new practice of tattooing moles on the face.

We have here, then, additional proof that atavistic phenomena are more frequent among prostitutes than among common female criminals, although in both groups tattooing is rarer than among males. Other differences between

dd. *Archivio di psichiatria*, XII.

ee. According to Parent-Duchatelet (p. 159, 169), about one quarter of the registered prostitutes of Paris were lesbians, a number that sounds about right for Copenhagen and Paris as well (see Bergh, *Vestne Hopital nel 1889*, p. 13).

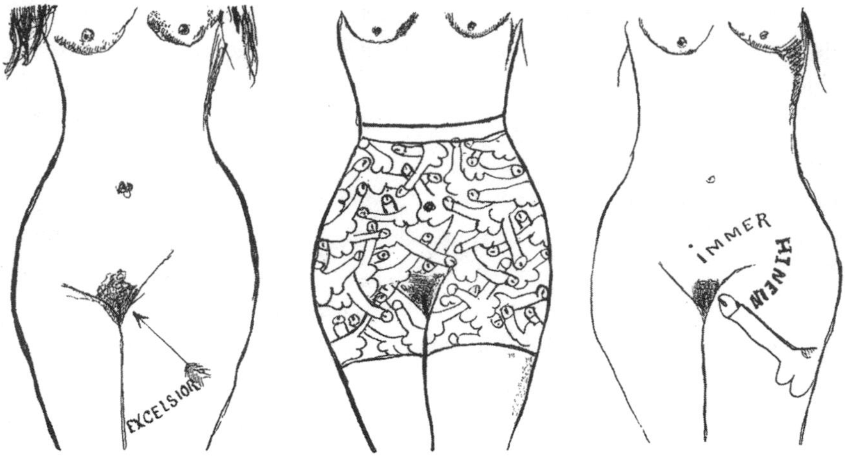

23 Tattoos of prostitutes—erotic torsos. *Source*: Lombroso, *Atlante*, 1897. *Editors' note*: Lombroso explains that the first design (*Excelsior*, or "Onward and upward,") comes from a French prostitute and the second from an eighteen-year-old Argentinian woman. The text of the third design, from a German woman's tattoo, reads "always inside" (*Atlante*, xv).

24 Tattoos of prostitutes—miscellaneous inscriptions. *Source*: Lombroso, *Atlante*, 1897. *Editors' note*: Clockwise from the upper left, Lombroso's comments read: Two linked hearts with a badly spelled motto, "Fidelity," tattooed on the shoulder of young Louisa, of Naples; The tattoo of a German criminal and prostitute, which reads, "I have learned to suffer without complaining"; The names of the barracks [*sic*] which a young prostitute frequented for twelve years (*Atlante*, xv).

women's and men's tattoos are the much greater lack of variety among the former; the absence of epigrams, obscene signs, and cries for vengeance; and the presence of only ordinary symbols and initials. Here we have another indication of women's lesser ingenuity and weaker imagination, for the main differentiating factor between their tattoos and those of men is intelligence. Even the female criminal is monotonous and uniform compared to her male counterpart, just as woman in general is inferior to man.

Once again, we must look for an explanation in atavism, an explanation that becomes doubly significant when we learn that even savage women were tattooed less frequently and more simply than their male counterparts. At Nouka Hiva, for example, it is a privilege of the more aristocratic women to be tattooed with fantastic designs, while plebeian females are restricted to simpler patterns.[ff] A chief's daughter was tattooed with a serpent entering her vulva, while another of his daughters had images of two men on her buttocks—evidently erotic allusions.[gg]

Modern woman's craving for self-beautification did not exist in primitive woman, who was a true beast of burden and reproduction. Even such a simple and primitive adornment as tattooing—which requires time and some effort—

25 Woman with autobiography written on her body. *Source*: Lombroso, *Atlante*, 1897. *Editors' note*: Lombroso collected prisoner art, including this example, which appeared originally on a cell water jug or wall.

ff. Scherzer, *Novara Reise*, III.
gg. *Archives d'anthropologie criminelle*, 1893.

was accompanied by religious rites, and had to be durable because it served as a record of descent and legal claims—was practiced only by and for men. Among women, for a long time its place was taken by blue and red painting of the hair, nails, and even teeth, probably starting at puberty. The elegant women of Baghdad dyed their lips, legs, and chests blue, outlining the curves of their breasts with blue flowers. In Burma, women's toenails and fingernails are colored red,[hh] while in Sackatu, indigo is used to dye the hair, teeth, feet, and hands. Even simplicity in tattooing is a sign of atavism in the criminal prostitute.[ii]

hh. C. Variot, *Les tatouages et les peintures de la peau, Revue scientifique*, III.

ii. The pornographic aim of some prostitutes' tattoos is now revealed by Laurent (*Les habitués des prisons de Paris*, 1890), where one reads of a woman who had herself tattooed with a blade of grass on her forehead and who told admirers that she had another, similar tattoo on her genitals, which she would exhibit to inflame their desires. Another woman had her thigh tattooed with the word *Excelsior*, along with an arrow pointing to her vulva. This is the only simultaneously pornographic and witty tattoo that I have found among women.

Part IV

Biology and Psychology of Female Criminals and Prostitutes

20
Menstruation, Fecundity, Vitality, Strength, and Reflexes

Menstruation

Menstruation is the most specialized of all female functions. In normal Italian women the onset of menstruation varies from 13 to 15 years (in Turin, the average is 13.3 years). Salsotto (op. cit.)[1] made the following observations on age of onset among Italian female offenders by crime type:

infanticide	median age of 13.4 years	precocious onset (10–12 years), 20%
poisoning	median age of 14.3 years	precocious onset (10–12 years), 10%
murder	median age of 14.2 years	precocious onset (10–12 years), 16%

Although these are just small differences, they do indicate retarded onset in female criminals (aside from those who commit infanticide) compared to the thirteen-to-fifteen-year average for normal women.

Reversing this pattern, 16 percent of our prostitutes experienced early onset of menstruation, while only 9 percent were notably late in age of onset. Rossignol (Icard, *La femme*, ecc.), in his study of fifty-eight girls who became prostitutes between the ages of nine and eleven, found that:

Thirty-three menstruated after first sexual intercourse
Twenty-seven menstruated before the age of ten
Nineteen menstruated before the age of eleven
Ten menstruated before the age of twelve
Two menstruated before the age of thirteen

During the menstrual period all experienced heightened erotic feelings.

In this regard, Tarnowsky's data are best because she made these comparisons herself, a woman working in her own region and under diverse conditions. Tarnowsky's precise findings thoroughly confirm the conclusion that prostitutes menstruate prematurely.

Menstruation strongly influences certain crimes.[2] Of eighty prisoners arrested for rebelling against or assaulting the guards, I found that only nine were not menstruating. Parisian women are likely to begin shoplifting while menstruating: among fifty-six such thieves studied by Legrand de Saulle, thirty-five were in the menstrual period, and for ten it had just ended. Legrand thus concluded that when hysterical young women steal bibelots, perfume, and the like, it is almost always during the menstrual period. Emet and De Gardane observed that in exceptionally lascivious women, menstruation is always abnormally prolonged, repeated, or abundant. Another characteristic of menstruation among prostitutes is its apparent irregularity.

Sexual Precocity

Sexual precocity among criminal women and prostitutes is evident in premature menstruation and even more in the early age when sexual relations begin.[3] In his *Inchiesta sulle cause della prostituzione delle minorenni in Francia* [Inquiry into the causes of prostitution among young women in France], Téophile Roussel finds that natural tendencies to vice sometimes lead girls who have not quite reached puberty into prostitution, in spite of their parents' efforts.[a] Of 2,582 women arrested for clandestine prostitution in Paris, 1,500 were minors. Roussel gives these examples to illustrate his point:

> The daughter of a Belgian engineer, well brought up and kept in boarding school until the age of sixteen, fled to Rotterdam to escape the vigilance of her mother and immediately entered a brothel.
>
> Another girl was sent by her rich and honest parents to boarding school at the age of eleven. When she graduated at the age of eighteen, she met a young man whom her parents rejected as a son-in-law. She fled her father's house to live with the young man; abandoned by him after ten months, she entered a brothel. She is said to be happy because she can satisfy her appetites, and she would not return even if her parents asked her back.

Sexual precocity is even more prevalent in Italy where, according to statistics collected by Grimaldi and Gurrieri, sexual activity begins even before the age of

a. Téophile Roussel, *Enquête sur les orphélinats et autres établissements de charité consacrés à l'enfance*. Mouillet, imprimeur du Sénat, 1882. [In the text, Lombroso gives an Italian title for this work, and it is that which we have translated here.—Eds.]

eleven—sometimes at the age of eight or nine, before the completion of sexual development and onset of menstruation. To be precise, sexual activity began:

In eight	one year before menstruation
In two	two years before menstruation
In one	four years before menstruation
In six	at the same time as menstruation

Sexual precocity is also evident among the prostitutes studied by De Albertis, who were deflowered at the median age of fifteen. He reports that one was deflowered at the age of nine by her father, another at age ten, two others at age twelve, six between thirteen and fourteen, eight from fifteen to sixteen, and only one at the age of forty-four.

My research has found the same results. In fact, 29 percent of my female thieves —a higher rate than among normal women—had first intercourse before the age of fifteen; 67 percent began sexual relationships between the ages of sixteen and nineteen; and only 2.7 percent had their first sexual experience after age thirty-five. Prostitutes have an even higher rate of precocious intercourse (45 percent), and none delayed intercourse until an advanced age. Thus the sexual precocity of prostitutes, which one might almost call a professional characteristic, is greater than in normal women and even female criminals.

It is now known that sexual precocity is an atavistic characteristic of animals and savages.

Fecundity

An opposite pattern seems to obtain for fecundity. Salsotto observed that among roughly 150 female criminals, 79 percent had children; among 20 poisoners, the rate was 80 percent; and among 130 murderers, the rate was 77 percent. I myself have found in Italy (where, unfortunately, the influence of ethnicity can confound results) these averages:

4.5 children for poisoners
3.2 children for murderers
2.0 children for women who commit infanticide

Thus only among the poisoners is fecundity above the average,[4] which fits with their sexual precocity and with the eroticism that frequently causes their crimes.

Among prostitutes, Andronico found 20 percent with children and Riccardi 34 percent. I will not try to explain this low fecundity rate in terms of atavism or degeneration, since we know that the lower animals have the highest birthrates. Instead one must explain prostitutes' low fecundity in terms of their great susceptibility to illnesses that affect the sexual organs, such as metritis, salpingitis, urethritis, and ovaritis, and in terms of the noxious remedies prostitutes use to cure themselves, particularly mercury and iodic compounds. Then too, alcohol abuse makes it difficult to carry a fetus to term, as do orgies and traumas, including coitus itself, which can lead to loss of the fetus. Moreover, the agitated, impoverished life of prostitutes excludes normal development of the ovule, even a fertilized ovule. It also makes it difficult to raise children—another side effect of this sad profession.

Vitality

Not only do women live longer than men; they also have more resistance to misfortune and deep grief. In the case of the female criminal, this well-known law seems almost exaggerated, so remarkable are her longevity and the toughness with which she endures hardships, even the prolonged hardships of prison. As is well known, the number of aged female criminals exceeds that of males. I know some women prisoners who have reached the age of ninety, having lived within penitentiary walls since they were twenty-nine without grave injury to health.

It is impossible to determine the average lifespan of prostitutes due to the scarcity of data and their nomadic habits. While Parent-Duchatelet failed to settle that issue, he did demonstrate that many prostitutes, when forced to abandon their trade by age and infirmities, become artisans, wives or friends of ragpickers and sweepers, and so on, or become attached to brothels, convents, refuges for beggars, hospitals, and prisons.

Mortality for prostitutes does not exceed the average. Indeed, when one allows for the special illnesses to which prostitutes are subject, such as bronchial and uterine consumption, syphilis, alcoholism, and so on, it becomes clear that their average mortality is relatively low.

"Many physicians," Parent-Duchatelet writes, "claim that prostitutes die of consumption or syphilis in early youth, but many others assert that they have iron constitutions, that their profession does not wear them out, and that they can resist anything." Facts confirm the latter view. There was Marion de Lorme, who lived to be 135 (from 1588 to 1723), so that when Parisians wanted to refer to something that resisted the onslaughts of time, they mentioned her as well as the towers of Notre Dame. She buried four husbands and was over eighty before losing her freshness of mind and body. Nino de Lenclos at age eighty still had the glossy black hair of her youth, white teeth, bright eyes, and a full form;

reportedly she excited a violent passion in the abbot of Châteauneuf, a youth of twenty.

Voice

As Parent-Duchatelet remarked, many prostitutes have a voice as masculine as that of a cart driver, especially if they are over the age of twenty-five or belong to the lowest class. While others have attributed this peculiarity to the habits of wine drinking and shrieking, Parent-Duchatelet attributed it to the effects of weather, exposure, and alcohol. He may be correct, but I myself have come to believe, as a result of Professor Masini's research, that what we are seeing here is a congenital trait: prostitutes' voices are masculine because they have a masculine larynx.

Handwriting

The few prostitutes with any education have a somewhat masculine handwriting. The same seems to be true of the true female born criminal, though the examples are too few to allow for definite conclusions.

Strength

The female criminal Perino d'Oneglia jumped from trees onto the roofs of houses to burglarize them, escaping in the same way and evading detection for years. I also know of a model (a tattooed, epileptic prostitute who killed the artist who painted her) who sometimes, especially when her vanity was wounded, became so violently agitated that five guards were unable to hold her down. The famous Bonhours, a prostitute who wore men's clothing, was as strong as a man and killed several men with a hammer. The celebrated Bell-Star, leader of a band of assassins, competed in a horse race in North America, dressed as a man and carrying off several prizes. With great justification Zola, in *Bête humaine*, gives the murderous virago Flora such strength of arm that she is able to derail a train in order to kill her lover and her rival.

It is proverbial that in farmhouses, the most agile and ready servant girls are the least honest.[5] As for prostitutes, their agility is proved by the great number of them who are dancers and tightrope performers; moreover, there is no coquette who does not fence.

Reflexes

We found reflex actions to be exaggerated in 25 percent of the criminals we examined, weak in 16 percent, normal in 54 percent, and absent in 5 percent. But the greatest number of anomalies was found, again, among prostitutes. Out of one hundred prostitutes, we found twenty with exaggerated reflex actions and twenty-one in whom reflex action was slight or absent entirely. Among criminals, most abnormal were the poisoners and murderers, in whom reflex actions tended to be slow, while least abnormal were the women who had committed infanticide.

Fifty percent of the murderers and 25 percent of the poisoners blushed at the mention of their crime. However, 45 percent of them met such allusions with absolute silence.

21

Acuteness of Sense and Vision

Touch

My initial investigations of touch showed that criminals are duller in this sense than honest women, as follows:

	criminals and prostitutes[6]	*normal women*
Delicate sense of touch	1.7 percent	16 percent
Dull sense of touch	26.2 percent	25 percent
Average sense of touch	51.6 percent	56 percent

In thirty-six female thieves, I found an average for touch of 3.75 in the index finger of the right hand, 3.73 in the index finger of the left hand, and 1.97 in the tongue; the comparable averages for women who had committed infanticide were 3.76 (right index finger), 3.46 (left index finger), and 2.75 (tongue).[7] Among 101 criminal women not differentiated by crime, I found these averages: 3.46 (right index finger), 3.67 (left index finger), and 1.9 (tongue). Criminal women have a duller sense of touch than criminal men, for whom the corresponding figures are 2.94, 2.89, and 1.9.

Prostitutes

My research on the sense of touch among prostitutes is thin and often contradictory. I found fifteen young prostitutes with a delicate sense of touch (1.90 right hand, 1.45 left hand, 1.48 tongue), but I also found sixty-eight mature prostitutes in whom touch was dull (3.04 right hand, 3.02 left hand, and 2.11 tongue). Gurrieri's studies of prostitutes, too, have revealed that some are even more sensitive than normal women. But we must keep three factors in mind: the influence of culture,[8] age, and degenerative characteristics.[b] In fact, twelve girls aged six to fifteen years had averages of 1.56 (right hand) and 2.57 (left hand); and among educated women dullness was lower (2), while among lower-class women it was 2.6. Dullness of touch is rather less frequent (16 percent) among honest women with no degenerative traits; a bit higher (28 percent) in those with some degenerative traits; and frequent (75 percent) in those who, though honest, have many such traits. Thus the differences I found might have arisen from the fact that I was comparing prostitutes with honest peasant women (as did Marro and Tarnowsky), or with honest older women, or with honest women who nonetheless had many degenerative characteristics.[9]

Sensitivity to Pain

Using the Lombroso algometer to determine sensitivity to pain, I found that the average among honest men was 42 mm compared to 45 among honest women.[10] The average among female thieves was 21.4 (right side) and 20.5 (left side); among prostitutes it was 19.0 (right side) and 21 (left side). These findings indicate a greater dullness of touch and rate of left-handedness in the latter group.[11] Indeed, 28 percent of the prostitutes showed complete insensibility to pain.

Gurrieri studied general sensitivity and sensitivity to pain in various body parts, finding that 10 percent of the normal women, compared to 7 percent of the prostitutes, felt the electric current in the palm of the hand when the points were 130 millimeters away. But when the points were 40 millimeters or more apart, 16 percent of the normal women, compared to 39 percent of the prostitutes, felt the current, demonstrating—as Tarnowsky has since confirmed—that prostitutes are more sensitive than normal women in the palm of the hand.

Gurrieri's results for other body parts appear in table 24. Thus the normal woman is much more sensitive than the prostitute, the latter being especially insensitive in the clitoris. Prostitutes are naturally more sensitive in the palm of the hand because the hands of female laborers and peasants (the normal women in Gurrieri's study) grow insensible through the thickening of the skin caused by hard work. But idleness refines the sensitivity of the palms of prostitutes. This greater sensitivity flows, then, not from the central nervous system or cortical areas, but from their profession. The opposite can be said of the clitoris, which grows insensible in prostitutes through overuse.

b. *Tatto, sensibilitá generale e dolorifica, e tipo degenerativo in donne normali, criminali e alienate. Archivio di psichiatria*, 1891.

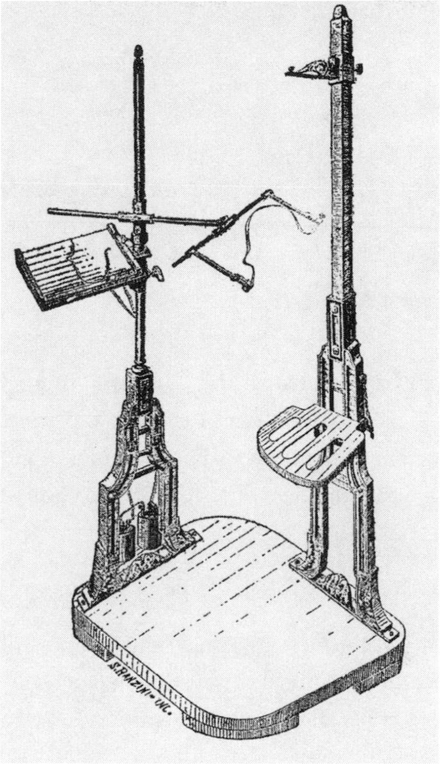

26 Craniograph. *Source*: Lombroso, *Atlante*, 1897. *Editors' note*: Criminal anthropologists used machines like this one, for measuring the head, to establish physical norms and detect anomalies.

Prostitutes' insensitivity to pain, which corresponds to that of the male born criminal, is confirmed by the ease with which lesbians and their lovers expose themselves to the most painful wounds without complaint.[12] Many are covered with scars (out of 392 prostitutes observed by Parent-Duchatelet, 90 had been treated for wounds). They also bear serious syphilitic lesions with indifference and endure with equal fortitude cauterizations of the external genitals and surgical operations. Professor Tizzoni lately told me about a prostitute whose leg he had had to amputate and who refused ether, begging only to be placed so she could see the operation, which she followed throughout as though she were a stranger, without uttering a cry. Such women are true *filles de marbre*.[13]

Gurrieri has noted a very significant fact: that prostitutes who have had children are the most sensitive to pain.[14] Their sensitivity of the tongue is 99 mm, compared to 76 among other prostitutes. Similarly, in those who have had children, the sensitivity of the clitoris is 102, compared to 97 in the others. But the same differences do not always occur in the breasts, tongue, and hand.[15]

Table 24 Sensitivity in Normal Women and Prostitutes

	general sensitivity				sensitivity to pain			
	fine		dull		fine		dull	
	norm.	pros.	norm.	pros.	norm.	pros.	norm.	pros.
throat	82 %	50 %	10 %	9 %	18 %	38 %	8 %	3 %
forehead and hand	4 %	4 %	20 %	49 %	6 %	5 %	20 %	16 %
tongue	14 %	3 %	28 %	55 %	4 %	13 %	—	2 %
clitoris	8 %	5 %	24 %	32 %	33 %	5 %	8 %	16 %

Taste

Fifty percent of the normal women and 15 percent of the criminals whom I studied showed great delicacy of taste, being able to detect 1 in 500,000 parts of strychnine. But among 10 percent of normal women, 20 percent of criminals, and 30 percent of prostitutes, we found a marked dullness of taste (1 in 100 parts of strychnine).

Sense of Smell

Dullness of the olfactory sense, which Dr. Ottolenghi tested with essences of cloves, turned out to be three times greater in criminals (occurring in 6 percent) than normal women (2 percent). Nineteen percent of born prostitutes lacked a sense of smell.

Hearing

In Tarnowsky's studies, the sense of hearing was normal in 86 percent of honest women, 74 percent of prostitutes, 68 percent of thieves, and 54 percent of women who committed homicide. It was weak in 14 percent of honest women, 24 percent of prostitutes, 30 percent of thieves, and 40 percent of homicide offenders. Two percent of prostitutes and thieves and 6 percent of women guilty of homicide lacked this sense entirely.

Field of Vision

In my clinic, Ottolenghi measured the field of vision of female born criminals, female occasional criminals, and born prostitutes. Only three in fifteen born criminals had a normal field of vision. Twelve of them had more or less limited fields of vision, and in nine cases the diagrams of the visual fields showed the deep peripheral recesses and broken peripheral lines that he had noted previously in the male born criminal and in epileptics (Ottolenghi, *Anomalie del campo visivo nei psicopatici*, ecc. Bocca, 1890).

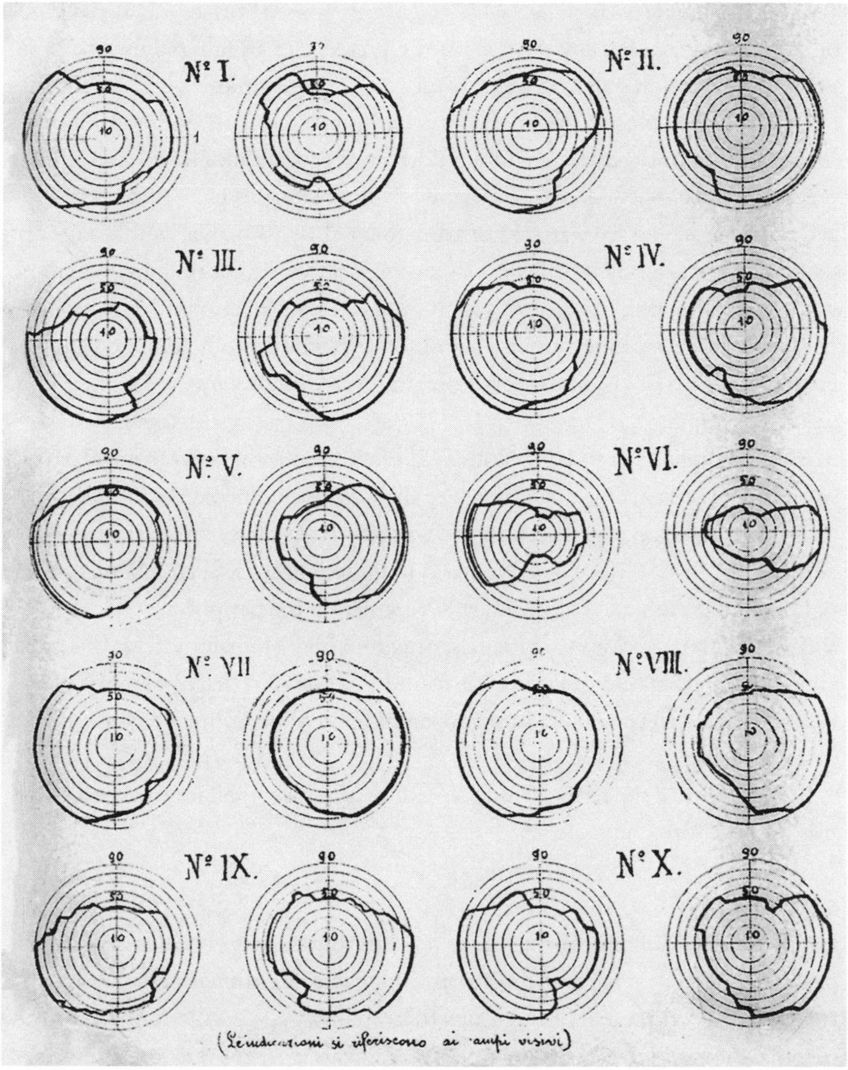

27 Field of vision of criminal women and prostitutes. *Source*: Lombroso, *La donna delinquente*, 1893. *Editors' note*: Lombroso discusses these cases in detail. For example, of number 3 he writes that this diagram charts the visual field of a forty-year-old thief who represents the complete criminal type. Her field of vision is limited and has an irregular periphery in both eyes, especially on the right. Of number 6 he writes, "Age thirty-nine; is a criminal type who killed her husband with the help of her lover and with great premeditation and indifference. Her field of vision is very limited and irregular around the periphery, especially around the left eye, partly as a result of syphilis" (*La donna delinquente*, 391).

My first example is a certain F. M., aged fifteen years, a born criminal, daughter of a thief who sent her out to steal on the pretense of begging alms. She practiced her profession only too well, stealing something almost wherever she was received. She had the face of an old woman, with marked cheek and frontal bones, small and very unsteady eyes, and wrinkles on her forehead. Her tactile dullness was remarkable. She was almost completely insensitive to pain; and every now and then she would have attacks of something close to mania, perhaps epileptic in character, during which she was sleepless and sang continually. When she was tranquil, her field of vision (Laudolt method) showed diminution (especially on the left side), asymmetry, and profound peripheral scotomata. When she was excited, her field of vision increased greatly in size but became in no way more regular.

Another typical case of anomalous field of vision was the born criminal M. C., who tried to poison a companion when she was nine years old and at the age of twelve succeeded. At age fourteen she was convicted of corrupting minors and of theft. Her field of vision was regular but limited on the left, anomalous on the right due to peripheral scotomata, and irregular on the periphery.

Among fifteen occasional criminals, only four had anomalous fields of vision. One quite regular field of vision was found in a girl of sixteen years, who foolishly attempted to poison her husband, an old brute, by putting copper sulphate in his polenta.

In sensitivity of the retina, born prostitutes are closer than female born criminals to male born criminals.

Summary

On the whole, dullness of the senses (except touch) and visual anomalies appear more often among prostitutes than among female criminals. However, these traits are less common in both groups than among male born criminals. Prostitutes have slower reflexes than male born criminals, perhaps due to the effects of syphilis on the nerve centers.

22
Sexual Sensitivity (Lesbianism and Sexual Psychopathy)

Excessive Sexuality

Some female born criminals and prostitutes have more sexual sensitivity than normal women, just as they menstruate earlier and lose their virginity at a younger age. However, they are far less sensitive sexually than men imagine when they themselves are sexually aroused.

Reviewing studies by Riccardi, De Sanctis, and Gurrieri, I found only 9 out of about 165 cases of women whose sexual tendencies were more exaggerated than those of the typical male.[16] I remember one case of an epileptic—a thief and prostitute—who started thinking about sex the minute she saw a male, squeezing her legs together. Magnan cites the cases of two women who from the time they were children engaged in oral and anal intercourse with their own brothers. Another woman spent all day masturbating and attempting to have coitus, falling into fits when someone tried to stop her. Tardieu tells us of a girl of fifteen-and-a-half years who, when boys were nearby, undressed and sat on their stomachs, forcing them to have sex; in a few months she had corrupted twenty young men. She also attempted to seduce a road inspector, and when he refused, she writhed on the ground yelling, "Oh, I want him so badly."[c]

Those who most clearly manifest exaggerated and unceasing lustfulness are both born criminals and born prostitutes; in them lasciviousness intermixes with ferocity, as in the examples of Messalina[17] and Agrippina.[18] Their eroticism differentiates them from normal women, in whom sexuality is weak and delayed, and makes them resemble males. In fact, in this respect the main difference between them and males is their even greater and sometimes bizarre sexual precocity.

c. *Les attentats aux moeurs*, 1884, 3d ed.

28 Messalina. *Source*: Lombroso, *La donna delinquente*, 1893. *Editors' note*: For Lombroso, Messalina—wife of the Roman emperor Claudius—epitomized the deadly combination of the born criminal and born prostitute. As this example illustrates, Lombroso drew on historical examples to supplement his contemporary anecdotes and measurements of criminals.

Due to her indecent speech and behavior, the young woman named Gabriella Bompard was expelled from boarding and convent schools. She was almost like a mature prostitute and told her father, "I will never marry because one man is not enough for me."[19]

Even born criminals for whom sex is not all-absorbing are livelier before puberty than normal women, but their vivacity gradually disappears. Almost all of them begin their careers by fleeing with a lover; and prostitution is always one of their many sins, although not the most serious. They feel a strong attraction toward men and are more curious than other women about the mysteries of sex. Allowing themselves to be courted, they fall in love, give themselves to prostitution, and elope. But since their level of sexual interest is lower than that of other female criminals, they eventually calm down. And then prostitution, previously a mere diversion, becomes a means of self-support from which they profit without joy in the pleasures they formerly badly abused.

Below-Average Sexuality

Among professional prostitutes, cases in which true love plays a role are rare. In professionals we find a precocity that relates to not true sexual passion, but rather vice. Of two women I studied who had lost their virginity early, one confessed that she had done so out of curiosity and because companions encouraged her to follow their example, while the other admitted that she had done it to earn money for better clothes. Even later in life, they never felt the slightest sexual pleasure. On the other hand, in the few cases of excessive sexuality, sexual experience begins well before puberty and indicates a really diseased character.

The graffiti I have collected from women's prisons[d] and hospitals for syphilitics indicate an excessive libidinousness in four out of seventy-eight examples. For example, one graffito read "Dear dickybird"; another said "Always thus" under a sketch of an immense penis; and a third said, "Bring me a bird to my taste and I'll bring one to you, and when I am free you will find that I am just as hot and tight as you want. Playfully, ______." But these graffiti were created by prostitutes who were also born criminals. In the graffiti of others, insofar as it exists, eroticism is latent, as in "I kiss my little brother" (Guillot), or else the writings express only sentimental love or desire for revenge.

Those prostitutes characterized by sexual insensitivity (I repeat) exist in rather large numbers, which fits with the finding that a great many of them are also deficient in the senses of touch and smell. This realization has entered public consciousness, with people referring to such women as *filles de marbre* and describing them in novels. Meunier's *La femme enfant*,[20] for example, depicts a girl who began prostituting herself when she was very young; after years of licentiousness, she still had the attitudes, thoughts, and emotions of a little girl. This infantilism, which contrasts so vividly with prostitutes' professional appearances, sometimes nevertheless closely accords with their retardation in menstruation.[21] Similar arrested development can be found in male criminals who go on to become pederasts.

Then too, many of those who give themselves passionately to lovers find little sexual satisfaction, but need to experience themselves as the female complement to the masculine. In general, aside from those who are both born criminals and prostitutes, frigidity is the rule, as it is in normal women as well, though to a lesser degree.

Sexual Psychopathy

Perversion is rather more frequent among prostitutes,[22] although less frequent than in the male criminal. Among 103 prostitutes, I found certain proof of lesbianism only in 5 cases—a finding that contrasts strongly with Parent-Duchatelet's conclusion that all elderly prostitutes are lesbians.

Of twenty-five women sentenced for corruption in Turin, nine had prostituted their daughters, five had had or attempted to have sexual relations with male chil-

d. *Palimsesti del carcere*, 1891. *Archivio di psichiatria*, XII.

dren, three had taught children of both sexes to have sex with one another, two had committed obscene acts in the presence of children, and three had had sex with a brother or father (Salsotto, op. cit.). Of five prostitutes who claimed to experience no pleasure in intercourse,[23] two enjoyed lesbianism.

According to Riccardi, many frigid prostitutes take pleasure in clitoral masturbation or in oral sex, which they prefer to [heterosexual] intercourse; and still more of them prefer lesbianism. Nor is there a lack, among born criminals and elite prostitutes, of sexual psychopaths who take pleasure not only in playing the male role, but also in torture, beating men, bloodying them, and turning them into slaves (masochism). Similarly, there is no lack of those who find pleasure in exciting children to have coitus with them or other children. However, to grasp how rare these cases are among women, note that according to French statistics, 7,286 males but only 76 females (1.1 percent) were accused of sexual attacks on children.[e] Moreover, of 196 cases of sexual psychopathy reported in the latest work of Krafft-Ebing[f]—the most classic and complete inventory of these matters—only 22 were female cases (11.2 percent). Moreover, women fell into only eleven of Krafft-Ebing's seventeen categories, those indicating the less serious sexual inversions, as shown in table 25.[24] The smaller proportions of women can be explained by the weaker influence of eroticism on women in general and by epilepsy, the central source of these anomalies.[25]

Masochism seems to come naturally to women, who are deeply under the sway of men, even in relatively advanced civilizations.[26] In fact, many women throw themselves at their lovers' knees. Slav women are often unhappy if they are not beaten, and in Hungary, peasant women feel unloved if they are not slapped.

"We women," reads a passage in Schiller's *Kabul und Liebe*, "can choose only between being mistress or servant; but the sensual pleasure of domination is miserable recompense compared to the much greater pleasure of being a slave to a man whom one loves."[27] On the other hand, I have located only one case of true masochism, of a Russian woman, thirty-five years old, from a neuropathic family that had already been struck once, by congenital paranoia. After excessive masturbation, the Russian fell into a state of cerebral-spinal neurasthenia. Although presently not attracted to women, she recalls that "between the ages of 6 and 8 I began to long to be whipped. This obsession never left me but was realized only in fantasy. In my fantasies, which were so intense as to seem real, it was a woman who beat me; I never desired to be whipped by a man. At the age of 10 I lost this

e. Tardieu, *Attentats aux moeurs*, 1873.
f. *Psicopatia sexualis*, 1892, VII Auflage.

Table 25 Sexual Pathologies

	men	women
sexual anesthesia	10	—
sexual hypertension	4	5
sexual paresthesia:		
(*a*) libidinous killings	6	—
(*b*) necrophilia	1	—
(*c*) sadism	11	2
(*d*) masochism	29	1
(*e*) fetishism	29	—
(*f*) acquired sexual inversion	8	2
(*g*) exhibitionism, rape, etc.	26	—
congenital sexual inversion:		
(*a*) psychical hermaphroditism	5	1
(*b*) homosexuality	19	3
(*c*) effeminization and masculinization	8	2
(*d*) androgyny and ginandria	1	2
cases linked to psychosis:		
(*a*) idiots, the insane, epileptics	15	—
(*b*) periodic madness	1	2
(*c*) hysteria	—	1
(*d*) paranoia	1	1

Editors' note: Ginandria or hermaphroditism is a condition in which a woman's external genitalia resemble those of a man. Lombroso's text makes it clear that he drew this data from Krafft-Ebing's *Psychopathia sexualis* (Stuttgart: F. Enke, 1892).

morbid inclination. Not until I was thirty-four and read Rousseau's *Confessions* did I understand the significance of my desire." Other sexual perversions, too, are rare in women and less intense than in men.

A unique case of perversion was related to me by Prof. Bianchi, who told of a wife who every night asked her husband to produce a series of rapid farts. There is also the case reported by Moraglia in my *Archivio* (XIII, p. 567)[28] of an eighteen-year-old with a head of thick black hair who instead of coitus preferred masturbation so long as she could be stimulated by the smell of male urine. She could differentiate male urine from that of women and was driven to masturbate on the site of urinals, or nearby, at the risk of being arrested, which in fact happened several times. In her room she recaptured the most intense sexual pleasure by holding a little bottle of male urine under her nose with her left hand, while masturbating with her right.

Lesbianism

Unlike other forms of sexual perversion, lesbianism—a phenomenon closely associated with prostitutes—is widespread among women. As Parent-Duchatelet observes, some authorities claim that all prostitutes (or nearly all) abandon themselves to lesbianism, while others hold that it is actually rather rare. He believes that this apparent contradiction stems from the rarity with which women admit to this vice. When asked about it, they respond briefly and impatiently, "I am a prostitute for men, not women!" Others whom I questioned added, "We do it, but it is nasty."

In a study that appears unassailable, Moll reports that about 25 percent of all prostitutes in Berlin are lesbians. In general, prostitutes maintain a certain reserve concerning lesbianism; they may curse one another foully, but do not refer to the vice itself even when they are personally involved. Around the age of twenty-five or thirty, prostitutes abandon lesbianism, according to Parent-Duchatelet—at least if they are not in prison.[29]

In Berlin, among lesbian couples who live together as heterosexuals, at least one is usually a prostitute, according to Moll.[g] The active and passive parties are always distinct. The more active partner is called the *father* or *uncle*, and as in marriage she gives herself all the advantages of masculinity, including a lot of freedom in relationships with men; this is the one who is most likely to be a prostitute. The passive partner is known as the *mother*, and woe betide her if she strays!

Women often seem to become lesbians over night, but recall that from childhood they were keen to play boys' games, dress as men, dance with women, smoke strong cigars, get drunk, ride horses, and fight. Some began smoking at the age of five; some loved to build machines and felt repelled by needlework. They assumed masculine roles when they knew they were not being watched.

Lesbians recognize one another, it seems, by certain signals of the eyes and mouth. Usually they confine their fancies to a single category—some prefer blondes, others brunettes—and they never change. Many are faithful for years—even for seventeen years. But the majority switch partners month to month, sometimes day to day.

The Nature and Causes of Lesbianism

Parent-Duchatelet, who is not always as correct in his analysis as he is precise in his information, explains lesbianism in terms of forced abstinence from men and residing with other women in prisons and brothels. But he does not take into

g. *Les inversions sexuelles*. Paris, 1893.

consideration the fact that lesbianism also occurs in the broader world, which has little in common with prisons and brothels. To show that it is in fact more widely spread, we have only to point out, as Sighele has sensibly noted,[30] that a great many novels allude to this vice.[h]

Lesbianism has various causes, the first and most significant of which is an excessive lustfulness, which seeks outlets in all directions, even the most unnatural. The second cause is the influence of the surroundings, especially the dwelling place. In prisons some women, being unable to satisfy themselves with a man, throw themselves on other women and become a center of corruption that spreads from the prisoners all the way to the nuns.[31] This is why the majority of prisoners, even though they are only criminaloids and thus not oversexed, will become lesbians under the influence of extremely lascivious born criminals. As Parent-Duchatelet noted, prison is the great school for lesbianism. There even the most reluctant women, if they remain for eighteen or twenty months, end up giving in to the vice. In this respect women prisoners resemble animals: when unable to satisfy their sexual needs with the opposite sex, they attempt to do so with their own. The same thing occurs in madhouses, in which the appearance of a single lesbian is sufficient to infect all the other inmates, even if none of them earlier showed signs of this tendency (Lombroso, *Il tribadismo nei manicomi*, 1888).

A third cause of lesbianism is the way in which the gathering of many women, especially if the group includes prostitutes or lascivious women, provokes imitative behavior, intensifying the vices of each individual and increasing collective vice. Prostitutes often pass their days in the nude, in constant contact with one another and often sleeping two or three in one bed. In the outer world, too, gatherings of women occur in boarding schools, during carnival orgies, and even during religious festivals. In brothels women hold competitions, betting on who has the most beautiful sexual organs; naturally this ends up in lesbianism. There are girls who at first resist, disgusted by this vice; they are therefore not born lesbians. Yet they succumb in a state of intoxication, or else they familiarize themselves with the practice little by little, eventually becoming occasional lesbians.

h. Diderot, *La Religieuse*, a novel about a devotee of lesbian love; Balzac, *La fille aux yeux d'or*, lesbian love; Théophile Gautier, *Mademoiselle de Maupin*; Feydau, *La comtesse de Chalis*; Flaubert, *Salammbò*. To this list Krafft-Ebing adds (op. cit., p. 76) Belót, *Mademoiselle Giraud, ma femme*. From the German literature Krafft-Ebing cites novels by Wilbrand, *Fridolin's heimliche Ehe*; by Emerich Graf Stadion, *Brick and brack, oder Licht in Schatten* [*sic*]; and by Sacher-Masoch, *Venus im Pelz*. In addition, Zola throws light on lesbianism in *Nanà* and in *La Curée*, and recently in Italy, Butti does the same in his novel *L'automa*.

Fourth, maturity and old age tend to invert sexual characteristics, which further encourages sexual inversions among women. Natural history (as we saw earlier) demonstrates that among animals there is a tendency for elderly females to adopt masculine sexual habits. In fact, aging is itself a form of degeneration. While it is true that lesbianism can be found among many young women, most of these live in brothels, where they succumb when tempted by provocative companions.

Fifth, among prostitutes and also some women of easy morals, another cause of lesbianism is apathy and disgust for men produced by physical and sexual maltreatment. Abused by men, they may turn to women when they feel sexual passion. (Fishermen do not eat fish, as the saying goes.) Then, too, women who truly love their paramours may from time to time experience male mistreatment, at which point they give themselves to women, hoping for more faithfulness and certainly kinder treatment. Thus did Nanà throw herself at women out of disgust for men's filthy lusts and the way fickle lovers abandoned her.[32]

"One of the causes of lesbianism," Sighele writes in "Coppia criminale" (*Archivio di psichiatria*, XII, p. 533), "is doubtless men's sexual perversions. Sadists (a term under which Sighele includes all men who practice unnatural sexuality) force prostitutes into repugnant acts that exhaust and nauseate them. These women, even though they hardly seem feminine, can feel only disgust for men who are not completely masculine. And thus is born lesbianism—a logical and natural outcome. To escape one dreadful situation, prostitutes fall on one another." The same thing happens with women who are not prostitutes.

Degeneration

Degeneration induces confusion between the two sexes, as a result of which one finds in male criminals a feminine infantilism that leads to pederasty. To this corresponds masculinity in women criminals, including an atavistic tendency to return to the stage of hermaphroditism. In women, this tendency to sexual ambiguity often begins before puberty, with many dressing like men, enjoying views of female sexual organs, and avoiding female work. According to Schule, one often finds cases of sexual perversion among the morally insane and epileptics.[33]

"Among women who love women, the relationships, *mutatis mutandis*, are basically the same. The dominant female feels like a man; she gratifies herself by demonstrating courage and virile energy, traits that please women. She wears her hair and clothes in masculine style and delights in appearing in public dressed as a man."[i]

i. Krafft-Ebing, op. cit.

I have observed an epistolary mania in female criminals, especially among lesbians. I remember one assaultive coquette who the minute she entered prison, began exposing herself and starting lesbian relationships with the female guards and other prisoners, scattering erotic letters in the process. Sometimes she sent five or six letters a day to the other prisoners in their cells, even though she could see them only briefly during exercise hour and on the way to mass.[34]

To demonstrate the presence of innate virility among female prisoners, it is enough to present a photograph of a couple whom I surprised in a prison. The one dressed as a male is simultaneously so strongly masculine and so criminal that it is difficult to believe she is actually female.

Even stronger proof comes from a case[j] in which the dominant partner demonstrated masculinity from early childhood.[35] R., a woman of thirty-one years, an artist, had masculine facial lines, a masculine voice, and short hair; she wore men's clothes and had a man's gait. Yet she also had a female pelvis and notably well-developed breasts, and she lacked hair on her face. In childhood she loved playing with boys and taking the part of soldiers and brigands. In contrast, she had no interest in girls' games or in women's work. In school she was especially interested in mathematics and chemistry; she became an artist and studied masculine beauty, but without allowing herself to be seduced. She could not stand female mawkishness, strongly preferring masculine objects. Women's talk bored her, with its chatter about makeup, ornaments, and flirtations. Nonetheless she loved to embrace and kiss women and to stroll under their windows, and she was torn by jealousy if she saw them with men. In general she felt no attraction for men, although she confessed that twice men did make a strong impression on her, so much so that she would have married them if they had asked, partly because she loved family life and wanted children. But she found women more beautiful, more ideal. Her erotic fantasies fastened solely on women. She felt she could never love a man deeply. Her father was neuropathic and her mother insane; when she was little she madly loved her own brother and tried to run away with him to America. Her brother, too, was very strange.

There are evidently cases of female hermaphroditism in which, although the organs are essentially female, there is a congenital tendency toward the masculine. Such cases constitute the nucleus of the lesbian group.

Nonetheless, the fact that one can collect only a few such cases in comparison to the hundreds of male cases shows that among women even erotic tendencies are less marked, and it demonstrates again the scarcity among women of sexual

j. Krafft-Ebing, op. cit.

29 Lesbian prison couple. *Source*: Lombroso, *La donna delinquente*, 1893. *Editors' note*: Himself a prison physician, Lombroso collected evidence for his theory while treating patients. This couple, whom he happened on while doing his rounds, provided him with evidence of women prisoners' supposedly unnatural virility.

psychopathies. Further, it explains why among women there is lesser variation: Their cortical center has much less influence on eroticism, giving them fewer opportunities for becoming excited and thus perverted. On the other hand, circumstances such as prostitution encourage lesbianism among women more than pederasty among men. The majority of lesbians are not born lesbians but rather occasional lesbians who borrow the virile traits of the criminal and the prostitute. This explains why the occasional lesbian is able to put up with, simulate, and inspire the love of men, even making that her exclusive profession. It would be impossible for the true born lesbian to do this, for she is disgusted by men, just as the pederast is disgusted by women.

23
The Female Born Criminal

There is a perfect correspondence between the anthropology and the psychology of the female criminal. In the majority, degenerative traits are but few or weak, but there is a subgroup in which such traits are almost more marked and numerous than in male criminals. Similarly, while the majority of female criminals are merely led into crime by someone else or by irresistible temptation, there is a small subgroup whose criminal propensities are more intense and perverse than even those of their male counterparts. These are the female born criminals, whose evil is inversely proportionate to their numbers. "Woman is rarely wicked, but when she is, she is worse than a man" (Italian proverb).

The extreme perversity of female born criminals manifests itself in two characteristics: the variety of their crimes and their cruelty.

Variety of Crimes

Many female born criminals specialize in not just one but several types of crime and often in two types that in males are mutually exclusive, such as poisoning and murder. Bompard, for instance, was a prostitute, thief, swindler, slanderer, and murderer; Trossarello was a prostitute, adulterer, killer, abortionist, and thief. In history we find Agrippina, an adulterer, incest offender, and party to homicide, and Messalina, a prostitute, adulterer, accomplice in homicide, and thief.

Cruelty

Second, the female born criminal surpasses her male counterpart in the refined, diabolical cruelty with which she commits her crimes. Merely killing her enemy does not satisfy her; she needs to watch him suffer and experience the full taste of death.

In the band of assassins known as La Taille, the women were worse than the men in torturing captives, especially female captives. The woman Tiburzio, having killed a pregnant friend, bit her ferociously, tearing away pieces of flesh and throwing them to the dog. Chevalier killed a pregnant woman by driving a pair of scissors through her ear and into her brain. A certain D., when asked why she had not stabbed her lover instead of throwing vitriol at him, answered by quoting a Roman tyrant: "Because I wanted him to feel the misery of death."

The very worst examples of such barbarity are provided by mothers in whom maternal affection—the most intense of all human sentiments—has been transformed into hatred. Hoegli beat her daughter and plunged her head into water to suffocate her cries. One day she kicked the girl downstairs, deforming her spine. Stakembourg, a loose woman, took to persecuting her daughter when she reached the age of forty-two and her lovers abandoned her. "I do not like girls," she used to say. She hung her daughter from the ceiling by the armpits, knocked her on the head with a brick, and burnt her with a hot iron. One day, having beaten the girl black with a shovel, she laughed and said, "Now you are nothing but a little Negro."

In short, while female born criminals are fewer in number than male born criminals, they are often much more savage. What is the explanation?

We have seen that the normal woman is by nature less sensitive to pain than a man. Because compassion is an effect of sensitivity, if one is lacking, the other will be too. We have also seen that women have many traits in common with children; that they are deficient in the moral sense; and that they are vengeful, jealous, and inclined to refined cruelty when they take revenge. Usually these defects are neutralized by their piety, maternity, sexual coldness, physical weakness, and undeveloped intelligence. However, when a morbid activity of the psychical centers intensifies their bad qualities, women seek relief in evil deeds. When piety and maternal feelings are replaced by strong passions and intense eroticism, muscular strength and superior intelligence, then the innocuous semicriminal who is always present in the normal woman is transformed into a born criminal more terrible than any male counterpart.

What awful criminals children would be if they had strong passions, physical strength, and intelligence, and if, moreover, their evil tendencies were aggravated by morbid psychical activity! And women are big children; their evil tendencies are more numerous and varied than men's, but usually these remain latent. When awakened and excited, however, these evil tendencies lead to proportionately worse results.

In addition, the female born criminal is, so to speak, doubly exceptional, first

30 Delinquent girls. *Source*: Lombroso, *Atlante*, 1897. *Editors' note*: Lombroso identifies anomalies in the faces of these five-and-a-half-year-old girls. The girl on the left, he writes, has swellings on her forehead as well as facial asymmetry. The girl on the right is marked by overdeveloped jaws and cheekbones (*Atlante*, xiii).

as a woman and then as a criminal. This is because criminals are exceptions among civilized people,[36] and women are exceptions among criminals, women's natural form of regression being prostitution, not crime. Primitive woman was a prostitute rather than a criminal. As a double exception, then, the criminal woman is a true monster. Honest women are kept in line by factors such as maternity, piety, and weakness; when a woman commits a crime despite these restraints, this is a sign that her power of evil is immense.

Eroticism and Virility

We saw how sexuality can be exaggerated in female born criminals; this is one of the traits that makes them similar to men. Due to it, all women born criminals are prostitutes. While prostitution may be their least significant offense, it is never absent. Eroticism is the nucleus around which their other characteristics revolve.

This exaggerated eroticism, which is abnormal in most women, forms the starting point for vices and crimes. It turns female born criminals into unsociable beings, preoccupied entirely with the satisfaction of their own desires, like lustful savages whose sexuality has not been tamed by civilization and necessity.

Affections and Passions/Maternity

One strong proof of degeneration in many born criminals is their lack of maternal affection. Lyons, the celebrated American thief and swindler, abandoned her children when she fled her country, leaving them dependent on public charity even though she was wealthy. Often female criminals will force their own children to become accomplices.

This lack of maternal feeling becomes comprehensible if we keep in mind the female criminal's masculine qualities, which prevent her from being more than half a woman, and her love of dissipation, which prevents her from carrying out her maternal duties. She feels few maternal impulses because psychologically and anthropologically she belongs more to the masculine than the feminine sex. Her exaggerated sexuality alone would be enough to render her a bad mother; it makes her egotistical and redirects her energies toward satisfying her pressing and multiple sexual needs. How, then, could she be capable of the abnegation, patience, and altruism that constitute maternity? While in the normal woman sexuality is subordinate to maternity, and a normal mother will unhesitatingly put a child before a lover or husband, among criminal women the opposite is true. Such women turn their daughters into prostitutes in order to keep a lover.

Another factor contributing to the female criminal's lack of maternal feeling is the organic anomaly of moral insanity stemming from epilepsy. This underlying cause of innate criminality tends to deflect women's feelings from their normal course, extinguishing maternal impulses first of all. Similarly, it extinguishes religiosity in nuns, turning them into blasphemers; and among military men it extinguishes loyalty, inspiring formerly loyal soldiers to savagely attack their superiors.[37]

Paradoxically, in some cases maternity and sexuality, instead of working against one another as usual, join together in incest, and the mother becomes the lover of the son, adoring him partly as a son and partly as a lover. This mixture of sexual and maternal love can be explained by the fact, established earlier, that maternal love has a sexual foundation; when nursing, the mother feels a little sexual pleasure and usually prefers a male baby. This factor, usually subordinate and of little importance, becomes exaggerated in an intensely erotic woman.

Here is proof of the anticriminogenic influence of maternity on women. In those in whom it has not been entirely extinguished, maternity works, at least for certain periods, as a potent moral antidote.[38] Thus Thomas, a vicious woman who passed only six honest months in her entire life, was transformed during that period by bearing a child. But when her daughter died, she fell back into the gutter.

Maternity never inspires crime, even among female born criminals. The sentiment is too noble to coexist with degeneration. But the sorrows of maternity can lead to madness and suicide.

Vengeance

The chief motive for female crime is vengeance. The inclination toward revenge that we noted even in normal women becomes extreme in criminals. Because their psychic centers are irritated, the smallest stimulus can provoke an enormous reaction. But usually the female born criminal revenges herself more slowly than men. She has to develop her plan little by little because her physical weakness and fearful nature restrain her even when her reason does not.

Hatred

In certain very serious cases, female born criminals have no motive whatsoever other than a small and distant complaint. These crimes originate in an innate and blind savagery. Adulterers and poisoners, in particular, tend to commit oddly pointless crimes.

A passion for evil for evil's sake is a characteristic of born criminals, epileptics, and hysterics. It is an automatic hatred, one that springs from no external cause

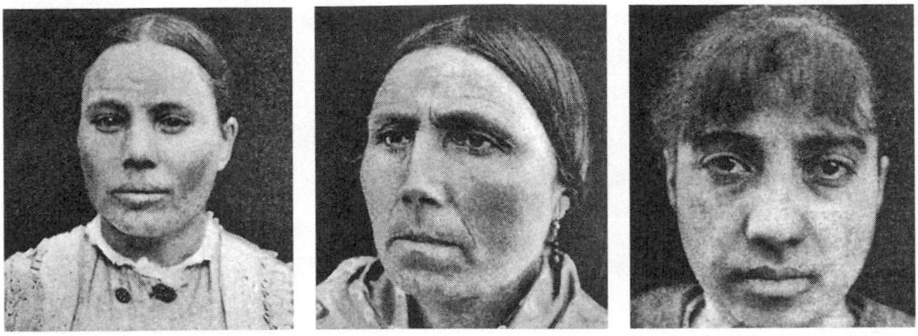

31 Homicidal women. *Source*: Lombroso, *Atlante*, 1897. *Editors' note*: Lombroso identifies these three murderers as born criminals by detecting multiple anomalies. The first, he writes, has swollen lips and a virile physiognomy. The second, who killed her father, has arched eyebrows, deep furrows in her forehead, a strange pattern of wrinkles, a receding forehead, overdeveloped cheek- and jawbones, and thin lips. The third, a husband killer, has swollen lips (*Atlante*, xi).

such as an insult or offense, but rather from a morbid irritation of the psychical centers which relieves itself in evil action. Driven by continuous irritation, such women need to discharge their aggravation on someone. Thus some unfortunate with whom they frequently come in contact becomes, for some trifling defect or difference, the object of their loathing and victim of their savagery.

Love

Although the female born criminal has intensely erotic tendencies, love is rarely a cause of her crimes. For her love, like hatred, is just another form of insatiable egotism. There is no self-abnegation or altruism in her love, only a drive for self-satisfaction.

The impulsivity and casualness of these women's passions are extraordinary. When they fall in love, they need to satisfy their desire immediately, even if that means committing a crime. Monomaniacal, as if hypnotized by desire, they think of nothing but how to satisfy themselves and rush to commit crimes even though if they were patient they might achieve the same goal without risk. Their affection is like that of children—intense but incapable of disinterested sacrifice or noble resignation. It can result in the kind of jealous tyranny more often found in the love of a man for a woman.

Greed and Avarice

Greed is a cause of crime in women, though less often than vengeance. Among dissolute female offenders, who need a great deal of money for their orgies and other pleasures but do not care to work for it, avarice takes the same form as in male criminals: both want to have large sums of money to waste. This inspires them to attempt or instigate crimes which can reap a rich harvest. Thus Bompard encouraged Eyraud to kill the porter, and thus Messalina had the richest citizens of Rome killed so she could appropriate their villas and wealth.

Dress

Another factor that pushes women into crime is a passion for objects of clothing and ornament. Madame Lafarge stole her friend's diamonds, not to sell them, but only to possess them, even though doing so involved grave risks.[39] According to Tarnowsky, many Russian thieves steal not out of need (they have jobs and are earning wages) but to obtain small luxury objects.[40]

In the psychology of normal women, dress and personal adornment play a role of immense significance. A poorly dressed woman feels she has disgraced herself. Children and savages have similar reactions. Among savages, dress is the earliest form of property, and thus we should not be surprised that it is also a frequent cause of crime.

Religiosity

Religiosity is neither rare nor weak in these born criminals. While Parency was killing an old man, his wife prayed to God that all would end well. G., when setting fire to her lover's house, cried out, "May God and the Holy Virgin do the rest." Pompilia Zambeccari vowed to light a candle to the Virgin if she succeeded in poisoning her husband.

Contradictions

The female born criminal does not lack a paradoxical and intermittent goodness which contrasts strangely with her usual depravity. Madame Lafarge was extremely kind to her servants. In her own neighborhood she was called the godsend of the poor, and she gave succor to the sick. Jegado was deeply affectionate to her fellow servants, but poisoned them the moment they offended her. Thomas gave alms to the poor, wept when they described their miseries, and bought presents and clothes for their children.

Such altruism is intermittent, however, and it does not last long. The kindness of criminal women is of an inferior sort, growing as it does out of selfishness. Charitable acts enable them to feel that others are at their feet; for once, their love of power is gratified by good behavior.

Sentimentalism

Although these women lack strong and true feelings, they do exhibit a kind of mawkish sentimentality, especially in correspondence. Trossarello wrote her lover letters full of affection and declarations of fidelity, even while betraying him. Criminal women are moral lunatics; having no noble, deep affections, they lapse easily into showy substitutes.

Intelligence

Criminal women exhibit many levels of intelligence. Some are extremely intelligent, while others are ordinary in this respect. As a rule, however, their minds are alert; this is evidently why, relative to men, they commit few impulsive crimes. To kill in a bestial rage requires no more than the mind of a Hottentot; but to plot out a poisoning requires ability and sharpness. The crimes of women are almost always deliberate.

M. (a case described by Ottolenghi) was capable of rapid and rich thinking despite her lack of schooling; in addition (and this is important given women's backwardness in the development of writing abilities), she felt a deep need to record the ideas that flooded her, scribbling some down, dictating others to her companions. Although she was only seventeen years old, she amply demonstrated her intelligence by organizing a vast and profitable prostitution ring.

Lyons, the famous American adventurer and thief, must have had a very superior intelligence. After enriching herself through burglary in America, she came to Europe to pursue the same system, solely out of love for her trade. Arrested *in flagrante* in Paris, she managed to get free through apologies and the intercession of the British and American ambassadors. Another example is Bell-Star, who for many years led a band of outlaws in Texas, organizing raids against the U.S. government itself.

More evidence that female born criminals are often strong intellectually lies in the frequently original nature of their offenses. For example, M. (Ottolenghi's case) enriched herself through a remarkable combination of prostitution, pandering, and blackmail. The superior intelligence of these criminals can be explained by the fact that they are often physically incapable of satisfying their perverse instincts. With sufficient cleverness, they can still achieve their ends; if not, they become prostitutes.

Writing and Painting

These two accomplishments are almost totally lacking in female born criminals. I have never found a drawing or tattoo alluding to crime and made by a female born criminal—not even an embroidery, a medium one might expect such women to favor. Nor are there many examples of their writing. We have found only three examples of memoirs by female born criminals: those of Madame Lafarge, of X, and of Bell-Star. Male criminals, on the other hand, are greatly addicted to these egotistical outpourings.

Method of Committing Crimes/Deliberation

More evidence of the mental ability of female born criminals lies in the deliberation with which many of them plan their offenses. The means they use to reach a goal, even a relatively simple goal, are often very complicated.

To kill her husband, Rosa Bent . . . prepared, in his room while he was sleeping, a great caldron of boiling water. When he suddenly woke up, she said that people were calling to him from the street, and when he rushed to the window, still half asleep, she pushed him into the caldron. Clearly, such complicated plans require a certain amount of imagination, which may take the place of physical force.

However, this deliberation often trips up even the cleverest criminals. Their elaborate plans turn out to be absurd and impossible, not to mention mad. Buisson, for example, was scratched by an old man while murdering him; as soon as she got home, she hanged her cat and proceeded to announce angrily to friends that the beast had clawed her face.

Instigation

The female born criminal does not always commit her crimes herself. Courage may fail her unless she has a man's strength, or her victim is another woman, or her crime is secretive as in poisoning or arson. It is not that such a woman shrinks morally from crime, but rather that she instigates an accomplice to commit it. Characteristically, her part in a joint crime is that of an *incubus*, to use Sighele's term; she incites her partner, deploying him with calculated evil.

Lasciviousness

Lasciviousness often plays a part in the crimes of these offenders, who tend to be lustful and immodest. It is natural that, in planning a crime, they often decide to use sexuality to achieve their ends.

Often the female criminal instigates her accomplice by promising sex. D. . . . , who gave herself to everyone, refused only one admirer, the weakest and most suggestible. When she had in this way reinforced his desire, she promised to give herself to him if he killed her husband.

Obstinacy in Denial

One peculiarity of female criminals, especially female born criminals, is the obstinacy with which they deny their crimes, no matter how strong the evidence against them. Male criminals confess when there is no longer any reason for denial; but women protest their innocence more strenuously as their claims increase in absurdity.

Madame Lafarge maintained her innocence to the end, proclaiming it in her memoirs. Jegado, despite the wealth of evidence against her, continued to assert that she knew nothing about arsenic and that her only fault lay in being too kind. She persisted in these claims to the end.

In court, these women sometimes change their defense argument completely, two or three times. Apparently unaware that such mutations raise doubts in judges' minds, they continue to assert their innocence with undampened ardor.

Revelation of Crime

In yet another of those contradictions that turn up in the study of criminal women, we find that while they often obstinately deny their guilt, they also often spontaneously reveal it. This complex psychological phenomenon is caused in part by that need to gossip and that inability to keep a secret which are characteristic of females. Gabriella Bompard, for instance, when she was traveling with Garanger, started telling him many things about Eyraud, and when they arrived in Paris, where all the newspapers were full of news about Eyraud and herself, she could not refrain from revealing her own and her accomplice's identity. In a different case, Faure, a woman who threw vitriol at her lover, would never have been discovered if she had not confessed to a female friend. When the crime is one of vengeance, there is of course an additional temptation to confess, beyond that of confiding in someone, because avengers take joy in their deeds. Another factor here is the typical foolishness and imprudence of criminals, who speak openly of their deeds without recognizing the risks.

Particularly curious is the way a woman will confess to her lover. She will tell him of her crime even if he himself is honest, unsuspecting, and incurious. Sometimes she forces him to accept written proof of her guilt, proof that can convict her and that, when her intense but fleeting love has cooled, can constrain her to commit another and even more serious crime to get rid of an inconvenient witness. Here again we have an example of the habitual recklessness of the female criminal. Failing to realize that her loves are always brief, she believes that this time it will be as lasting as it is intense. This blindness, together with that lack of morality that causes her to regard the worst crimes as insignificant lapses, is the only way to explain her behavior.

But in other cases, driven by jealousy and a desire to revenge herself on a lover who has abandoned her, the female criminal will accuse her accomplice. Or, if she fears detection, she may betray her partner in hope of cutting a deal for herself. Female fickleness also plays a role here. A woman adores a man as if he is a god and is willing to die for him—for a few months. But then her affection turns to hatred, and she hands him over to justice without hesitation.

Summary

In general, the moral physiognomy of the born female criminal is close to that of the male. The atavistic diminution of secondary sexual characteristics which shows up in the anthropology of the subject appears again in the psychology of the female offender, who is excessively erotic, weak in maternal feelings, inclined to dissipation, and both astute and audacious. She dominates weaker people, sometimes through suggestion, sometimes through force. Her love of violent exercise, her vices, and even her clothing increase her resemblance to a man. These virile traits are often joined by the worst qualities of woman: her passion for revenge, her cunning, cruelty, love of finery, and dishonesty, which can combine to form a type of extraordinary wickedness.

It goes without saying that these characteristics are not found in the same proportion in every case. However, when muscular strength and intellectual power come together in the same individual, we have a female criminal of an indeed terrible type. A typical example is offered by Bell-Star, the female outlaw who several yeas ago terrorized all of Texas. Her education had developed her natural proclivities: as the daughter of a guerrilla chief who had fought for the South during the Civil War, she had grown up in the midst of fighting. At the age of eighteen she became head of her own gang, ruling her companions partly through superior intelligence, partly through courage, and to some extent through womanly charm. She organized attacks of great daring against cities and government troops; nor did she hesitate, the day after one of these raids, to enter a nearby town unaccompanied, dressed (as usual) like a man. Once she slept in the same hotel as the district judge without him suspecting her identity or even her sex. Her wish to die in her boots was granted when she fell in battle against government soldiers, directing the action until her final moment.

Bell-Star exemplifies the law we have formulated: that the female born criminal, when a full type, is more terrible than the male.[41]

24
Occasional Criminals

The born criminal offered us a type of intense depravity; but in the far more numerous type to which we now turn, perversity and vice are attenuated and the great virtues of woman, such as modesty and maternity, still prevail. Offenders of this type are occasional criminals, and they comprise the great majority of female offenders.

Physical Characteristics

The key characteristic of occasional criminals is their lack of prominent degenerative traits. Of all female criminals, 54 percent lack physiological anomalies.[42] Even in terms of sensitivity many of them show no abnormality, with 15 percent being acute in their sense of taste and 6 percent in their sense of smell.

Moral Character

The same is true of their moral character. Guillot unintentionally described this type when writing about female prisoners: "The guilty woman, with a few exceptions in which all vices are combined,[k] is more easily moved to penitence than men, recovers the lost ground more quickly, and relapses into crime less frequently."[43] Guillot quotes a lady visitor to St. Lazare who said of the female prisoners: "When one knows them, it is easy to love them," thus demonstrating that their natural perversity is not excessive. "The writings on prison walls in the male cells," Guillot continues, "express violence, impiety, threats, and obscenities; but those in the female cells are far more reserved, expressing only repentance and love."

k. Born criminals.

Moreover, in these occasional criminals the sense of chastity is very strong. In France, they are horrified by the idea of being sent to St. Lazare, where they might come into contact with prostitutes. The born criminal, in contrast, cannot despise prostitutes, for she herself is promiscuous.

Guillot notes the strong maternal love of the occasional offender, which contrasts with the complete lack of love in the born criminal that we have already amply documented. "In St. Lazare," writes Guillot, "maternal jealousy often breeds rivalries and jealousies. Every mother wants her own child to be considered the handsomest and strongest. The birth of a child turns the whole prison upside down; and prisoners who defy the regulations even when threatened with solitary confinement become docile as lambs when threatened with separation from their baby."

Other positive traits further demonstrate the closeness of the occasional female offender to honest women. For instance, women of this type are excessively affectionate toward and trusting of their lawyers (especially young and handsome lawyers). For them, as Guillot has noted, the lawyer is a type of protector on whom they rely fully (if somewhat naively) and who arouses in them an almost filial respect. One prisoner wrote on her wall, "I am in prison, charged with theft of 2,000 francs; but it doesn't matter—I have a lawyer." Here one sees that need for protection by and trust in the other sex which is typical of women but entirely lacking in the semimasculine, tyrannical, and selfish born criminal, who demands neither help nor protection from others but only the satisfaction of her own desires. Among occasional offenders, love, too, is much more profound and disinterested than among born criminals—in whom, in fact, it is merely a shallow impulse arising from unrestrained selfishness.

To understand fully the occasional offender's degree of criminality, we must study the factors that lead them into crime. These factors fall into several categories.

Suggestion

In many cases, the occasional offender is led into crime reluctantly, through the suggestion of a lover or, less frequently, her father or a brother. As a prison nun once observed to us, pointing to her charges, "These are not like men. They do not commit crimes out of evil passions but to please their lovers. They steal or compromise themselves for men's sakes, sometimes without having any direct interest in the crime." Then too, as Sighele has remarked,[1] one characteristic of occasional

1. *Coppia Criminale*, 1893, ed *Archivio di psich*, XIII e XIV. Torino.

crime is the length of time it takes for the suggestion to bear fruit, together with the woman's uncertainty in the execution of the crime and her speedy remorse once it has been committed.

M. R., who showed no sign of serious forms of degeneration, was an honest and industrious woman who resisted her father, who wanted to rape her, and her brother, who wanted her to support him through prostitution. However, she fell in love with a down-at-heel character and fled home in his company. They were soon reduced to misery, with her unable to find work and him refusing to look for work, and eventually he suggested that they should burglarize a jeweler's establishment, threatening to abandon her if she refused. She resisted for a time but, after a day or two without a penny, she agreed, only to prove herself so awkward and clumsy in the execution of the crime that she was quickly arrested. In prison, she fully confessed, demonstrating penitence.

Most women who commit abortion do so under suggestion; women who commit infanticide, on the other hand, are closer to the female offenders whose crimes are caused by passion. Abortion, as Sighele has well observed, is rarely the act of the woman alone; generally, her lover forces her to do it to avoid the scandal of a baby. Desirata Ferlin, a sickly girl, sweet but weak, suffered rape and incest by her own father; becoming pregnant, she agreed to an abortion under pressure from him. But when arrested, she refused to speak against her father and, when pushed, even defended him.

Sometimes the suggestion comes from not a despotic lover but a friend. A woman discovers she is pregnant and wants to avoid the compromising condition, but has no clear idea of what to do. Then she meets a friend who was once in the same fix and who gives her the address of an expert midwife, assuring the first woman that the procedure is simple and safe. No one will find out about it. Thus the troubled woman is persuaded, with her original vague desire turning into firm resolution.

In other cases, poverty and the demands of an already large family suggest abortion as a solution to unwanted pregnancy. "Why bring another unfortunate being into the world?" reasons the mother who loves the children she already has and would love the new one, too, were it not destined to add to the family's poverty.

Women who are persuaded by others to commit crimes certainly have a latent tendency toward crime. However, that tendency is too weak to manifest itself spontaneously, as it does in born criminals. While occasional criminals are indeed offenders, they are offenders on a reduced scale, and they have only some of the born criminal's traits. In one case, maternal feelings may be weak and the morals undermined by a tendency to fall in and out of love and thus be dragged into crime. In another case, the offender may be close to the normal woman, resorting to crime only with great struggle and afterward experiencing intense regret. There is a series of gradations from the born criminal at one end of the scale to the honest woman at the other, with varieties of occasional criminals in between.

While the suggestion that leads female occasional criminals into trouble nearly always emanates from a man, it sometimes comes from a woman. Giulia Bila was bound to Maria Moyen, a doubtful character, by affection of extraordinary intensity and was so completely under her friend's influence as to agree to carry out the vengeance planned by Maria against a lover who had abandoned her. Giulia was just as furious with the betrayer as Maria, who always painted him in the darkest colors, and Giulia felt such hatred that she quickly adopted Maria's suggestion of throwing a bottle of vitriol in his face. But no sooner had she done so than she was filled with horror. Allowing herself to be arrested, she swore, weeping, that she had not been in control of herself when she committed the act; and of course that was true.

Why do such friendships exist in the world of criminals but not among normal women? Latent animosity among normal women impedes their friendships; but perhaps even more important is the fact that friendship does not exist without suggestion, and suggestion occurs only between two individuals separated by a considerable psychic distance.[44] Normal women are monotonous; they resemble one another, which makes suggestion, friendship, and domination of one by the other impossible. Among criminals, however, degeneration produces a great variability, sometimes to the extent of monstrosity; this creates that inequality of character, which is a prerequisite to suggestion. The born criminal, with her semimasculinity and extreme perversity, can thus act on a criminaloid in whom evil instincts are merely latent.

Education/Frustrations

A factor that drags honest women into crime with increasing frequency is the way society is starting to give them access to higher education while at the same time, bizarrely, refusing to allow them to practice their profession or earn a living.[45] Many sufficiently intelligent women find themselves with nothing to show for the expense and effort of their education. Reduced to misery, aware that they deserve something better, and blocked from matrimony by men's distaste for well-educated women, they have no alternative but suicide, crime, or prostitution. Those who are chaste kill themselves, while the others sell themselves or steal.

Macé writes that many teachers end up in the St. Lazare prison for stealing gloves, veils, umbrellas, handkerchiefs, and other articles needed for good appearances at school but which they cannot afford to buy. They have been driven to steal by the exigencies of their profession. "The number of instructors," he writes, "who have no pupils is so great that a teaching certificate, instead of bringing in income, drives them to suicide, theft, and prostitution."

Excessive Temptation

Property crimes in particular can be committed by normal or nearly normal women out of an excess of temptation. We have already seen that in normal women respect for property is not particularly strong. This is confirmed by Richet, according to whom objects brought to the Paris lost-and-found department are nearly always brought in by men. It is further confirmed by a cultivated lady, Mrs. R, who told us confidentially that women have great difficulty playing games without cheating. Such weak respect for property naturally succumbs to strong temptations. Offenders will even regard their crimes as escapades; and of course it is true that such offenses can be committed without deep depravity.

Shoplifting, which has become common since the establishment of huge, fashionable department stores, is a form of occasional crime in which women specialize. The temptation stems from the immense number of articles on display; these excite the dreams of women who can afford only a few of them, an excitement made all the easier in that, as we have seen, for women ornaments are not luxury items but rather necessities, powerful tools of seduction. It is the department stores, with their hundreds of identical items and thousands of varieties of fashion, that lure women into crime, and not the small shops, where the temptations are fewer and problematic customers can be easily identified. An inspector of the French department store chain Au Bon Marché told Joly that out of one hundred female thieves, 25 percent are habitual offenders, 25 percent steal out of need, and 50 percent are what he called *monomaniacs*—women of often good social position and ample means who cannot resist the temptation of so many beautiful things laid out before them.[46] Of this group, a certain proportion are true kleptomaniacs.[47]

Ladies who cannot afford to buy things or do not need to will go to the end-of-season sales, just as engineers go to exhibits of machines—out of curiosity. Little by little fever possesses these women, and they end up either spending far beyond their means or committing a dexterous theft.

Nearly all household stealing by maids falls into this category of occasional crime. Torn from the countryside to work in the town houses of those who seem to be millionaires, badly paid, frequently handling the grocery money and precious objects—inevitably their innate womanly greed is awakened. Pilfering while making change from the groceries or sorting the silverware seems to them more a subterfuge than lawbreaking. "Forty-nine percent of female thieves," Tarnowsky writes, "are domestic servants." This statistic confirms our concept of the occasional criminal.

Given women's organic inability to resist stealing, shoplifting quickly becomes a habit if the opportunities repeat themselves. The occasional offender becomes a habitual offender, and the maidservant joins the ranks of those who, in large cities, steal systematically and continuously from employers.

Abandonment and Corruption in Childhood

Childhood neglect and parental abandonment contribute very strongly to the making of female occasional criminals. After periods of idleness in prison they may find it impossible to learn skills for a job, or their criminal records may make it impossible to find a job; thus they become habitual offenders. Children need good examples and moral instruction in respect for others' property. Parental desertion is particularly fatal for female children, who are innately less honest than male children, even when well-educated and raised with every advantage.

Insults and Blows

Other occasional crimes committed with some frequency by women are insults and injuries to others, especially companions.[48] Due to women's latent antipathy for one another, trivial events give rise to fierce hatreds; and due to women's irascibility, these occasions lead quickly to insolence and assaults. Such incidents happen daily between neighbors, competing shopkeepers, building superintendents and renters, and building superintendents and maidservants. Women of high social station do the same thing, but their more refined forms of insult do not lead to law courts.

Begging

In men, begging is nearly always a sign of degeneration, a form of congenital crime that results from vagabondage and laziness; but begging can be an occasional crime among women. As we have already seen, women are less inclined than men to commit suicide out of poverty; this is partly because when reduced to extreme need, women resort more easily to begging. Perhaps they are less proud, or perhaps maternal love blocks them from suicide.

According to Macé, the police often lack the courage to arrest women for begging. Even police officers, who are not known for liberality in application of the law, realize that it would be inhuman to treat these occasional and involuntary offenders as if they had the innate degenerative tendencies of the veritable vagabond.

Typical Local Crimes

It is the occasional nature of most female offenses that explains why, despite the monotony that characterizes all aspects of femininity, the crimes typical of women vary by country. The ethnic variations in female criminality are greater than those of any other aspect of female psychology; but this is because the social life of various countries offers diverse opportunities for crime.

In Sweden, for example, infanticide is common. In that country, women are used to pulling sledges, tiring work that throws them into constant contact with brutal men on journeys away from the cities and the protection of the authorities. Frequently raped and impregnated, they resort to infanticide to save their reputations. The blame lies not with them but with their type of work. These offenders are close-to-normal women who, under other circumstances, would not have broken the law.[49]

Similarly, shoplifting was for a time a French speciality, at least as long as department stores were a French speciality. Even now, this problem is worse in France than elsewhere, to judge from the fact that almost all the discussions of the topic come from French authors. According to all observers, the French shops are the largest and most attractive in the ways they display items for sale; thus they are the most tempting.

Another location-specific occasional crime is abortion in the United States, where it is so common that public opinion no longer treats it as an offense. The physicians and midwives who specialize in abortion publicly advertise through wall posters and newspapers. This acceptance is undoubtedly due to the ever-increasing activity of women in American professions and businesses, a phenomenon that flows naturally from the development of capitalism. It transforms maternity into a veritable disgrace and abortion into a social necessity. Public opinion is so supportive that in the United States abortion is no longer deemed a dishonorable or criminal act.[50]

Summary

Occasional criminals, who constitute the majority of female offenders, can be divided into two categories, one including mild sorts of born criminals, the other criminals who are close to normal women. Indeed, the second category even includes some normal women in whom circumstances have brought out the basic immorality latent in all women.

To the first category belong above all the suggestible offenders and those guilty of violence against the person; the second group includes property offenders. For the latter, theft often seems as inconsequential as it does to children; in their eyes, it is a somewhat bold act for which one might have to personally apologize to the owner but not to deal publicly with the judicial system. They regard theft as an individual, not a social crime—which of course is just how it was regarded during primitive periods of human evolution and how it continues to be viewed today by savage people.

25
Crimes of Passion

An analysis of crimes of passion disproves yet another widespread but false belief about women.[51] In crimes of passion woman proves herself inferior to man, not so much numerically as in her tendency to resemble first the born criminal, then the occasional criminal, while the male offender in this category is truer to type. Moreover, premeditation and savagery play a greater part in women's than men's crimes of passion. Otherwise, however, men's and women's crimes of passion parallel one another.

Age

As one would expect, in crimes of passion by women, youthful offenders predominate, as they do among men. The age at which the crime is committed is usually that of the fullest sexual development: Vinci was twenty-six years old, Provensal eighteen, Jamais twenty-four, Daru twenty-seven, Laurent twenty-two, and Noblin twenty-two; also young are women who commit political crimes through passion.[52] Less frequent but not unusual are cases in which crimes of passion for love are committed at a relatively advanced age, especially by women whom youth and sexual passion passed by quickly. Lodi, whose conduct was good until she reached middle age, finally fell in love with another servant, at his instigation robbing her master of 20,000-francs worth of bonds, which she turned over to her lover without keeping a cent for herself. Dumaire killed her lover when she was thirty years old; Perrin tried to do away with her husband at age forty.

Degenerative and Virile Traits

Aside from the greater development of their lower jaws and their greater degree of virility,[53] female offenders from passion have no special physiological marks or degenerative characteristics. Indeed, Charlotte Corday, among others, was very beautiful.

Remarkably, female offenders of this type also have some masculine moral traits, including love of firearms. Raymond always carried a dagger and pistol, having (according to her husband) acquired the habit in Hawaii, where all the women do the same. Nonetheless, it is difficult to understand why she should have continued to do so after so many years of living in Paris. An eyewitness described Souhine as haughty, energetic, and resolute of character. Dumaire, according to an observer at her trial, was firm, outspoken, and logical.

Many offenders of this class are passionate politically, which is rare in women generally; they become religious or patriotic martyrs.[54] Daru was a Corsican and Noblin a Basque, meaning that they belonged to semiprimitive populations in which women usually have virile traits. Moreover, both showed muscular force in the commission of their crime, for Daru killed her lover with knife blows, and Noblin strangled her rival.

Positive Affections and Passions

Women who commit crimes of passion are far more ardent in their affections than normal women, and they never show the born criminal's lack of family feeling. B., who was virile in appearance but had few abnormal traits, was an extremely affectionate wife and exemplary mother, and so honest that after her arrest, neighbors signed a document attesting to her probity. Daru adored her children, supporting them by working like a slave while her husband squandered everything on drink. Even when in extreme need, Jamais remained honest and pure, writing to her distant lover, "I keep myself for you alone." Dumaire made a fortune through a somewhat dubious marriage, but after being widowed generously helped her relatives.

Passions as Motives for Crimes

The passion that most often leads women into crime is love. Lacking the frigidity of normal women, offenders by passion experience love with the intensity of an Heloise,[55] delighting in self-sacrifice for the man they adore and for whose sake they are even willing to endure social opprobrium and violate the law.

For her lover's sake, Vinci sacrificed the long hair which was her only beautiful trait. Jamais sent money and gifts to her soldier lover, even though she was toiling to support herself and her two children. Disinterestedly but passionately, Dumaire helped Picart pay for his studies, asking not for marriage but only that she might continue to live with him. And Noblin was so devoted to Sougaret that despite her own fundamental honesty, she would not leave him when he turned out to be a criminal. To please him, she consented three times to an abortion, and she herself finally committed an offense that was completely incompatible with her innate goodness.[56]

Such intensity in love explains why these criminals fall into relationships that are illicit from the social point of view, even though nothing negative can be said about the women's own purity. Virginity and marriage are social institutions, adapted (like all customs and institutions) to the average person, in this case, to the sexually frigid normal woman. But offenders by passion love too ardently to comply with such rules.

While the woman whom passion leads to crime is very different from the born criminal, who violates the laws of chastity from lust and love of idle pleasure, nonetheless such good, passionate women are fatally inclined to love bad men. They fall into the hands of frivolous, fickle, and sometimes depraved lovers who later abandon them, often adding to betrayal the even greater cruelties of scorn and slander.

Having sacrificed her hair and thus become ugly for her lover's sake, Vinci was taunted and eventually replaced by her rival. Jamais, too, was abandoned, in this case after she lost her job and could no longer provide her lover with money. Raymond discovered an affair between her husband and best friend; although she forgave them, she later discovered that the relationship continued and found letters from the friend full of insulting remarks about herself.

To the causes of crimes by passion we need to add the unjust scorn which the world heaps on a woman it condemns for sinning but whose problem is really an excess of love in a society dominated by egotism. Derision, often accompanied by inhuman condemnation by relatives, adds to their already great grief. Jamais, for instance, was rejected by her dying father who refused her final kiss. Provensal received a letter from her brother denouncing the way she had dishonored her family and become a stranger.

Our analysis is confirmed by statistics showing that illegitimate births and infanticides vary inversely instead of paralleling one another in their rates of increase, as might be expected. In other words, infanticide is most frequent where illegitimacy is rarest. When illegitimacy is treated with enormous severity, infanticide becomes more frequent, for the fear of dishonor pushes women into crime. There are more infanticide arrests in the countryside than in cities, evidently because towns offer more opportunity for concealing the crime. In sum, some crimes of passion are caused by public opinion and prejudice;[57] they remind one of the vendettas of barbarous times when to avoid dishonor, men had to avenge wrongs to themselves and family members.

Maternal and Family Affection

A less frequent cause of crime is injury to a woman's maternal or domestic affections. Du Tilly, a most loving mother and wife, found herself abandoned by her husband for a milliner and insulted by them both. In her eyes, the family honor and her son's inheritance were being undermined little by little, but what tormented her most was the idea that, should she become sick and die, her husband would then marry the other woman. To thwart this potential marriage, she decided to disfigure her rival with vitriol.

Daru, a very honest woman, and her son fought continually with her drunken husband. One day when the husband threatened her and the children with a knife, she took them and fled the house. She returned when her husband was asleep to murder him with a knife.

Given that maternal love is women's strongest feeling, it may seem strange to find that crimes from maternal love are unusual.[58] But maternity works as a sort of moral vaccine against evil, dampening a mother's resentment because her main fear is separation from her children. Maternity has an anticriminogenic effect on her children as well because many mothers, far from wanting vindication, encourage their children to ignore injuries against them; again, they fear losing their children. Moreover, maternity is preeminently a normal physiological phenomenon while criminality, no matter how derived from passion, is pathological, and the two are rarely able to combine. Maternity is intense even in normal women and therefore cannot become an aggravating factor in crime. In contrast, love is weak in normal women; when intense, love is always pathological and therefore capable of pushing women into criminal behavior.[59]

On the other hand, maternity is an important cause of madness. Out of one hundred cases, the proportion driven mad by domestic sorrow is as follows:

	men	*women*
Italy (1866–1877)	1.60	8.40
Saxony (1875–78)	2.64	3.66
Vienna (1851–59)	5.24	11.28

In Turin, deaths of children cause three times as many women (twelve) as men (four) to go mad, and grief over sterility has driven three women but no men insane.

The possibility of maternal passionate crimes is limited by yet another factor: women consider their children to be almost part of themselves, nurturing them and personally resenting injuries against them, especially when they are small and cannot take care of themselves. However, when the child grows up and can care for himself, he separates from his mother and she, while still following his life with affectionate interest, no longer feels duty-bound to protect or avenge him. A wrong against her child will still trouble her profoundly, but it will no longer excite her as it did when he was a baby. In this respect human mothers reenact a phenomenon that occurs in simpler form in the animal world, in which mothers abandon offspring as soon as they can walk or fly away. Maternal passionate crimes, being thus possible only when the children are small, are perforce rare, for the child, not yet having entered the struggle for life, has not yet formed enemies, received blows, or been persecuted. A bad or indifferent father is almost the only person against whom mothers need to protect their infants; and luckily there are few of these.

Clothing and Adornment

A curious, exciting cause of crime that is related to and sometimes even confused with maternal love or family feeling is that passion for dress so characteristic of the female-born criminal. Du Tilly confessed that one of the things that angered her most was her husband's practice of dressing up his mistress in her garments. Raymond was exasperated by the frequency with which her husband gave jewelry to his lover, while at the same time treating her with obstinate stinginess.

Similarities to Male Criminals

Up to this point the parallels between male and female criminals from passion have been nearly perfect, but there are other traits which, while they are essential to the males, are found in only some of the women. For example, in only some of the women does provocation lead immediately to an explosion of crime by passion. It did so in the case of Guérin, who on hearing that her husband was at Versailles with his mistress, rushed there and stabbed him. Similar examples of rapid action are offered by Provensal and Jamais.[60]

Then too, only some women sincerely and violently repent after their crime. Noblin ran screaming through the village streets to give herself up to the authorities. Daru attempted suicide, but, courage failing, turned herself into the police.

Finally, we occasionally find such women lacking self-assurance in the way they execute their crimes. Both Jamais and Provensal fired many shots without aiming, thus barely grazing their intended victims.

Differences from Male Criminals

None of the women in the preceding examples was entirely spotless. Most had wicked traits, which makes them different from the exaggeratedly good male criminal-by-passion and brings them closer to the female born criminal or criminal by occasion.

Often, in fact, their explosion of passion is not truly violent, but rather they brood over their crime for months and years, alternating periods of hatred with tolerance and even friendship for their victims. Often, too, they premeditate longer than male counterparts. Colder and more cunning, they execute their crimes with a skill and intricacy that are psychologically impossible for the true male criminal-by-passion. Nor does sincere penitence always follow the offense; indeed, what follows is often exultation, and the offender rarely commits suicide.

Discovering her husband's affair with the maidservant, Laurent fired the girl; but memory of the insult rankled in her mind, and after *six months* she hunted the girl down and killed her. No male criminal by passion would have waited so long for vengeance. The use of vitriol, too, as in the Du Tilly case, is incompatible with the true crime of passion in its refinement of cruelty and need for coolness, for the fluid must be well aimed, which no one could accomplish in a state of extreme moral turbulence. Even Daru, one of the best examples of offenders of this type, waited until her husband was asleep to kill him.[61] In many of the female cases, we find not the sudden fury of passion that blinds even a good man, transforming him temporarily into a killer, but a slower and more tenacious ferment of cruel instincts which leaves time for premeditation.

It may be objected that the women we have described are by nature very good; and indeed, they are very similar to normal women. But this apparent contradiction disappears when we reflect that even the normal woman is deficient in moral sense and has slight criminal tendencies such as vindictiveness, jealousy, envy, and malignity, which are usually neutralized by women's weaker sensitivity and lesser intensity of passion. However, if a moral woman is but slightly more excitable than usual or exposed to a serious provocation, then her latent criminal tendencies gain the upper hand. Being colder than men, women become criminal not through intensity of passion but through the explosion of a latent tendency to crime that has been activated by circumstance. Their deeds are attributable partly to passion and partly to innate depravity; but this does not negate their general goodness.

In some cases passion is a very important factor but in itself impotent to cause crime without the additional push of a man's suggestion. Lodi stole at her lover's insistence and only after he threatened to leave her if she did not obey. In such cases, the criminal tendencies are more latent than usual but nonetheless profound and tenacious; passion must be reinforced by suggestion. A man who commits a crime from passion may have a strong natural repugnance for the crime which is momentarily broken down by his emotion; but someone who needs both passion and suggestion to commit an act of violence—who premeditates the act—must have a lower degree of organic repulsion for evil deeds. The latent wickedness of the normal woman makes possible a hybrid form of criminal impulse in which suggestion plays a role.

Crimes of Passion from Egotism

Egotistical criminal impulses provide an excellent illustration of the fact that women's crimes of passion result from a slow fermentation of the wickedness latent in normal women. Those crimes that we call *passionate-egotistical* involve women who are honest, good, and loving, but impelled by self-centered jealousy. Such crimes, although they originate partly in passion, lack serious cause and are also entirely unprovoked by the victim; in this sense the offenses are unmotivated, like those of the born criminal. Bedridden for five years with an incurable disease, Perrin became extremely jealous of her husband, perpetually reproaching him for infidelities. Having decided finally to put an end to the situation, she called her husband to her bedside and wounded him with a revolver hidden under the sheets, declaring later that she premeditated this act for a long time.

In such cases the motive for crime is the noble feeling of love, and the offenders are naturally good women. They are impelled to crime by an outbreak of the wickedness latent in every woman and by a jealousy that takes the happiness of others as a personal injury. Their own inability to be happy makes them unwilling to have anyone else marry the man they are leaving. But their motives are comprehensible, and in other circumstances every one of them would have remained a fine woman. In this respect they are like children, since their crimes are those that might be committed by big children with developed intelligence and passions. We are here concerned, then, with crimes of passion that originate entirely in egotistical feelings such as jealousy and envy and not in those sentiments which Spencer calls *ego-altruistic*, such as love and honor, which drive men to crimes of passion.

It is worth noting Marro's observation[m] that jealousy causes madness in 17 percent of female cases, compared to 1.5 percent of male cases. This proves how powerful jealousy is in women.

m. *La pazzia nelle donne*, 1893.

26
Suicides

To complete our study of crimes of passion, we must examine suicide. Legal considerations aside, there are so many similarities between crimes of passion and suicide that the two seem like two branches of one tree.

Suicide occurs four or five times less frequently among women than men, as shown in table 26.

Suicides from Physical Suffering

The number of suicides attributable to physical pain is much greater among men than women. Women feel pain less than men and consequently are less often driven by it to suicide.

Poverty

Extreme poverty is another factor that drives more men than women to suicide. The probability of falling into poverty is the same for one sex as the other; that is, loss of income usually affects both the husband and wife, or both a father and daughters. However, women cope better than men with poverty, for a variety of reasons. One is that women, who form the average type of the species, can better adapt themselves to changing social conditions. As Max Nordau remarks, the difference in nature between a duchess and a washerwoman is only superficial, so that a duchess can adapt herself to a new environment and become a washerwoman much more easily than a man can adapt under analogous circumstances.[62] Then too, women have fewer needs and a lower degree of sensitivity, which makes them better able to endure both moral suffering and physical privation.

Moreover, in cases of financial ruin, the woman is often only indirectly respon-

Table 26 Suicide Rates by Sex

	men	women		men	women
Italy (1874–83)	80.2	19.8	Scotland (1877–81)	70.0	30.0
Prussia (1878–82)	83.3	16.7	Ireland (1874–83)	73.0	27.0
Saxony (1874–83)	80.7	19.3	Switzerland (1876–83)	85.0	15.0
Wurtemberg [*sic*] (1872–81)	84.6	15.4	Holland (1880–82)	81.0	19.0
France (1876–80)	79.0	21.0	Denmark (1880–83)	78.2	21.8
England (1873–82)	75.0	19.0	Connecticut (1878–82)	70.0	30.0

Editors' note: Lombroso does not give the numbers on which the rates are based.

sible and as a result is less remorseful than the man. Once again, maternity has a beneficent influence, for a mother who sinks into poverty is less affected by grief at the ruin than alarmed by the need to provide for her children. The father, on the other hand, wracked by regret, is thus more likely to forget about the innocent victims of his mistakes and faults. Finally, women have less pride than men, which makes it easier for them to beg, while men often prefer death to begging. And women, with their weaker moral sense, sometimes have recourse to prostitution.

It follows that many more factors must come into play before women can be driven to suicide by extreme poverty.

Love

Love contributes heavily to suicide, just as it does to crime. Statistics show that women are more likely than men to commit suicide as a result of problems in love. The passionate woman flies to suicide as a relief from the disillusions and pains of love. This keeps the number of crimes of passion by women low due to the well-known inverse relationship between suicide and crime.

The predominance among women of suicide over homicide for love meshes perfectly with my view of the nature of womanly love. For women, love is a form of slavery, a willing sacrifice of their entire personality. When women end the agony of unrequited love through suicide, they will often use their last words to express their self-sacrificing devotion to the man who has wronged them. Desertion awakens no resentment; rather, they act as though they had lost him to death. Their only consolation is to die in turn.

Here is the reason why one so rarely finds a woman turning to crime due to passionate love. When pure, strong passion exists in a woman, it drives her to suicide rather than crime. In other cases, if her natural latent store of depravity is released, or if a masculine disposition infuses her feelings with violence, then she has the capacity for murderous assaults. This capacity is never found in the woman who is truly a woman; her true crime of passion (if *crime* is the right word) is suicide.

Double and Multiple Suicides

In a double suicide, the predominant partner is almost always the woman. When two lovers commit suicide, usually in consequence of violating social laws, the woman is the more resolute of the two. In the Bancal-Trousset case, for instance, it was she who, after reading *Indiana*,[63] conceived the plan of dying with her lover. Bancal was opposed, but she scolded him, saying, "You don't love me enough to make this sacrifice," and Bancal finally gave in. However, on the appointed evening, he balked at opening her veins, and she had to urge him on. When she fainted, Bancal, horrified, tried to stop the bleeding, but Trousset insisted that he give her poison, and, when that was not enough, told him to stab her. "You have to finish it," she said, "kill me now."

Whatever moralists and theologians may say, in this money-conscious, grasping age of ours, such incidents, far from horrifying us, bring tears to our eyes and fill us with compassion. They demonstrate that people can still feel idealistic, unselfish passions and even die for them.

It is not difficult to understand the physiology of suicide for love. Recall that love is a result of an attraction that is strengthened by the reproductive organs and by the repugnance to separation induced by the molecules of these organs.[64]

A type of suicide peculiar to women is that of the mother who, driven to despair by poverty or other circumstances, kills a young or sickly child and then herself. Arresteilles, who adored her twenty-nine-year-old son, an epileptic idiot, feared that after her own death the rest of the family might not take care of him adequately; thus she killed him and herself. Berbesson killed a daughter whom she loved dearly but who had gone mad and was about to be sent to an asylum; unable to bear the separation, the mother then killed herself. When the child is still young enough to be dependent but old enough to be susceptible to suggestion, the mother may not actually kill him but rather persuade him to commit suicide along with her.

Double suicides in two women are extremely rare. We have found only one case, and that incomplete, in the instance of Olga Protaffow and Vera Gerebessow, intimate friends who lived together in dire poverty. Exhausted, Vera made her friend promise to kill her if their circumstances had not improved within two months. Olga promised, and when the two months had elapsed, reluctantly kept her word. The rarity of such an act is explained by the weakness of friendship among women.

Table 27 Suicides from Madness by Sex

	men	women		men	women
Germany (1852–61)	30.17	50.77	Belgium	41.22	81.94
Prussia (1869–77)	23.50	44.0	France (1856–68)	15.48	13.16
Saxony (1875–78)	26.59	48.40	Italy (1866–77)	16.30	27.50
Austria (1869–78)	8.20	10.80	Norway	17.90	28.40

Editors' note: Lombroso does not give the numbers on which the rates are based. The dates covered by the statistics for Belgium and Norway are omitted in the original.

Suicides from Madness

Fifty percent or more of female suicides are attributable to madness. The statistics appear in table 27. In women, violent passion is more likely to lead to madness than to suicide or to crime. Being less variable than men, women remain more normal; but when they are anomalous, they are usually more so than men, becoming double exceptions. This is why in their case suicides from passion, which indicate only slight variations of character, are rare, while suicides from madness, which happen when the anomaly is more intense, occur more frequently.[65]

27
The Born Prostitute

Prostitutes are both sexually frigid and sexually precocious. They present us with a real tangle of contradictions: an eminently sexual profession, practiced by women in whom sexuality has almost been extinguished; and women who, despite their weak sexual drive, devote themselves to vice at an age at when they are barely physically ready for sexual intercourse. What, then, is the origin of prostitution? Psychologically, as I will show, it originates not in lust but moral insanity.

Moral Insanity/Family Feelings

As Tarnowsky has already recognized, in some cases prostitution stems from moral insanity. My own careful studies show that moral insanity occurs frequently among born prostitutes, so much so as to be a defining characteristic of the type. Signs of moral insanity can be found in the prostitute's lack of natural feelings, such as family affection, along with her wickedness as a child, jealousy, and ruthless taste for revenge. More evidence of moral insanity lies in the fact that among prostitutes, the normal woman's difficulty in forming friendships with other women becomes an absolute impossibility.

Additional proof of moral insanity comes from statistics showing that very few prostitutes enter the profession through noble motives. Among 5,144, Parent-Duchatelet found only 89 who took up prostitution in order to support old or sick relatives or a large family.[66] Others took up prostitution due to poverty and abandonment by relatives or a lover. But for the majority of prostitutes, poverty and abandonment are only catalysts, while the underlying cause is their lack of modesty and moral insanity, which push them first into debauchery and then the brothel. This is especially true of abandonment, because the passionate woman who errs for the sake of love and is then vilely abandoned does not become a prostitute but rather kills herself or, through self-sacrifice, keeps herself honest. Nor can poverty toss women in the arms of vice if their sense of modesty is not already weak or they are not already predisposed by cravings for riches and pleasure.

Maternity

Another and very serious indication[67] of moral insanity—so important that we must consider it separately—is the lack of maternal feelings that makes the born prostitute the twin sister of the female born criminal. Lesbians, especially, are completely indifferent to maternity and indeed terrified of pregnancy.

Prostitutes rarely have children (only 34 percent); those in elite brothels, in particular, use every available method to prevent pregnancy. One might hypothesize that they avoid pregnancy out of professional necessity and the difficulty for them of caring for children. However, for most women maternity is a physiological drive. Unsatisfied, it leads to physical and psychological decline.

Criminality

Like moral insanity, criminality—which is no more than a variant on moral insanity—is often linked to prostitution. Prostitutes' most common offense is theft, particularly complicity in theft. For example, according to Lecour, older prostitutes frequently commit blackmail. Sighele describes how a prostitute works with her pimp to blackmail clients: She lures the client and the pimp, playing the part of a husband or brother, surprises them in flagrante, forcing the client to cough up money if he wants to avoid scandal. Another fairly common crime among prostitutes, who are quick to anger, is stabbing.

Alcoholism

Prostitutes' passion for liquor equals that of male criminals and ends up weakening them or even ruining their muscular reflexes. Out of nine cases, Marro found that to have happened in seven; two had begun drinking in infancy, and one, a favorite child of drunken parents, consumed seven liters of brandy a week even before puberty (Marro, *Caratteri*, p. 438). Of sixty prostitutes studied by Gurrieri and Fornasari, eleven were alcoholics and thirty smokers, and twelve had fathers who were heavy drinkers.

Greed

Another mild form of criminality among prostitutes, in addition to theft and blackmail, may not reach the level of actual crime because the profession encour-

32 Margherita and Louisa. *Source*: Lombroso, *La donna delinquente*, 1893. *Editors' note*: These degenerates were ages twelve and nine, respectively, at the time they were photographed; on the basis of these images and the girls' case records, Lombroso concludes that the one on the left, Margherita, is a born prostitute, and that Louisa, on the right, is a born criminal. Margherita masturbated from the age of four on and performed oral sex on her brother; she also had a violent temper. Louisa began stealing at the age of three and, while in an insane asylum, she masturbated in public and allowed another inmate to insert a piece of wood into her rectum (*La donna delinquente*, 346–48).

ages them to satisfy themselves without breaking the law. That is the unrestrained greed which marks even the most intelligent of born prostitutes.

Prostitutes (writes Macé) think of their clients as money and often talk about them that way ("Here comes my *scudo*, my *luigi*).[68] I studied the case of one Perino, a thief from childhood, who gave up stealing as soon as she became a prostitute.[69]

Modesty

Lack of modesty is the most salient trait of these unfortunates. Some authors such as Parent-Duchatelet tend to deny (or at least minimize) this in view of the fact that prostitutes cover their pictures of the Madonna when they abandon themselves to lust and are ashamed to have sex in front of companions. But the behavior that some commentators interpret as modesty is in fact nothing more than superstition, vanity, fear of the Madonna, and simulation.

Especially strange is a vicarious form of modesty shown by many prostitutes: shame at undergoing vaginal examinations when the vagina is unclean, especially during menstruation. In this respect they sometimes manifest a resistance even greater than that of the honest woman. Yet one must remember that *modesty* derives from *putere*, the disgust of putrefying vaginal secretions.[70] The original love greeting—the first form of the kiss—was a sniff, the residuum of the sniffing that we see in animals when they meet one another. Similarly, for many savages the greeting is not, "How are you?" but rather, "How do you smell?" Therefore, prostitutes' behavior in this regard probably echoes modesty as it originally manifested itself in savage women: fear of arousing disgust in man.

In sum, prostitutes' modesty is completely immodest.

Moral Insanity and Innate Prostitution

Thus the born prostitute—lacking maternal and family feeling, unscrupulous in the pursuit of her desires, and mildly criminalistic—presents the complete type of moral insanity. This fact, too, helps explain her lack of modesty, for immodesty is characteristic of morally insane women. In women the entire force of moral evolution is directed toward the creation and reinforcement of modesty; thus moral degeneration (in other words, *moral insanity*)[71] necessarily obliterates that virtue, just as in the male, moral degeneration erases the loftiest civilized sentiments, such as respect for human life. Linked to both lack of modesty and moral insanity—almost crowning them—is the ease, indifference, and even joy with which prostitutes accept participation in the world's most infamous profession, one that banishes them from society.

This point resolves the apparent contradiction between prostitutes' profession and their sexual frigidity. Unusually intense sexual desires do not necessarily lead women to prostitution; women with this makeup will make a lot of demands on their husbands, and when seized by desire, they may supplement the husband with others, even giving in to men they hardly know. But they will not prostitute themselves. Thus their modesty still exists, even though overcome from time to time by strong sexual excitement. On the other hand, when women, despite their innate sexual coldness, become prostitutes, the determinative cause is not lust but moral insanity. Lacking modesty, indifferent to the infamy of vice, even attracted to all that is forbidden by a taste for the pathological, they give themselves to prostitution because it offers a way to support themselves without working. Sexual coldness is in fact an advantage for them, almost a Darwinian adaptation. For a sexually excitable woman, prostitution would be exhausting. But for prostitutes, coitus is an insignificant act, morally and physically. They sell themselves to men because they get money in return.

The fact that the germ of prostitution lies not in lust but moral insanity also explains prostitutes' sexual precocity, which is nothing more than an aspect of that general early propensity for evil which one finds in the morally insane. From early childhood, the morally insane demonstrate a morbid tendency to do everything that is forbidden.

Thus the origin of the born prostitute lies in moral insanity. The following secondary traits in the moral physiognomy of the prostitute confirm that the born prostitute and the morally insane woman are in fact one.

- Intermittent goodness. Prostitutes, like female born criminals, intermittently exhibit goodness; at certain moments this goodness carries them far from their habitual egotism.[72]
- Intelligence. In intelligence prostitutes exhibit extreme variation, ranging from those who are almost idiots or half-wits to those who border on brilliance. However, most prostitutes in childhood show themselves incapable of learning. Inattentive and insubordinate, they get nothing out of school, and no school can hang onto them. Here is another proof of their moral insanity.[73] Just as weak intelligence and brilliance can be found side by side in the morally insane, so, too, in prostitutes one can find a strong intelligence that is nonetheless narrow and riddled with gaps.
- Jargon. Prostitutes have their own jargon. *Miché* is their name for a client. *Little kneeling girls* is their term for young lesbians who turn tricks.[74] *The owl* is a brutish female; *rail* is a term for a police inspector; and *guardians of the dead* is a term for those who disrupt the life of the brothel. *Gougnottes* are lesbians. *The tip of the pen* refers to oral sex; *the paw of the spider* means manual masturbation; and *pulling the petals off the rose* designates anal masturbation. *Flea workers* are lesbians who put on homosexual shows (Taxil, op. cit.).
- Religiosity. Like criminals and most other degenerates, prostitutes are very religious. Strolling through the most crowded quarter of Naples, one finds a candlelit image of the Madonna before every brothel. When a client enters their room, they rush to cover their personal image of the Madonna so she cannot see them.
- Affection for animals. Another trait common to both prostitutes and the morally insane is excessive love of animals—a strong contrast to prostitutes' scanty love for human beings. Love for an animal is a purely egotistical sentiment because the creature is a slave which one need not respect or make sacrifices for. Love for a human, on the other hand, is both an ego-

tistical and altruistic sentiment; one must sacrifice many selfish desires for the sake of the beloved.

- Love. Prostitutes have lovers, their *souteneurs*, and at first glance nothing is odder than the ties of affection that bind lost women to those evil creatures. In this respect prostitutes differ from female born criminals, who, as we have seen, are incapable of strong and lasting affections. This difference manifests itself in the prostitutes' need to lean on a man. A characteristic of women in general, this need is felt deeply by prostitutes, most of whom, due to their minimal intelligence and rather drab personalities, succumb easily to men's suggestions.[75] Female criminals, on the other hand, have forceful personalities and intensely egotistical, evil passions; thus they seek in their lovers not masters but slaves.
- Gluttony, voracity, and tendency to drink. One of prostitutes' liveliest tastes is for eating; often they are extraordinary gluttons. If one recalls the weak intelligence of most prostitutes and their sexual coldness, one can understand how, with two of life's most important functions (intelligence and reproduction) in decline, the only remaining one is the most fundamental, nutrition. It develops with unheard-of vigor, almost as if to compensate for the weakness of the other two.[76] Gluttony links prostitutes with children; during childhood, before the awakening of intelligence and sexuality, one's entire existence is still focused on the stomach. Gluttony also links them to idiots, in whom weak intelligence is accompanied by voracious appetite. Thus gluttony indicates profound degeneration.

  Most prostitutes are drawn to strong liquor, albeit to different degrees. Their tendency to drink, acquired at an early age (and therefore another sign of precocity), in the long run reduces them to the level of brutes. They begin drinking to dull their senses; little by little they get used to it; and eventually the habit becomes so strong that they fight off anyone who tries to help them.
- Vanity. Prostitutes are characteristically vain, although in various ways. One might almost say that their vanity bears an inverse relationship to its objective reality. However, they are less vain than male criminals, with their ridiculous pomposity.
- Laziness. One of the prostitute's dearest loves is laziness. Insensible to boredom, they spend entire days in their homes or brothels, stretched out on the bed or seated, doing nothing and remaining unwearied by this inertia that for a normal woman would be worse than hard labor. In fact, they

loathe work, and this is one of the factors that pushes them into the life of prostitution, together with that fondness for diversion, good times, and orgies which they share with the criminal. Their incapacity for continuous and regulated work is linked to their obsessive need to distract themselves with orgies, which in turn is linked to their passion for dancing. For nearly all prostitutes, dancing was the first step toward their life of infamy. To go dancing they will run away from home and abandon their jobs; to be accompanied to a dance, they will strike up a relationship with a stranger and end up by giving themselves to him. This alternation between the extremes of laziness and agitation is characteristic of degenerates and recalls the lazy life preferred by savages, who alternate it with those orgies of movement that constitute their dances.

- Volubility, thoughtlessness, improvidence. Prostitutes' volubility, like their laziness, is proverbial. It and their thoughtlessness stem from their weak attentiveness. Since concentration is one of the final and most difficult victories of mental evolution, it almost disappears in degenerates.[77] Along with thoughtlessness comes the prostitute's proverbial improvidence. Over and over again we find even high-class coquettes who, with a certain degree of high-spiritedness and intelligence, earn lavish sums only to squander them on mad purchases, heedless of the fragility of that beauty on which their present fortune depends. Prostitutes of the second or third grade are even less likely to peer beyond their present difficult circumstances into the shadowy future. This is why so few prostitutes, even the most able and lucky, grow rich.
- Lies. Like criminals, prostitutes tend to lie incorrigibly and pointlessly. This habit flows partly from their disreputable position in society and partly from an awareness of the low opinion that others have of them. Moreover, they are all in fact fleeing from something: paternal authority, judicial investigators, or the police. Thus they end up falsifying even in unimportant matters.

Equivalents of the Born Prostitute in Higher Social Classes

It would be easy to prove that most prostitutes come from the poorer classes. One need only glance at table 28 (compiled by Parent-Duchatelet) on the causes of prostitution, while keeping in mind that most of the causes listed there are only apparent, with the fundamental cause lying in individual degeneration.

It is clear from this table that those who are prostitutes from poverty, who are

Table 28 Causes of Prostitution

determining causes	born in Paris	born in cities	born in small towns	born in the country	born in other countries	total
poverty	570	405	182	222	62	1441
death of parents or abandonment	647	201	157	211	39	1255
to support aged or infirm parents	37	—	—	—	—	37
to raise orphaned siblings	29	—	—	—	—	29
widows or abandoned women, to raise a numerous family	23	—	—	—	—	23
widows who come from provinces to Paris to find resources	—	187	29	64	—	280
brought to Paris by soldiers, shop clerks, students, etc.	—	185	75	97	47	404
servants seduced and fired by employers	123	97	29	40	—	289
concubines who have lost their lovers and have no other means	559	314	180	302	70	1425
totals	1988	1389	652	936	218	5183

Editors' note: Lombroso's text makes it clear that this table is derived from Alexandre Parent-Duchatelet's *De la prostitution dans la ville de Paris* (Paris: Baillière, 1836).

widows from the provinces seeking resources in Paris, who are girls brought by soldiers, workers, and so on, and so on, and finally who are domestic servants and ex-concubines can come from none other but the most impoverished class. They comprise 3,839 out of the total of 5,183 cases. The Goncourts, too, observed that nearly all of the great coquettes of the last century came from the common people.

Without denying that poverty and bad education contribute to the making of occasional prostitutes, one would be foolish to believe that the phenomenon explaining innate prostitution in the lower classes does not manifest itself as well in the upper classes, in forms that are different but substantially the same. The lower-class woman who becomes the inhabitant of a house of prostitution has her upper-class counterpart in the incorrigible adulterer. It would be disingenuous to hold that the only prostitutes are those who live in brothels. The appearance of the born prostitute varies depending on social class; but she is fundamentally the same in high society as in the most revolting brothel.

Prostitution and Criminality

We now have firm facts to resolve the hotly debated issue of the relation between prostitution and criminality.

The psychological and anatomical similarity of the male criminal and the born prostitute could not be more complete: Both resemble the moral lunatic, and therefore all three are identical, according to logic. Male criminals and prostitutes exhibit the same lack of moral sense, hardness of heart, youthful appetite for evil, and indifference to public opinion which lead the former to become a convict and the latter a fallen woman. Moreover, they show the same improvidence, restlessness, and tendency to idleness; the same taste for immediate gratification, orgies, and drink; and the same (or almost the same) sort of vanity. Prostitution is nothing more than the female form of criminality.

Prostitution and criminality are analogous or, one might say, parallel phenomena, to such an extent that they meet at their extremes, with mild crimes like theft, blackmail, and stabbing occurring frequently among prostitutes. The prostitute is, therefore, psychologically a criminal. If she does not commit actual crimes, it is because she is physically weak, or intellectually backward, or able to get what she needs by easier methods. In accord with the law of minimum effort, she prefers prostitution.

In women, criminality generally takes the form of prostitution. Women who are born criminals are extraordinarily anomalous; exhibiting more extreme wickedness than male criminals and a masculine character, they are therefore very rare. As a result, we must look for true female criminality in prostitution. This explains why mild forms of crime predominate among prostitutes. Being identical to criminals, they lead the same lives, insofar as their strength allows. Beyond that, in them degeneration expresses itself in the specific form of prostitution. We knew a girl, P., who was a thief from childhood but then, when she grew up, became a prostitute.

These women do not commit crimes, and they are rarely dangerous to society. Indeed, their special form of criminality—prostitution—is socially useful as an outlet for male sexuality and a preventive of male crime. Sometimes criminality works in useful ways. Criminal behavior and prostitution are two forms, one masculine and one feminine, of criminality.[78]

28

The Occasional Prostitute

Not all prostitutes are afflicted with moral insanity, and thus not all of them can be called born prostitutes. Some are occasional prostitutes.

Physical and Psychological Characteristics

About 63 percent of all prostitutes have few or almost no degenerative traits. Of these, 55 percent were neither early nor late in menstruation, 45 percent have children, 16 percent have normal reflexes, and 39 percent have normal sensitivity to pain.

Occasional prostitutes diverge more from the normal type of woman than do occasional criminals. While the criminaloid, especially the thief, is almost always closer to the normal woman than to the born criminal, the occasional prostitute is closer to the born prostitute than to the normal woman. Vice and other psychologically abnormal traits play but a small role in her makeup, yet she remains, at base, notably abnormal.

Maxime Du Camp tells the story of one such prostitute whose character presented a strange mix of vicious and good qualities.[79] Arrested for streetwalking at the age of fourteen, she said that her mother did not want her in the house, that she had never been taught a trade, and that prostitution was her only means of support. She became pregnant and had a daughter to whom she was devoted, but who, due to the hardships of their life, died one night of cold. The mother's desperation was extreme; when arrested, she wrote a moving letter to the police chief, saying: "Remember that my mother sent me to the foundlings' hospital and that my darling daughter died in my arms. I implore your pity." Freed, she found an honest workman who was struck by her many good qualities and married her. But the prostitute's life into which she had been thrown by circumstance had developed bad habits in her, and after a while she left him to return to it. Rearrested, she was again reclaimed by her husband; but on release she disappeared in the maze of police headquarters and sneaked off. Thus habitual latent vices, reinforced by use, prevailed over good and normal feelings (such as maternity) that under other circumstances might have assured her of an honest life.

In many occasional prostitutes one finds the frivolity, volubility, incoherence, and improvidence of the born prostitute and the same anomalous and degenerate traits, but in smaller proportion. In them modesty is certainly less strong than in normal women; but nonetheless it exists. That is one difference between them and the born prostitute; another is their lack of joy in evil for evil's sake—the fact that they have not abandoned themselves to vice solely through fondness for it. To push them into this way of life, an occasion was necessary, one that was more or less strong depending on the strength or weakness of their anomalies. In addition, their moral sense, without being completely intact, is firmer than that of the born prostitute. They are horrified by their way of life, even though their efforts to break free are rarely sufficient to succeed.

In sum, without the negative circumstances that caused them to fall, occasional prostitutes would have joined the ranks of those frivolous, brainless women who can be found in large numbers in all social classes, especially the upper ones. Without being excessively wicked, even while loving their children and family, they allow themselves to be easily led into adulterous and above all stupid adventures. They then sincerely repent, but when temptation recurs, they will fall again if nothing stands firmly between them and relapse. They are chatterboxes who lack a complete moral sense and intelligence but whose social lives are neither extremely deleterious nor perverted; in this they contrast with morally insane women, who are driven from one debauch to the next by their unhealthy pleasure in vice.

Maternity

While the born prostitute is neither psychologically nor (in many cases) physically a mother, occasional prostitutes love their children tenderly. Often they love relatives deeply as well. Some ply their infamous trade in order to help family members. "It must be said," writes Carlier, "that some prostitutes have honorable motives for requesting legal registration.[80] One may worry about feeding her parents or other relatives; another, widowed and resourceless, thinks only about rearing her little ones. Still others, without going quite so far, enter the trade to help their families. Those who were orphaned may use the income from their shameful profession to feed younger brothers and sisters, exhibiting an entirely maternal devotion and deeming it worthy."

Shame and Remorse

When they are not working, occasional prostitutes are ashamed of their trade. They lack both the cynicism and the impudence of the born prostitute. This proves that they took up their evil way of life only when a complex of circumstances overwhelmed their virtue, which was none too strong to begin with. Modesty has not been totally obliterated in these women but survives in several intermittent signs.

The circumstances that push these women into prostitution vary; we will examine the main ones.

- Loss of virginity. Many occasional prostitutes are thrust into this work for which they have no affinity and even extreme distaste by losing their virginity through a first mistake, such as a seduction not followed by matrimony, or by a first disgrace, such as a rape. As long as they are virgins, their moral sense is reinforced by fear of the unknown; they are afraid to make the serious decision of giving themselves to a man for the first time. But when a young girl has lost her most precious treasure, the worst step has been taken. Feeling incapable of restoring her honor through work, she looks instead to profit from her disgrace. And thus the occasionals turn to the life of prostitution rather than honest work. "Once a door is open, it is difficult to close," remarked one girl who had been raped by her employer at the age of fourteen and afterward took up prostitution.

  In these women, it is not so much that honesty safeguards virginity as that virginity safeguards honesty. Nonetheless, they are women who, had they not experienced this disgrace or made that mistake, would have remained honest. As Marro has wisely observed, loss of virginity has a huge influence on woman's psyche, revolutionizing her from head to toe. Once the spell is broken—once that veil that hid the knowledge of good and evil has been torn—those whose moral sense was weak in the first place and who are now socially shunned easily decide to ignore other considerations as well.
- Violence and shrewdness. To society's shame, many occasional prostitutes are recruited through violence and traded as black slaves were.[81] They are enlisted by some scoundrel who, pretending to find them work as waitresses or something similar, takes them to foreign countries where they have neither friends nor supports. He shuts them up in brothels where everything encourages them to give in: cajolery, threats, liquor. Most lack

the energy of that girl described by Grandpré, who seized a knife and threatened to kill the man who refused to let her leave a house of ill repute. Most are raped and maliciously prevented from leaving their brothel-prison. They end up by adapting to the prostitute's life, and they continue with it because escape is so difficult.

- Poverty and bad examples. Sometimes the cause is poverty, bad example, or even instruction by corrupt parents. When modesty is weak, prostitution is too easy a means of earning a living for poor women not to resort to it. This is especially true if education and training have not developed those feelings of modesty that, in infants, are still embryonic. Of course, the entirely honest woman would prefer death to prostitution; at the other extreme, the born prostitute has an organic need for vice. In between is the occasional prostitute, pushed by poverty but likely to have remained honest had she been economically comfortable.

Into the "occasional" category fall those prostitutes who, again in contrast with the born prostitute and her innate love of wickedness, give themselves to this work as they would to any other trade, practicing it methodically and regularly, even taking care to register properly. While it is true that they are deficient in modesty, prostitution seems to them like an ordinary job. Since their lack of modesty is unaccompanied by other signs of moral insanity, one must regard it as not a sign of innate degeneration but rather an acquired trait. The sense of modesty is poorly organized in their brains.

For them, in other words, prostitution is less a morbid tendency toward an asocial life than a job like any other, practiced because other work pays too poorly or because they do not know how to do it. Under more favorable circumstances, they would never have become prostitutes, despite the weakness of their sense of modesty, which cannot be normal since their horror for this trade was not strong enough to repel them from it.

Summary

The occasional prostitute is therefore psychologically more abnormal than the occasional criminal. My theory both explains this difference and is reconfirmed by it. In my view, prostitution and not criminality is the main way in which degeneration manifests itself among women. Female born criminals are rare and monstrous exceptions, and criminaloids are often just women in whom dreadful living conditions have brought out that basic immorality that exists in all women, even the normal ones. Theft and fraud, for example, are not in and of themselves indications of great perversity in women because respect for other people's property is not one of women's strongest traits, and thus to commit such violations does not require serious degeneration. Modesty, in contrast, is the strongest female sense, after maternity; it is the goal toward which the entire psychological evolution of woman has focused its energy for centuries. Therefore the woman who, without originally lacking modesty, easily loses it, must be more profoundly anomalous that the woman who, under the pressure of great temptation, loses her respect for the property of others. The latter is nearly normal, the former more anomalous. This is the reason why the occasional prostitute almost always presents traits that resemble those of the born prostitute, though in attenuated form, while the criminaloid, who is almost normal, has very little in common with the born criminal, who is a double exception and from time to time a monstrosity.

29

Insane Criminals

Statistics

In Italy in the decade 1870–79 there were 7.3 female criminals for every 100 male criminals. But in roughly the same period (1871–86), there were 5.6 insane female criminals for every 100 male insane criminals.[n] From a study by Sander and Richter, we find that out of 1,486 insane men, 13.9 percent were criminal, while out of 1,462 insane women, just 2.6 percent were criminal.[o][82]

The smaller proportion of female insane criminals can be attributed to two factors: women's lesser degree of alcoholism (drink supplying the largest contingent of insane male criminals) and the lesser prevalence of epilepsy among them, together with the tendency of epilepsy to express itself in women in either prostitution or lasciviousness. These offenses, while indecent, are nonetheless neither particularly criminal nor dangerous, and thus they do not attract a lot of public attention.

As to the nature of insanity in criminal women, table 29 gives Italian data for the years 1870–79. Here we find a clear predominance of forms of mental disorder produced by prison life such as melancholy, hallucinatory monomania, and suicide, and of congenital problems such as imbecility and idiocy that ought to rule out incarceration.[83] On the other hand, criminal women have few of the mental diseases such as epilepsy and moral insanity that are common among male criminals.

While there is little insanity among the minor offenders who form the great majority of incarcerated women, the opposite is the case among the most serious

n. V. Rossi, *I pazzi criminali in Italia*, 1887.

o. Dr. Sander und Richter, *Die Beziehungen Zwischen Geinterstorung* [*sic*] *zerbrechen*. Berlin, 1886.

Table 29 Types of Insanity in Criminal Women (Italy, 1870–79)

melancholy and paranoia	33 cases	megalomania	2 cases
mania	22 cases	suicide	4 cases
imbecility and idiocy	10 cases	moral insanity	4 cases
hallucinatory monomania	7 cases		

Table 30 Insanity Rates by Sex and Crime Type

	insane female criminals	(number of cases)	insane male criminals
murder	26 percent	(130)	40 percent
poisoning	25 percent	(20)	—
assault	30 percent	(10)	26 percent
robbery	20 percent	(10)	23 percent
swindling	15 percent	(20)	23 percent
arson	80 percent	(4)	85 percent
rape	16 percent	(25)	33 percent
theft	0 percent	(90)	31 percent

Editors' note: Lombroso's original text makes it clear that data on women for this table come from a study by Salsotto of 409 cases in the Turin prison, although he does not cite this study here. He further states that he has added comparative data on men from a study (also uncited) by Marro. The figures in parentheses show the number of cases on which the female percentages were based. No comparable figures are given for the male percentages. The surprisingly large number of women convicted of rape is probably comprised mainly of women who were accomplices of male rapists. We have rearranged the table to make it more readable.

offenders, as shown in table 30. Clearly, insanity prevails among the worst female offenders, and there is some parallelism with the males.

The majority of insane female criminals are married while the majority of their male counterparts are single. A similar pattern turns up in the data from all countries.

Premeditation

One essential trait of the most serious cases of moral insanity and epilepsy in women is premeditation. The crimes of insane women are sometimes even more remarkable than those of ordinary female offenders in terms of skill, premeditation, steps taken to establish an alibi, and efforts at covering up.[84]

The madness of the female insane criminal grows particularly acute at the times of menstruation, menopause, and pregnancy. In this respect, she merely exaggerates women's normal state. To quote Icard,[85] "One woman, every time she menstruated, felt drawn to big department stores and shoplifting. Another girl, every time she had her period, castrated the first animal she could lay her hands on." Brouardel has recorded many examples of pregnant women with incendiary or homicidal impulses. One of his cases concerns a pregnant mother of five children who sent poison to one child at school and then, arranging for the youngest to be brought to her from the wet nurse, threw him and the other three down a well. "When she is pregnant," writes Icard, "woman is capable of anything. Excellent mothers will cut the throats of children they love passionately; and others, ordinarily good, will pose as victims and make up infamous calumnies against their loved ones. Chaste women will talk and act with disgusting obscenity." "During pregnancy," writes Cabanis (tomo III, p. 344), "a type of animal instinct dominates woman and can drive her to any excess. The same thing can happen at the first resumption of menstruation and during the period of nursing."

Another characteristic of the insane woman (and, by extension, of the insane criminal woman) is exaggerated sexuality. While sexuality usually diminishes in insane men, I have always found it heightened in insane women. I have seen an old woman of eighty years who masturbated with a brass crucifix. Another old woman filled her vulva with knives, bits of cloth, and eggshells. A third masturbated in front of others with candles and eggs. And while lesbians, even if they are prostitutes, will conceal their practices, they will openly have sex with one another in madhouses. It is quite common there (I have found it in ten out of two hundred cases), even in prepubescent girls, and they will do it without a trace of their usual pretenses of love and jealousies (*Arch. di psych.*, VI, p. 219).

Marro writes[p]: "Most women who are insane during menopause exhibit erotic delirium. They have bizarre ideas about marriage, pregnancy, and giving birth to monsters. They are subject to sudden obscene delusions. One hallucinates about a crowd of lovers who abuse her in endless succession; another is seized by delirious jealousy; yet another thinks that little devils are hanging on her apron, grabbing at her, pinching her, and giving her hot little bites. These sexual hallucinations constitute one of the worst forms of delirium."

Nymphomania transforms the most timid girl into a wild and shameless reveler. She looks at every man with longing and flirts outrageously, even to the point of violence. Often she is extremely thirsty, with a dry mouth and bad breath, and she swings her hips almost as if in intercourse. She tends to bite everyone she meets, as if rabid, so much so that she is sometimes repelled by liquids and feels that she is being strangled. I was consulted in one case in which this morbid eroticism ap-

p. Marro, *La pazzia nelle donne. Ann. di fren.*, 1891, p. 28.

peared in a previously chaste woman after a bout of diphtheria. This case remains unique (Lombroso, *Amore nei pazzi*, 1880).

Insane women tend to surpass insane men in their sexual aberrations and tendencies. After long years of observation, I think that Hergt (*All. Zeits. Psych.*, XXVII) did not exaggerate when he calculated that two-thirds of insane women suffer from hypertrophy of the cervix, ulcers of the vagina, and other gynecological disorders, all of which inflame the uterine reflexes, weaken psychological activity, encourage convulsions, favor abnormal sensations, and transform these sensations into illusions, hallucinations, and obscene acts.

A third characteristic of insane women is that they are more perceptive and more impulsive than male counterparts.[86] Moreover, Krafft-Ebing observes that in women madness can be more turbulent and indecent in its manifestations than in men. Briefly, we find in insane criminal women, although to a lesser extent than in female born criminals, an inversion of the qualities that most characterize the normal woman: reserve, docility, and sexual apathy.

30

Epileptic Criminals and the Morally Insane

Epileptic Criminals

The same relationship that we have found in men between moral insanity and epilepsy also appears among women. The main difference is that epilepsy and moral insanity are much rarer among female than male prisoners. Marro reported that motor epilepsy occurs about one-third less frequently in female than male criminals. Rarer still in women is psychological epilepsy, or epileptic insanity. Epilepsy is relatively infrequent not only among female prisoners but also women who are inmates of insane asylums.[87]

The extraordinary difference between male and female rates of epilepsy can only be explained by women's cerebral cortex. Although their cerebral cortex is as irritable as men's in its motor centers, it is much less so in its psychological centers, precisely because there are fewer of these.

Moral insanity, too, is more prevalent among men than women; and moral insanity is closely linked to both inborn criminality and epilepsy. The relative rarity among women of epileptic insanity and moral insanity helps explain why women are so much more often merely occasional criminals and why, even when they are criminals from passion, they so seldom commit crimes in one of those sudden impulses which are always partially epileptoid. It also helps explain why women who commit ordinary crimes premeditate and gloat in a way incompatible with offenses that spring instantaneously from an epileptic seizure. Further, women's lower rate of epilepsy sheds light on the slow reactions of the female offender; and while it indirectly confirms our theory of the link between congenital criminality and epilepsy, it works as well to explain sexual differences in offense rates.[88]

In the few instances of female born criminals, I have always been able to find signs of epilepsy, as in male born criminals. In the most serious female offenders, motor forms of epilepsy are rarer than in men while the psychological forms predominate. One example is that of Maria Br.: age 47; face of the Mongolian type; cranial capacity 1,426; sense of touch somewhat dull; slight insensibility to pain; vision affected by peripheral scotomata in the internal superior quadrant. From youth she had drunk five or six litres of wine a day,[89] plus eight glasses of liquor. At the age of twenty she stole a thousand lire, which she squandered on fancy clothes and drink. Later, she wounded a lover who had deserted her for another woman. This woman has no idea that she is epileptic, yet many times when working in the kitchen she has cut her hand without realizing it. She has become dizzy for no reason and fallen to the ground; and on three occasions she had psychological fits. On one of these occasions, when ordered by her mistress to carry the night soil to the latrine, she instead headed toward the bureau and attempted to open the drawers, complaining that she was unable to do it. On another occasion, she made a chain of three clean shirts and hung them from the kitchen chimney, not to hide them but only because she had no idea what she was doing. On the third occasion, she tried to light the fire with a fifty-lire note and would have succeeded if her mistress had not snatched it from her hand. She has no direct memory of these fits, just as she had no consciousness of them at the time, and relates the incidents as they were told to her.

Prostitutes

Less than 1 percent of prostitutes have epilepsy, according to Parent-Duchatelet's statistics. This is lower than the average for the most serious born criminals, but higher than that for ordinary born criminals. In only one case (and it was complicated by hysteria) have we been able to find the complete epileptic type in prostitutes.

Here, then, is another of those contradictions which we have encountered so frequently in our work but which becomes largely comprehensible when we reflect on the shamelessness, lasciviousness, and semi-imbecility of morally insane women and prostitutes. These women reembody the atavistic traits of the primitive woman. When one considers the passive and regressive work of prostitutes, it is easy to understand how moral insanity would trigger this atavistic behavior, even if there is not always the additional complication of psychological epilepsy or cortical irritation, which leads to more serious crimes and striking sexual perversions.[90]

Morally Insane Women

In 1888 in Italian insane asylums there were 148 cases of moral insanity, of which 105 were male and 43 female, or 40.9 women for every 100 men. Noncriminal morally insane women have several traits in common with prostitutes: anger, excessive hatred, obscenity, and a tendency to lesbianism.

A unique case of what might be called "altruistic" obscenity among morally insane women is presented by the example of X. di Legrand, who, under pretext of protecting her son against syphilis and other illnesses, initiated him into carnal love herself, little by little, reasoning that he would not suffer thereby. When she became pregnant, she wanted to abort so she would not spoil her good looks and through that drive her son away; if he left she planned to commit suicide. Moreover, she brooked no criticism, saying "I have been absolved by God, who is infallible."

Catt. di Bonvecchiato, to conceal her lesbianism, pretended to be paralyzed and summoned nymphomaniacs to assist her. She made up a hundred illnesses to avoid working in the asylum, and she turned the hysterics on her ward into a veritable association of false accusers.

I knew a woman of outstanding family who wrote verses and was in fact very well educated but gave herself to everyone, from the grandest dignitary to the lowliest street sweeper. With extraordinary finesse she accused her husband of adultery and of wanting to lock her up to be free for his other loves; she even took this story to the authorities. In the asylum she boasted that she had never passed a day without making love, and she teased the officials for being like her in this respect. Moreover, in the asylum she succeeded, despite advanced age, in initiating intrigues and false accusations. Her only perversion was dumping her feces and urine on her food, which she might do on the same day that she wrote with tremendous lyricism about the purity of platonic love.

Another woman walked around the ward half-dressed in front of the nurses. She described her husband's obscene demands and her own body in intimate detail. Sometimes she touched and ate feces, an act that was often accompanied by obscenity, and she washed her eyes with urine. But in front of doctors and judges she knew how to justify her oddities. For instance, when asked why she washed her eyes with urine, she said that this was a way of healing them, and that everyone used this cure, and so on. She even succeeded in instituting legal proceedings against her husband.

31
Hysterical Criminals

Hysteria is one of the most common disorders in insane asylums, and it is the disorder that most differentiates insane women from insane men. In Italian asylums in 1888 there were only 4 hysterical men, but 788 hysterical women. At the most general level, hysteria relates to crime because it leads to sensational trials that have little real value.

The Psychology of Hysteria

At least half of hysterical women are normal in intelligence, but they are easily distracted. Due to their profound egotism and total self-absorption, they adore scandal and public attention. They are extremely impressionable and as a result subject to sudden anger and unreasonable likes and dislikes. Their will is always unstable; they delight in speaking evil; and if they cannot attract attention through baseless trials and outrageous forms of revenge, they embitter the life of their associates with continuous quarrels and disputes. Hysterics specialize in false accusations and false testimony, stirring up lawyers and the authorities against those they accuse. These symptoms often begin in childhood.

The characteristics of hysteria that are of most interest here include:

- Hypnotic suggestibility. Hysterical women are hypnotized easily. Their will is replaced by that of the hypnotizer, who can make one side of the patient's brain act quite contrary to the other side. In hallucinatory suggestion, the organs are modified just as in real suggestion. For example, if the patient is asked to think of an imaginary bird on the top of a tower, her pupils will dilate, and when she is instructed to follow the bird's descent, her pupils narrow.[91] Hysterics can be persuaded that they are made of glass, that they are birds, or that they have changed their sex, and they will act accordingly. The hypnotizer can impart to them ideas that are fixed, strange, impulsive, and even criminal; he can induce them to kiss a cranium, for example, or to kill a third party at some future point in time. While hypnotized, people forget what they did earlier in hypnotized states; offenders cannot recall their crimes until they are hypnotized again.

- Mobility of mood. Hysterics pass with astonishing rapidity from laughter to tears, "like children," writes Richet, "whom you will see laughing immoderately before their tears are completely dry."
- Special handwriting. Hysterics have a special handwriting, or rather a special tendency to vary their handwriting, which is sometimes very large and other times very small, according to their emotional condition (Binet). This same peculiarity can be observed in epileptics.
- Compulsive lying. "The biblical phrase *Homines mendaces*," writes Charcot,[92] "seems made for them; they simulate suicide and illness, they write anonymous letters. Lying without need and without limit, they cultivate lying as an art form." One girl told the authorities that she had thrown a man into the river. The water was about to be dragged for his body and the girl to be brought to trial when a doctor revealed that her entire story was a fable, invented out of hysteria.
- Tranquility. Another curious trait of hysterics is their tranquility, even in the face of serious illnesses. It sees them through paralysis and blindness without fear, irrespective of whether they have hope of being cured.
- Theft and arson. Hysterics commit theft and arson most frequently when they are menstruating.
- Eroticism. Hysterics are remarkably erotic. Out of eighty-three hysterics, Legrand found that 12 percent had become prostitutes even though they did not need to; two had committed monstrous violations of morality; and one mother had tried to force her daughter to masturbate her. It strikes me that all hysterical criminality in fact revolves around sexuality. Of twenty-one women who made false accusations, nine brought charges of rape, four of violence by their husbands, and one of being violently coerced to commit an unnatural sexual act. Accusations of rape by minors are almost always accompanied by erotic details that would be repugnant to adults. In light of these facts, I would say that in hysterics the sexual instincts are often exaggerated to the point of hallucinating intercourse, or are transformed into lesbianism. Most paradoxical of all is the way hysterics com-

bine sexual coldness with an obsession about sex, a phenomenon that also appears among drunks and lascivious old men.

- Anonymous letter writing. Hysterics have a mania for writing anonymous letters or letters with a faked signature, some of which they address to themselves. Sometimes they even persuade themselves of the authenticity of these fabrications, becoming victims of their own deceit. Almost all of their accusations of assault are supported by anonymous or forged letters.

Delirium

Hysterics, like epileptics, often suffer from delirium, either melancholic or monomaniacal. The maniacal form of the disorder is accompanied by hallucinations, impulsiveness, constant agitation or a need for movement, and desires to smash whatever lies in their way. These symptoms will appear in a flash in someone in good heath, last just a short time, and leave without a trace. Suddenly a person will run from a ballroom and throw herself into the river. A girl will break all the dishes and pour boiling water over her brother's head and then fly from the house to the woods, where she may be found building a stone altar for the celebration of her imaginary marriage. These crises, like those of epilepsy, come and go.

Suicide and Flights

Hysterics attempt or simulate suicide more often than they actually commit it. Their attempts are usually spontaneous and causeless, and they are made suddenly and very publicly, in contrast with other suicides. One hysteric will take poison after calling the police, while another will jump into the river when a boat is passing.

Another characteristic of hysterics (this, too, one that they share with epileptics) is the tendency to run away on strange trips. They are only partially conscious when they do this. They will disappear from home for three or four days, sometimes for a bout of prostitution, sometimes only to wander around, and when they return they either say nothing or boast about their adventures.

False Accusations

Many hysterics accuse their servants of theft, either to savor their disgrace and imprisonment or out of hatred and feminine vanity. The most common form of calumny is the charge of rape, an accusation made frequently against fathers and guardians, but above all against priests and physicians. Usually the accusation is so absurd that no one believes it; yet often it works, and the means used to make it work is in many cases a letter, anonymous or otherwise.

An unmarried woman, twenty-five years old and of good family, pursued a priest with erotic letters, writing, for instance, "My beloved, where are you? How are you? No one knows us. With ardent kisses, Laura." Shortly thereafter she accused the priest of making love to her.

Maria V., aged twenty-three, was found unconscious, slashed in a regular manner over her entire face and body, her hands tied, her mouth gagged, her eyes blindfolded with the ribbons of her cap. She accused four young men, describing in detail how they had reduced her to this condition when she resisted their assault; but in court the case was shown to be a hysterical invention (*Ann. d'hyg.*, vol. 1). Another woman burnt her hand with hot coals in order to accuse someone else of having done it.

Stealing

Another offense frequently committed by hysterics is stealing. Legrand du Saulle's study of 104 women apprehended for shoplifting in Paris found that 50 were hysterics.

C. H., a jealous woman, traveled to a neighboring village to keep an eye on her husband. Although she did not locate him, she got the idea of stealing chickens from the house where she was staying. She took twenty-one of them and sold them so cheaply that the merchant himself accused her of theft. Thereupon she confessed, ate a big meal, and chatted with everyone about her crime. When arrested, she threatened to kill herself.

A certain A., the daughter of mentally disturbed parents, at age fifteen, while she was menstruating, imagined herself surrounded by enemies. She fled to the fields, stole whatever she could find there, and threatened to burn everything and poison people. After ten to fifteen days she quieted down, declaring she had been overtaken by an irresistible impulse. For eight years she seemed cured, but with pregnancy her symptoms returned, along with erotic tendencies, and she became a prostitute.

Multiple Crimes/Murder

The impulses of hysterical women are like those of big children. They lack the strength to do greater evil,[93] as do all women, but in other respects hysterics can surpass other women, becoming terrible, worse than men.

Some hysterical women commit a variety of crimes. One will stab, rob, poison, burn, and testify falsely. Another will become a prostitute, steal children, spread false accusations, and steal. A classic example is offered by Z., who was simultaneously a thief, prostitute, murderer, and false accuser. Her story, in its general outlines, is the same as that of all women who are morally insane or born criminals. She came of a bad family: her father drank, her sister was a prostitute, and her mother (a foundling) was helpless and whiney. Z. had been branded by bad heredity: very thick, black hair, black eyes, a big mouth, prominent cheekbones, and frontal microcephalia. As soon as she started school she became a torment to her companions, and somewhere between the ages of fourteen and seventeen she took up prostitution. Placed in a shop, at age fourteen she quarreled with fellow workers and committed obscene acts. When she left that job, she took some things and then accused the owner of adultery; she also claimed that two other workers had been stealing. Pilfering some lace and hiding it under a bed, she blamed an innocent companion, whom the employer fired. She also tried to poison another employer who had always treated her kindly; and in a sort of delirium of perversity she reached the point, typical of hysterical women and born criminals, of doing evil for absolutely no reason at all. She would cut bell ropes, or cover her own belongings with filth and then point her finger at her mistress.

Z. formed a passionate affection for a beautiful but none-too-moral woman named Lodi, but even in this case she was dominated by consuming envy. When she turned against this friend, she made up frightful lies against her, demonstrating a fierce but baseless hatred. Then Z. became the mistress of an old man from whom she stole until, despite his fear of her, he sent her away. But she contrived to return one night, and that night the old man was killed by blows on the head.

In prison, Z. showed unusual piety. As soon as she was processed, she asked to go to confession, where she dictated prayers in verse to the Madonna. In court, she lied shamelessly, contradicting herself without blushing.

Comparison of Hysteria with Epilepsy

Readers will have noticed the many analogues between hysteria and epilepsy. The convulsions of hysteria so closely resemble epileptic fits that the only way to distinguish them is by the scarcity of urine in the former; by the fact that hysterics have hysterogenic zones, especially in the ovary, pressure on which will sometimes cure an attack; by hysterics' responsiveness to a continuous electrical current and their lesser responsiveness to bromide; and by the fact that hysterics are less likely to run a fever.

Hysterics may lack the epileptic's degenerative traits, but they nonetheless have all the epileptic's functional peculiarities, including dullness of the senses. Convulsions and other typical symptoms of epilepsy may be absent, but the psychological phenomena are common. Hysteria affects the sexual organs; so does epilepsy, though to a lesser degree. When hysteria starts in youth, it is quite incurable, and thus it corresponds, physiognomically as in other aspects, to epilepsy and innate criminality.

Hysterics parallel epileptics, infants, born criminals, and the morally insane in the variability of their symptoms, their restless and constant desire for change, their need to do evil for evil's sake, their senseless lying, and their causeless irascibility. Hysterics, like epileptics, may have a mania for letter writing. Another similarity lies in persistent or intermittent piety, which drives some members of both groups to attain saintliness (St. Paul, St. Theresa).[q]

Calumny

That which distinguishes hysterical women from all others, even epileptics, is the intensity and success of their calumnies.[94] The reason is simple. Women—even wicked women (and most of those are hysterics)—have less strength than men and consequently less capacity for crimes of violence. Thus they tend to channel their evil into calumny. Moreover, they are more susceptible than men to autosuggestion, which rapidly transforms ideas into action. Like hypnotized subjects (see my *Studi sull'ipnotismo*, 3d ed.), suggestible subjects will proclaim what is false with the same intensity as an honest person will affirm what is true. This is particularly the case with women; like children, they have but a weak sense of what is true and easily brush truth aside.

Hysterical women provide us with the most tragic cases of calumny, swindling, and triumphant lying. These cases are familiar in both daily life and the halls of justice, where hysteria masks falsity with a vitality that, unfortunately, it does not bring to knowledge of the truth. The most striking thing about the psychological anomalies of hysterics is how closely they resemble those of epileptics and female born criminals. The key difference is that hysterics are cleverer at telling lies. Although they are extremely susceptible to suggestion, this factor should never be allowed to mitigate their guilt, because usually it propels them toward evil, not good. We saw this in the case of Gabriella Bompard, who fell into the hands of an honest man but constantly deceived him.

An even more remarkable example is offered by the following case: A young married woman who prostituted herself stole a client's wallet. When he realized what had happened, he returned, but she professed to be astonished and offended by his accusation. The police investigated, finding the sum, intact, hidden in her chimney. She was led off to prison, where fear and anger brought on such a strong hysterical reaction that four people had trouble holding her down. After a few

q. Vedi, *Uomo di genio*, part IV. [Here, Lombroso cites his own *Man of Genius*.—Eds.]

hours, I appeared on the scene; a simple pressure on the eyeballs and the application of a small magnet rid her of all traces of convulsion. However, there followed a profuse uterine hemorrhage, probably induced by her psychological distress. When a warm enema did not work, I hypnotized her and ordered through suggestion that the hemorrhage should cease. As if by magic, it disappeared, just as the convulsions did earlier, and when both symptoms returned two days later, they were cured immediately by the same means. The nuns in charge of the prison thought I might be an emissary of the devil!

Now, here was a chance to try hypnotism as a means of getting a confession of guilt. I continued my experiments in suggestion for some time and was able thereby to chase away a headache and mood of deep melancholy. Briefly, I even thought I had achieved complete domination of the patient. However, when I ordered her to confess her guilt, she immediately resumed reciting the string of lies she had told (in vain, of course) to the magistrate, saying that the customer had invented the story of the stolen wallet to avenge himself for rejection by her younger sister, that the money the police had found had been earned honestly, and so on.

In this case, then, suggestion was strong enough to cure convulsions and a hemorrhage but not to extract a secret that the patient wanted to hide. Nor could suggestion alter by even a hair her tendency to lie. Thus I would say that mendacity must have a more organic basis than the other manifestations of hysteria.

Hysterical Prostitutes

Since hysterics and born criminals differ only in hysterics' stronger propensity toward lying, their volubility, and their preoccupation with sexual matters, we can see immediately that epilepsy is found infrequently in prostitutes because it has been replaced by hysteria. Legrand du Salle noted that 12 percent of prostitutes were hysterics who entered the work simply out of dilettantism, without any pressure from poverty. Similarly, Tarnowsky found that 15 percent of prostitutes were hysterical.

We know that psychological hysteria, like epilepsy, can manifest itself without true convulsions. It is quite likely that the number of prostitutes who are basically hysterics is much larger than we had previously suspected.

Appendix 1
Comparing Three Editions of *La donna delinquente*

La donna delinquente (Lombroso's original text of 1893), *The Female Offender* (the English-language translation of 1895), and *Criminal Woman, the Prostitute, and the Normal Woman* (the present edition) differ fundamentally along key dimensions. In effect, they constitute three distinct texts.

La donna delinquente, la prostituta e la donna normale (1893)

La donna delinquente consists of 640 pages of text and backmatter, a seven-page preface signed only by Lombroso, and eight *tavole*, or full-page illustrations. Three of the *tavole* display multiple photographic images of criminals' heads; three display multiple line drawings; and one is a chart diagramming the field of vision of criminals and prostitutes. Eighteen other illustrations are set into the text. The text itself falls into four parts:

- Part 1: "The Normal Woman," subdivided into seven chapters and covering 180 printed pages
- Part 2: "Female Criminology," subdivided into three chapters and covering 80 pages
- Part 3: "Pathological Anatomy and Anthropometry of Criminal Woman and the Prostitute," subdivided into nine chapters and covering 110 pages
- Part 4: "Biology and Psychology of Female Criminals and Prostitutes," subdivided into twelve chapters and covering 250 pages

The chapters are divided into subsections which themselves usually bear subtitles. Frequently, Lombroso introduces statistical material into the text, captioning tables when they fill a page, but more often presenting the numbers without a label. To document his extensive references, he sometimes gives his source in a footnote, and at other times he inserts the citation directly into the text. (More often than not, however, he fails to cite his sources.) Lombroso also uses page notes for substantive comments. This edition includes a detailed table of contents but no index.

After its initial publication, *La donna delinquente* was apparently reprinted in Italian twice, in 1894 and 1903, before being reissued in 1913 in a new edition by his daughter Gina Lombroso-Ferrero.[1] A 1915 edition (perhaps identical with that of 1913) was reissued in 1923 and 1927. *La donna delinquente* was published in German (1894), French (1896, 1906), and Russian (1897, 1902, and 1909), as well as in the English translation of 1895 described below.

Guglielmo Ferrero, credited as coauthor of *La donna delinquente*, was still a student and less than twenty years old when Lombroso invited him to collaborate on the project. This was in 1889,[2] more than a decade since Lombroso had begun publishing books on the born criminal and had been appointed to a chair in legal medicine and public health at the University of Turin. According to Delfina Dolza, the biographer of Lombroso's daughters, Lombroso had been on the lookout for talented young men and, having met Ferrero occasionally, "became so enthusiastic about his intelligence as to ask him to associate himself with his work on *La donna delinquente*."[3] Ferrero, a law student in Pisa, moved to Turin, where he became part of the Lombroso family's circle of liberal intellectuals. Although Ferrero is listed as coauthor, Lombroso's far greater scholarly stature, the dominance of his ideas and style in the book, and the fact that he alone signed the preface suggest that Ferrero's role was actually that of a trusted research assistant with whom the older man generously shared full credit. After completion of *La donna delinquente*, Ferrero left Italy to study abroad and publish on other topics, but later he returned and, after a ten-year engagement, married Lombroso's younger daughter Gina.

The Female Offender (1895)

The Female Offender, excerpted and translated by someone who remains unidentified, runs to 313 pages, roughly half the length of *La donna delinquente*. Nothing in the volume indicates that it is only a partial translation. Few if any readers could have known that they were reading excerpts from a longer whole.

Nor, of course, could readers have understood *how* the English version related to the Italian original. *The Female Offender* omits Lombroso's preface, all of part 1 ("The Normal Woman"), all of part 2 ("Female Criminology"), and three chapters within part 4 ("Sexual Sensitivity," "The Born Prostitute," and "The Occasional Prostitute"). Without notice, *The Female Offender* also omits the following material:

- "Breasts and Genitals," from part 3, chapter 6 ("Other Anomalies");
- "Menstruation, Precocity, and Fecundity," from part 4, chapter 1 ("Menstruation, Fecundity, Vitality, Strength, and Reflexes");
- "Erotism and Virility," from part 4, chapter 4 ("The Female Born Criminal").

In addition (and again without notice), *The Female Offender* moves Lombroso's final chapter, "Hysterical Offenders," to an earlier position in the book.

Taken together, these omissions and changes seriously distort the original. For example, for over a century, no English-language readers realized that to reach his conclusions about criminal women, Lombroso had in fact used a control group of "normal" women. Moreover, *The Female Offender* masks its distortions of Lombroso's original. The edition's major drawback, however, is that it simplifies Lombroso's arguments, making it impossible for readers to grasp the complexity of his thought. Lombroso himself considered its cuts "absurd."[4]

For the most part, *The Female Offender* translates Lombroso accurately but listlessly into sanitized and sometimes confusing English prose. Lombroso's original, hastily written like most of his works, presents many problems of interpretation; instead of confronting these, the translator of *The Female Offender* (who evidently had no criminological background) reproduces them, for example by translating an Italian pronoun of ambiguous referent into an equally ambiguous English pronoun. Worse yet, *The Female Offender* translation silently excises most passages concerning sexuality and drains even short phrases of sexual content. (In a passage describing a woman referred to as "M. R," for instance, it reports that she "resisted the profligate designs of her father."[5] Following the original, our translation reports that M. R. "resisted her father, who wanted to rape her [*stuprarla*].")[6] As a result, *The Female Offender* constitutes a pedestrian, bowdlerized, and sometimes incomprehensible text.

The Female Offender is organized into eighteen chapters covering roughly the same ground as parts 3 and 4 of *La donna delinquente*. The first nine chapters of *The Female Offender* correspond exactly in order and substance to the first nine chapters of *La donna delinquente*, part 3 and deal with anomalies in the bodies of female criminals. There follow two chapters, corresponding in part to *La donna delinquente*, part 4, chapters 1 and 2, on physical characteristics of female criminals. The remaining chapters of *The Female Offender*, corresponding very roughly to the remainder of *La donna delinquente*, part 4, but in abbreviated fashion, deal with types of female offenders. Like the original, this translation has no index.

Originally published by Unwin in London and Appleton in New York, *The Female Offender* replaced Lombroso's own preface with an introduction by W. Douglas Morrison, an English cleric who wrote about crime and criminals. (Morrison's introduction, however, said nothing about female offenders.) This English edition was reprinted fourteen times between 1897 and 1980, after which a New Mexico press brought out a "new and expanded edition" which was actually one-third the length of the Appleton original.[7]

Criminal Woman, the Prostitute, and the Normal Woman

To select material for inclusion in the new edition, we developed the following criteria:

- Complete coverage of Lombroso's arguments and adherence to the order in which he presented them
- Clear representation of Lombroso's procedures, including his use of tables, illustrations, and citations
- Reduction in bulk of the original to make the new edition readable and affordable

About half of this new edition is given over to previously untranslated *La donna delinquente* material, while the other half consists of a compressed and retranslated version of the material covered by *The Female Offender*. We have included Lombroso's own preface and added explanatory footnotes, a glossary, and an index. Professor Tamar Pitch of the University of Camerino and Maria Grazia Rosilli of Rome helped us translate particularly difficult passages.

To help readers compare the three editions and understand our approach to this translation, we here include, in their entirety, the *La donna delinquente* and *The Female Offender* versions of part 4, chapter 10, "Insane Criminals" (this volume, 227–30). We chose this chapter for the comparison because it is relatively short and shows how the two earlier editions handled citations and tabular material. In what follows, readers will first find an exact transcription of Lombroso's "Pazze criminali" (part 4, chapter 10, pages 589–96 of *La donna delinquente*); thereafter they will find an exact transcription of *The Female Offender*'s "Criminal Female Lunatics" (chapter 17, pages 289–97).

Pazze criminali

La donna delinquente, PART IV, CAPITOLO X (589–96)

1. *Statistica*.—In Italia dal 1871 al 1886 si notarono 1753 pazzi criminali e 96 pazze-ree, per cui queste darebbero il rapporto di 5,6 % maschi, quota inferiore nella frequenza alla popolazione criminale, in cui nel decennio 1870–79 le ree stanno ai maschi come 7,3 a 100.[a]

Dallo studio di Sander e Richter si rileva che sopra 1486 maschi pazzi si ebbero delinquenti 13,9 % mentre su 1462 femmine pazze si ebbero delinquenti 2,6 %.[b]

In un recente studio fatto col Busdraghi uno di noi trovò:

Su 100 incendiari pazzi		63 maschi	37 femmine
Su 100 omicidi	"	75 "	25 "
Su 100 ladri	"	62 "	38 "
Su 30 stupratori	"	30 "	0 "[c]

E si tratta di impazziti fuori del carcere.

Questa minore proporzione della pazzia nelle ree si deve certo al minore imperversare dell'alcoolismo che, come vedremo, da la quota massima dei pazzi criminali, alla minore diffusione dell'epilessia e alla forma che quella tende più facilmente ad assumere della prostituzione e della lascivia che, per quanto indecente, è sempre meno criminosa e meno pericolosa, e non provoca clamorosi processi o gelose reclusioni.

Infatti 99 su 1000 delle nostre ree pazze erano prostitute e 212 domestiche o senza professione.

Delle 24 pazze criminali di Sander 11 sono ladre, 6 prostitute, 2 mendicanti, 2 truffatrici.

Quanto alle forme di alienazione, in Italia si notarono nel decennio 1870–79:

Melanconia e monomania persecutoria	33
Mania	22
Imbecillità e cretinismo	10
Monomania allucinatoria	7
Megalomania	2

a. V. Rossi, *I pazzi criminali in Italia*, 1887.

b. Dr. Sander und Richter, *Die Beziehungen Zwischen Geinterstorung Verbrechen*.—Berlin, 1886.

c. *Uomo delinquente*, vol. II.

Suicidio	4
Follia morale	4

con evidente predominio (monomania allucinatoria, melanconia, suicidio) di forme melanconiche generate nelle carceri e per causa della detenzione, o di quelle congenite (imbecillità e cretinesimo), che dovrebbero escludere preventivamente dalle carceri, e con scarsezza o assenza di epilessie e follie morali, che tanto prevalgono nei rei.

Anche nelle donne oneste è più frequente la forma melanconica e la mania con furore, almeno secondo Esquirol. In Italia, però, se le melanconie vi furono inferiori ai maschi come 1657 a 3414, la mania è in aumento come 1836 a 1843, specie quella con furore.

Però, se nei reati minori che formano la quota più grande di carcerati scarseggiano, nei reati più gravi le malattie mentali giungono a una proporzione assai grande. Infatti su 409 ree studiate da Salsotto nell'ergastolo di Torino, se ne ebbero 53, ossia 12,9 % così ripartite: epilessie 11 (2,6 %); isterismo 19 (4,9 %); alcoolismo 13 (3,1%); cretinismo e idiozia 10 (2,5%).

E per i vari reati secondo i delitti si avrebbe avuto (aggiungendo i confronti coi pazzi rei maschi datici dal Marro):

il 26 %	nelle	assassine	(130)—	pazzi	rei	di	Marro	40 %
" 25	" "	avvelenatrici	(20)—	"	"	"	"	—
" 30	" "	feritrici	(10)—	"	"	"	"	26 "
" 20	" "	grassatrici	(10)—	"	"	"	"	23 "
" 15	" "	truffatrici	(20)—	"	"	"	"	23 "
" 80	" "	incendiarie	(4)—	"	"	"	"	85 "
" 16	" "	stupratrici	(25)—	"	"	"	"	33 "
" 0	" "	ladre	(90)—	"	"	"	"	31 "

con evidente prevalenza nei reati più gravi: assassinio, avvelenamento, incendio, e un certo parallelismo coi maschi.[d]

d. Quanto alle varie specie:

Su 130 assassine:	
5 epilettiche	4 %
9 isteriche	7,2 %
6 alcooliste	5 %
1 sonnambula	0,9 %
2 cretine	1,8 %
2 idiote	1,8 %
1 delirio religioso	0,9 %
Su 100 infanticide:	
2 epilessia	2 %
3 isterismo	3 %
3 idiozia	3 %
3 Alcoolismo	3 %
Su 10 feritrici:	
3 isteriche	30 %
Su 10 grassatrici:	
1 epilessia	10 %
1 esterismo	10 %
Su 20 avvelenatrici:	
2 isteriche	10 %
2 epilettiche	10 %
1 alcoolista	5 %

Anche in Inghilterra, a Broadmoor, il maggior numero venne dato dalle omicide e feritrici, 103 su 141; poi vengono i delitti d'incesto, 19; i parricidi, 6, ed i furti con effrazione, 3.

Il massimo delle alienazioni (vedi *Uomo delinquente*, vol. II) è dato anche nelle pazze ree dalle coniugate, mentre nei maschi è dato dai celibi; il che conferma i dati trovati nei criminali sani di tutti i paesi.

Il massimo numero delle entrate delle pazze criminali nei manicomi è nell'estate, 25; segue l'inverno, 21; la primavera e l'autunno, 11–14; press'a poco le cifre del maggior numero dei criminali. Per cui già da questi dati si sospetta che l'andamento delle criminali pazze segua quello delle criminali in genere. E altrettanto si può dire dei caratteri della pazzia, la quale non si distingue in costoro se non per esagerare i caratteri della criminalità.

2. *Premeditazione, ecc.*—Infatti, i casi più spiccati di pazzia morale o di criminalità congenita presentavano, benchè meno evidenti che nei maschi, quel carattere essenzialissimo che noi abbiamo trovato dell'epilessia (vedi cap. seg.). E l'abilità nel commettere il delitto, premeditando, cercando fin l'alibi e dissimulando, vi è grande quanto e più che nella criminale.

L'abilità della Eufrasia Mercier nel condurre a termine una serie di falsi complicatissimi per impossessarsi dell'eredità della Ménétrier, per ucciderla e farne sparire il cadavere è delle più straordinarie; tant'è che, malgrado gli interessi degli eredi ed una delle migliori polizie d'Europa, non si venne a conoscere il crimine se non dopo due anni, e solo per la denuncia di un suo nipote. Eppure si trattava di una monomane mistica, religiosa, pazza probabilmente fin dalla nascita, figlia di un pazzo religioso che credeva poter guarire tutti gli ammalati; con sorelle e nipoti affetti dalla stessa pazzie (Ball, *De la responsabilité partielle*, 1886).

Una ricca signora, d'anni 26, senza eredità, presa da melanconia attonita, da onesta che era prima, rubò ai pazienti che essa medicava come infermiera, delle biancherie, facendovi sparire le marche; protestava di pentirsi e poi tornava subito alle sottrazioni (Savage).

"Vi sono (dice Savage) ladre patholgiche che rubano con conscienza di causa, che provano, specie vicino ai mestrui, dei bisogni irresistibili, come di rubare, di rompere oggetti, di immergere la mano in certi liquidi; nulla le arresta pel soddisfacimento dei loro desideri; se non hanno altro modo, se lo procurano con violenza. Ve ne hanno il cui appetito non poteva essere soddisfatto che con cibi rubati."—Si veda per altre prove il vol. II dell'*Uomo delinquente*.

Su 20 truffatrici:		Su 4 incendiarie:		Su 25 stupratrici:	
2 isteriche	10 %	3 cretine	80 %	3 alcooliste	12 %
1 epilettica	5 %			1 isterica	4 %

Uno dei caratteri speciali alla rea-pazza, che non è però se non una esagerazione dello stato normale, è l'acutizzazione all'epoca mestruale, nelle gravidanze e nelle menopause.

"V'era (dice Esquirol) una donna che diveniva pazza all'epoca mestruale e guariva durante la menopausa."

Algeri notò in 97 pazze su 151 un'agitazione maggiore all'epoca dei mestrui.

"Schroter notò in 26 su 16 in quell'epoca una tale esacerbazione da rassomigliare ad un attacco d'epilessia" (Icard, pag. 72).

"Parecchie pazze (scrive Ball) tranquille sentono venire la furia, *la rage*, all'epoca mestruale, e reclamano assistenza."

"Una donna, ogni volta che aveva i mestrui, si sentiva tratta nei grandi magazzini, e rubava. Una ragazza, ad ogni epoca mestruale castrava il primo animale che le veniva alle mani, senza avere negli intervalli alcun delirio" (Icard).

Su 500 femmine studiate da Tilt, pervenute all'epoca critica, 333 avevano irritabilità morbosa, tristezza, ecc.

Kraepelin nel periodo climaterico scoprì una donna con relativa frequenza di eccitamenti erotici, sentimenti di gelosia e delirii assurdi di persecuzione o di peccato.

Altrettanto discasi dell'influenza della gravidanza. Lebon cita una donna che ad ogni gravidanza aveva la smania di uccidere il marito che pure amava, e Gall racconta di un'altra che, incinta, si sentì spinta a uccidere il marito, lo assassinò, ne salò il cadavere e ne mangiò. Brouardel notò spesso nelle gravidanze degli impulsi incendiari ed omicidi, e narra di una donna incinta, madre di cinque fanciulli, che inviò del veleno ad uno di questi che era in pensione, e mentre aveva mandato a cercare il più piccolo che era a balia, si gettò cogli altri tre in un pozzo.

Marc ricorda di una donna ricca, moglie di un magistrato, che, incinta, non aveva potuto resistere alla smania di prendersi un pollo messo in mostra da un pasticciere.

"Insomma, in questo stato (scrive Icard, op. cit.) la donna è capace di tutto. Eccellenti madri possono scannare i figli che pure amano passionatamente; altre, prima buone atteggiarsi a vittime e inventare calunnie le più infami contro i loro cari; donne caste fare atti e tenere discorsi schifosamente osceni."

"Durante la gravidanza (scrive Cabanis, tomo III, pag. 344) una specie d'istinto animale domina la donna che può trascinarla a qualunque eccesso. E altrettanto può accadere nel ritorno della prima mestruazione e nell'allattamento."

Un altro carattere spiccato della donna alienata, e quindi della rea-pazza, è l'esagerazione sessuale.

Mentre nei maschi pazzi il senso genetico tace quasi sempre, nelle alienate io l'ho trovato sempre eccitato. Ho visto una vecchia di 80 anni che si masturbava perfino con un crocifisso di ottone. Un'altra vecchia si riempiva la vulva di coltelli, de cenci, di gusci d'uova; una terza si masturbava in mezzo alle altre con delle candele e con delle uova.

E mentre il tribadismo anche nelle prostitute si tien celato, si mostra ed eseguisce all'aperto nei manicomi e vi è diffuso in larga scala (io lo trovai in 10 su 200) perfino nelle impuberi e senza nemmeno quegli accenni di platonismo, di gelosia, che in parte lo idealizzano (*Arch. di psich.*, VI, 219).

Marro scrive[e]: "La massima parte delle impazzite all'epoca della menopausa, presentano delirii a fondo erotico. Ora sono idee di nozze strane, di gravidanze, di parti straordinari; ora sensazioni di atti lascivi subiti. Ad una arrivano ogni volta a frotte gli amanti, che ne abusano con successione non interrotta; un'altra è colta dal delirio di gelosia; ad un'altra sono i diavoletti che le si appiccicano al grembiule, le fanno ogni sorta di gherminelle, punzecchiandola, pizzicandola; una varietà massima di delirii, di sensazioni allucinatorie sul fondo madre della sensualità."

"Nella mania (scrive Schüle) le donne si sfogano in un continuo cicaleccio che è un misto di percezioni vere e false, e specialmente di momentanee concezioni fantastiche, accompagnate da smorfie e da millanterie erotiche; hanno tendenza a denudarsi, a prendere atteggiamenti cinici, a imbellettarsi con vivande, con urina e con feci."

La ninfomania trasforma la ragazza più timida in una baccante che non può paragonarsi per impudenza nemmeno alla prostituta. Ogni uomo che incontra è fatto mira alle sue brame, lo provoca colle arti della più raffinata civetteria, e alla peggio perfino colla violenza: spesso ha sete violenta, bocca arsa, alito fetido, agitazioni dei fianchi quasi assistesse al coito, e tendenze a mordere chi incontra, sicchè pare un'idrofoba, tanto più che qualche volta ha orrore dei liquidi e senso di strangolamento.

Io assistetti ad un caso in cui codesto orribile amore comparve in donna onestissima come effetto di una difterite, e il caso è restato unico (Lombroso, *Amore nei pazzi*, 1880).

Più frequente è una forma più mite in cui si osserva solo nella donna una eccessiva pulitezza o sudiciume e tendenza a denudarsi e stracciarsi i vestiti, a parlare di nozze proprie ed altrui (Emminghaus, *Allgemeine Psichopathologie*, 1878): od ha una taciturnità triste, ostinata; davanti agli uomini ha respiro più frequente,

e. Marro, *La pazzia nelle donne.—Ann. di fren.*, 1891, pag. 28.

il polso più rapido, la fisionomia più vivace; dapprima riservata, poi abbandona ogni ritegno e non pensa, non parla che di lascivie: sfugge le donne e perfino le maltratta quando non è presa da impulsi tribadici. Io ne conobbi una la quale si vantava di aver avuto 44 amanti e quando veniva davanti agli studenti li provocava sfacciatamente al concubito (o.c.).

Le femmine alienate in genere, in tutte queste aberrazioni sessuali, come nelle tendenze veneree, superano i maschi d'assai ed io dopo lunghi anni di osservazione credo non abbia esagerato l'Hergt (*All. Zeits. Psych.*, XXVII) che calcolava come due terzi delle pazze soffrano: ipertrofia del collo uterino, ulceri dell'orificio, aderenze utero-vaginali, ovariti, sia, secondo Flemming, come complicanza di turbata circolazione addominale, sia per l'iperestesia ed irritazione del midollo spinale, che, rendendo sempre più vivi i reflessi uterini, più debole l'attivitá psichica, promuove convulsioni, favorisce le sensazioni abnormi e le trasforma in illusioni, allucinazioni, e in atti osceni impulsivi o in delirii.

Un terzo carattere speciale delle pazze è la maggiore acuzia, la maggior impulsività, per cui nelle statistiche italiane la mania con furore vi è in proporzione maggiore, come 669 a 524, che nei maschi pazzi.

Krafft-Ebing osservò che la pazzia nelle donne assume generalmente un aspetto turbolento ed indecente più che nell'uomo.

In complesso, troviamo nelle alienate ree, come nelle criminali comuni, ma in quelle ancora più spiccatamente, invertiti i caratteri più specifici della donna: la ritenutezza, la docilità e l'apatia sessuale.

Criminal Female Lunatics

The Female Offender,
CHAPTER XVII (289–97)

1. *Statistics.*—In Italy, between the years 1871–86, there were 1,753 criminal male lunatics and 96 criminal female lunatics, being 5.6 women against 100 men, which is a lower proportion of women than that found among criminals, these being for the decade 1870–79 as 7.3 women against 100 men.[f]

From Sander and Richter's observations we learn that out of 1,486 male lunatics 13.9 per cent. were criminal, while out of 1,462 female lunatics the criminals were 2.6 per cent.[g]

f. V. Rossi, "Criminal Lunatics in Italy," 1887.

g. Drs. Sander and Richter, "Die Beziehung Zwischen Geisterstorung and Verbrechen," Berlin, 1886.

In some recent investigations made together with Busdraghi, one of the writers found the following figures:—

Out of 100	incendiaries	63	males	37	females
"	homicides	75	"	25	"
"	thieves	62	"	38	"
"	guilty of rape	30	"	0	"

And these had all gone mad out of prison.

This smaller proportion of lunatics among female criminals is certainly ascribable to two causes—one being the minor degree of alcoholism (drink, as we shall see, furnishing the largest contingent of male criminal lunatics), and the other, the smaller prevalence of epilepsy, together with the tendency which that disease when existent in women has to assume the forms of prostitution or lasciviousness, both offences which, however reprehensible, are less criminal and less dangerous, and therefore do not lead to sensational trials and jealous reclusion. Ninety-nine out of a thousand of our female criminal lunatics were prostitutes, and 212 servants, or of no profession.

Out of 24 female criminal lunatics observed by Sander 11 were thieves, 6 prostitutes, 2 beggars, and 2 swindlers.

As to the nature of the madness, the following results are given for the decade 1870–79, in Italy:—

Melancholia and monomania of persecution	33
Mania	22
Imbecility and idiotcy [*sic*]	10
Hallucinatory monomania	7
Megalomania	2
Suicide	4
Moral folly	4

showing an evident prevalence of the forms (hallucinatory monomania, melancholia, suicide) generated by prison life, and on account of detention, or of those congenital affections, such as imbecility and idiotcy, which ought to guarantee the subject from incarceration; while the diseases so common in the male criminal, such as epilepsy and moral folly, are rare.

Esquirol says that even among moral women the most common forms of madness are melancholia and furious mania.

In Italy, however, the female melancholics were inferior to the male as 1,657 to 3,414, but the female maniacs (especially furious maniacs) are as 1,843 to 1,836.

If among the minor criminals, who form the largest proportion of the incarcerated, there is but little madness, the contrary is the case among the worse [*sic*] sorts of criminals.

Salsotto studied the cases of 409 female criminals in the prison of Turin, and found that 53, or 12.9 per cent., out of the number were affected as follows: Epilepsy 11 (2.6 per cent.), hysteria 19 (4.9 per cent.), alcoholism 13 (3.1 per cent.), and idiotcy 10 (2.5 per cent.).

The proportion of the different crimes to madness was as follows (adding the figures given for male criminal lunatics by Marro):—

26 p.c.		in murderesses	(130)—	male criminal lunatics			40 p.c.	
25	〃	poisoners	(20)—	〃	〃	〃	—	
30	〃	wounders	(10)—	〃	〃	〃	26	〃
20	〃	guilty of assault	(10)—	〃	〃	〃	23	〃
15	〃	swindlers	(20)—	〃	〃	〃	23	〃
80	〃	incendiaries	(4)—	〃	〃	〃	85	〃
16	〃	guilty of rape	(25)—	〃	〃	〃	33	〃
0	〃	thieves	(90)—	〃	〃	〃	31	〃

Here there is an evident prevalence of madness among the worse criminals, and a certain parallelism with the males.[h]

At Broadmoor the greatest number of lunatics are to be found among the homicides and wounders (103 in 141); next comes incest, 19; parricides 6, and burglary 3.

h. The various species of mental disorder were distributed as follows:—

Out of 130 murderesses—			
5 epileptics,	being	4	per cent.
9 hysterics,	〃	7.2	〃
6 drunkards,	〃	5	〃
1 somnambulist,	〃	0.9	〃
2 crétines,	〃	1.8	〃
2 idiots,	〃	1.8	〃
1 religious maniac,	〃	0.9	〃
Out of 100 infanticides—			
2 epileptics,	〃	2	〃
3 hysterical,	〃	3	〃
3 idiots,	〃	3	〃
3 drunkards,	〃	3	〃
Out of 10 wounders—			
3 hysterics,	〃	30	〃
Out of 10 guilty of assault—			
1 epileptic,	being	10	per cent.
1 hysteric,	〃	10	〃
Out of 20 poisoners—			
2 hysterics,	〃	10	〃
2 epileptics,	〃	10	〃
1 drunkard,	〃	5	〃
Out of 20 swindlers—			
2 hysterics,	〃	10	〃
1 epileptic,	〃	5	〃
Out of 4 incendiaries—			
3 crétines,	〃	80	〃
Out of 25 guilty of rape—			
3 drunkards,	〃	12	〃
1 hysteric,	〃	4	〃

The greater number of female lunatics are married women, while the greater number of male lunatics are single (*see* "L'Uomo Delinquente," vol. II); and this fact confirms the observations made on healthy criminals in all countries.

The lunatic asylums for females receive more inmates in summer (25) than in winter (21), while the figures for spring and autumn are respectively 11–14. The statistics of male criminals are about the same.

We may conclude that the history of female criminal lunatics is that of female criminals in general. And the same may be said of the characteristics of their madness, which simply serve to accentuate the nature of their crimes.

2. *Premeditation.*—Although to a less marked degree than in the male, the graver cases of moral insanity or congenital criminality in females present all the most essential features of epilepsy (*see* following chapter). And the ability displayed in the commission of the crime, its premeditation, the steps taken to establish an alibi, and the efforts at dissimulation, are equal and sometimes greater than similar phenomena in the simple criminal.

One of the most extraordinary instances of ability was given by Euphrasie Mercier, who carried through a series of most complicated forgeries in order to gain possession of the fortune of Madame Ménétrier, then killed her victim, and destroyed all trace of the corpse; doing the whole thing so well that, in spite of all the efforts of the rightful heirs and one of the best police systems in Europe, the crime was only discovered at the end of two years, when a nephew of the murderess revealed it. And yet Mercier was a mystic and a monomaniac, religious, but mad probably from her birth, being the daughter of a religious lunatic, who believed that he could cure all illnesses. And her sisters and nephews and nieces were afflicted with the same delusions (Ball, "De la Responsabilité partielle," 1886).

A lady of wealth, aged 26, with no hereditary history, after becoming a prey to fixed melancholia, stole sheets, &c., from patients whom she tended as a nurse, and effaced the marks to escape detection. She protested remorse, but relapsed again immediately (Savage).

There are (says Savage) pathological female thieves who steal, knowing what they do. They feel, especially at certain periods, an irresistible temptation to thieve, or to break things, or to plunge their hands into particular liquids. Nothing will deter them from the accomplishment of their desires, which they achieve, if by no other means, then through violence. There are women whose appetite can only be appeased with stolen food. (*See* also vol. ii. of "L'Uomo Delinquente.")

One peculiarity of the female criminal lunatic, which is, however, only an exaggeration of her normal state, is that her madness becomes more acute at particular periods, such as menstruation, menopause, and pregnancy.

Esquirol, Algeri, Schroter, and Ball have all noted instances of this peculiarity, which sometimes exhibits symptoms resembling epilepsy. In other cases there will be morbid irritability, melancholy, erotic excitement, delusions as to sins committed, persecutions undergone, &c.

Brouardel has recorded many examples of incendiary and homicidal impulses in pregnant women, and relates the case of one, the mother of five children, who sent poison to one child who was at school, and after despatching orders for the youngest one, who was with a wet nurse, to be brought to her, threw herself with the remaining three down a well.

"In short," writes Icard, "when in this state a woman is capable of anything. Passionately loving mothers will cut their children's throats; and others, naturally good, will pose as victims, and invent infamous calumnies against their dear ones; while chaste women will talk and act in the most indecent manner."

"A kind of animal instinct reigns supreme in the pregnant woman (writes Cabanis, vol. III. p. 344), and may drive her to any excess. And the same phenomenon is possible at the first return of menstruation, and during the nursing period."

We see, then, that another characteristic of the female lunatic, and consequently of the criminal lunatic, is an exaggeration of the sexual instincts. These which in male lunatics are almost always in abeyance, lead in women, even in very old women as in quite young girls, to the most disgusting and unnatural excesses. ("Arch. di. psich.," vol. VI. p. 219.)

Marro writes,[8] "The majority of female lunatics at the period of menopause are subject to erotic delirium. They have ideas of strange marriages and monstrous births, and are subject to sudden obscene delusions. One will be seized with a delirium of jealousy; another feels herself swarmed over by little imps, who hang on to her apron, play her every kind of trick, pinching and pricking her. Hallucinations, in short, abound, presenting every variety of delirium springing from the one basis of sensuality." "Under the influence of mania" (writes Schüle) "women relieve themselves by incessant chatter, in which there is a mixture of true and false perceptions, and especially of momentary fantastic ideas accompanied by grimaces and erotic gestures."

Nymphomania transforms the most timid girl into a shameless bacchante. She tries to attract every man she sees, displaying sometimes violence, and sometimes the most refined coquetry. She often suffers from intense thirst, a dry mouth, a fetid breath, and a tendency to bite everybody she meets, as if affected with hydrophobia, and sometimes she even shows a horror of liquids, and feels as if she were being strangled.

One of the writers knew of a case in which these morbid erotic symptoms appeared in a woman, previously absolutely chaste, after an attack of diphtheria. The instance remains unique (Lombroso, "Amore nei pazzi," 1880).

More common is a milder form of the same mania in which the subject shows either an excessive cleanliness or an excessive dirtiness, also a tendency to strip herself, or tear off her clothes, or to talk of her own marriage, or that of other people (Emminghaus, "Allgemeine Psichopathologie," 1878). Sometimes she is taciturn, melancholy, obstinate; the presence of persons of the opposite sex heightens her breathing, makes her pulse beat more rapidly, gives her a more animated expression. At first reserved, she will later throw off all restraint, and only think and talk of sexual things.

Female lunatics in general surpass their male prototypes in all sexual aberrations and tendencies, and, after long years of observation, I am disposed to agree with Hergt ("All. Zeit. Psych.," XXVII.), who affirmed that two-thirds of female lunatics suffer from maladies of the reproductive organs, which, by increasing reflex action and impairing psychical activity, bring on convulsions and produce abnormal sensations, which are transformed into illusions, hallucinations, delirium, or obscene impulses.

A third characteristic of the female lunatic compared with the male is greater acuteness and impulsiveness, so that in the Italian statistics furious mania in women is as 669 to 524 in men.

Krafft Ebing remarked also that in women madness is usually more turbulent and indecent in its manifestation than in men. Briefly, in female criminal lunatics we find to a more marked degree that which we had already noted in the ordinary female criminal, namely, an inversion of all the qualities which specially distinguish the normal woman; namely, reserve docility and sexual apathy.

Appendix 2

Illustrations in the Earlier Editions

This is a complete list of the illustrations in Lombroso's original, *La donna delinquente* (LDD), and in the first edition (1895) of *The Female Offender* (TFO). The former book includes more images than does the latter. In only two instances does TFO include images that did not appear in Lombroso's original: It inserts a photographic portrait of Lombroso opposite the title page; and it substitutes two views of the infamous Gabriella Bompard for a single image in LDD.

The following material uses these codes:

[ ] Brackets indicate that we have added a caption to an image that appears in LDD without a formal title

* Asterisks indicate images that appear in both books

Italic print indicates images that are reproduced in this new translation

Note that in addition to the images indicated below in italics, this new edition includes images taken from Lombroso's *Atlante* (*Atlas*) of 1897.

Messalina (title page of LDD). The image of Messalina appears on the title page of LDD and is repeated later as figure 11. It is omitted from the title page of TFO, which instead displays on the facing page a photograph of Cesare Lombroso.

Anomalie vulvari in Ottentotte ed in Europee (following 20 in LDD)

Polisarcia Abissina. Cuscinetto posteriore in Africane (following 20 in LDD)

Donne di genio Europee e Americane (opposite 160 in LDD)

Cranii di criminali Italiane (opposite 282 in LDD)

* [Cranio di Carlotta Corday (top view)] (on 287 in LDD). TFO caption: Skull of Charlotte Corday (opposite 34 in TFO)

* [*Cranio di Carlotta Corday (profile)*] (on 288 in LDD). TFO caption: Skull of Charlotte Corday (following 34 in TFO)
* [*Cranio di Carlotta Corday (front view)*] (on 289 in LDD). TFO caption: Skull of Charlotte Corday (following 34 in TFO)
* *Fisionomie di criminali Russe* (following 305 in LDD). TFO caption: Physiognomy of Russian Female Offenders (opposite 76 in TFO)
* [*Profile of an elderly woman*][9] (on 322 in LDD). TFO caption: Old Woman of Palermo (opposite 72 in TFO)
* *Fisionomie di criminali Francesi, Tedesche e Russe* (following 324 in LDD). TFO caption: Physiognomy of Fallen Women, Russian[10] (following 100 in TFO)
* [*Bar graph of prehensile feet*] (on 333 in LDD). The TFO bar graph is also untitled (on 84 in TFO)
* *Fisionomie di criminali Francesi, Tedesche e Italiane* (following 340 in LDD). TFO caption: Physiognomy of French, German, and Russian Female Offenders[11] (opposite and following 102 in TFO)
* *Gabriella Bompard* (on 343 of LDD). TFO caption: Gabrielle Bompard[12] (opposite 96 in TFO)
* *Berland* [*side view*] (on 345 in LDD). TFO caption: Berland (opposite 98 in TFO)
* *Berland* [*front view*] (on 345 in LDD). TFO caption: Berland (opposite 98 in TFO)
* *Thomas* [*side view*] (on 345 in LDD). TFO caption: Thomas (opposite 98 in TFO)
* *Thomas* [*front view*] (on 345 in LDD). TFO caption: Thomas (opposite 98 in TFO)
* *Messalina* (on 346 in LDD). TFO caption: Messalina (following 98 in TFO)
* [*Margherita*] (on 347 in LDD). TFO caption: Margherita (opposite 100 in TFO)
* [*Luisa*] (on 347 in LDD). TFO caption: Louise (opposite 100 in TFO)
* *Femmina negra* (on 360 in LDD). TFO caption: Negro Woman (opposite 112 in TFO)
* *Fanciulla patagona* (on 360 in LDD). TFO caption: Red Indian Woman[13] (opposite 112 in TFO)
* *Campi visivi di ree e prostitute* (opposite 390 in LDD). TFO caption: Field of Vision of Female Offenders (opposite and following 144 in TFO)
* Campo visivo della ragazza criminale F. M. (in stato tranquillo) (on 392 in LDD). TFO caption: Field of Vision of F. M. in a Tranquil State (following 142 in TFO)

*Campo visivo della ragazza criminale F. M. durante un accesso epilettico psichico a tono sentimentale esaltato (on 392 in LDD). TFO caption: Field of Vision of F. M. during an Epileptic Attack (opposite 142 in TFO)

[*Prison lesbian couple in "masculine" dress*] (on 423 in LDD)

Notes

Editors' Introduction

1 For more on the dissemination of Lombroso's thought in the English-speaking world and on *The Female Offender*'s role in this diffusion, see Rafter 1992. Another important vehicle for the transmission of Lombroso's theory to English-speaking countries was Havelock Ellis's *The Criminal* (1890).

2 The phrase *la donna delinquente* is best translated as "the criminal woman," not as "the female offender," "the delinquent woman" or "the female delinquent." At the time the book was originally published, *delinquente* and *criminale* were synonyms in Italy, although in the United States there was already a tendency to reserve the term *delinquent* for reference to youthful criminals and other offender types deemed less than fully responsible (for more on these distinctions and their import, see Rafter 1997). We decided to use *criminal woman*, not *criminal women*, in the title of this new edition because the former more accurately reflects Lombroso's original. The plural *women* would be more in line with current feminist thinking and its rejection of the nineteenth-century idea of the eternal woman, but the singular form of the noun better conveys the essentialism of Lombroso's thinking about female nature.

3 Lombroso 2005.

4 Goring [1913] 1972; Beirne 1993, 212.

5 Gould 1981, 126–27.

6 Lombroso-Ferrero [1911] 1972.

7 Rafter 1997; Gibson 2002; Wetzell 2000.

8 Becker and Wetzell 2004.

9 Italian books on Lombroso published between 1975 and 2000 include: Baima Bollone 1992; Bulferetti 1975; Colombo [1975] 2000; Dolza 1990; L. Guarnieri 2000; Leschiutta 1996; Lombroso 1995; Mazzarello 1998; Rondini 2001; and Villa 1985.

10 Chen 1992; Drapkin 1977; Gadebusch Bondio 1995; Lombroso, Reig, and Reig 1975; Mella, Alvarez, and Arias 1999; Quiroz Cuarón 1977. Also see Mucchielli 1994.

11 Nicole Rafter and Susan Erony, curators, 1998 (May 11–30), *In Search of the Criminal*

Body: Science and Myth in Criminological History, an exhibit at Northeastern University, Boston, Mass.; Susan Erony and Nicole Rafter, curators, 2000 (September 26–November 5), *Searching the Criminal Body: Art/Science/Prejudice, 1840s to Present*, University Art Museum, State University of New York, Albany. See also Erony and Rafter 2000; McKay 1996.

12 Regener 1999.

13 Dolza 1990; Harowitz 1994. Also see Gibson 1982; Gibson 1990; Horn 1995; and Rafter 2001.

14 Editions of *L'uomo delinquente* had been published in 1876, 1878, 1884, and 1889. The fifth and final edition appeared in 1896–97, after the publication of *La donna delinquente*.

15 Lombroso devotes all of part 3 of *Criminal Woman* and the first three chapters of part 4 to documenting stigmata.

16 See this volume, 112.

17 See this volume, 113.

18 See this volume, 114.

19 See this volume, 134.

20 See this volume, 146.

21 See this volume, 186–87.

22 See this volume, 182.

23 See this volume, 183.

24 See this volume, 183, 185.

25 See this volume, 36.

26 See this volume, 42. Lombroso's apparent readiness here to acknowledge female superiority among lower forms has the rhetorical advantage of suggesting that he is impartial in his views and indeed happy to acknowledge women's strengths where they do occur.

27 See this volume, 45.

28 See this volume, 46.

29 See this volume, 64.

30 See this volume, 77.

31 In an essay on *La donna delinquente*, David Horn (1995, 115) makes the same point when he writes: "The normal woman, a figure that had no real counterpart in Lombroso's studies of male criminality, was ostensibly constructed as a background against which the female offender might become distinct, visible, and legible. . . . [But] this aim was largely frustrated; on the contrary, the portrait of the normal woman contributed substantially to locating *all* women within the domain of the social expert." Thus Horn titles his essay "This Norm Which Is Not One."

32 See this volume, 147–48.

33 Also see Ellis [1906] 1936, 267, suggesting that Lombroso was "developing the results reached in the important study of the Jukes family, by Dugdale" when he put forth his "doctrine that prostitution is the vicarious equivalent of criminality."

34 See this volume, 185.

35 Author's preface, this volume, 35.

36 For a particularly thorough American evaluation by one of Lombroso's contemporaries, see Wines 1895. For other examples of criticism, see Aschaffenburg 1913; Kellor 1901; Lydston 1904; Nye 1976; Parmelee 1911; and Tarnowsky 1889. Dolza (1990, 34) speaks of Lombroso's "infantile naiveté" and of "the frenetic rhythm that characterized his existence," traits that no doubt contributed to his evidentiary gullibility. Also see Villa (1985, 133) on an "extremely negative" judgment of Lombroso's experimental work, made by professional colleagues in 1875 ("Lombroso was treated practically like a charlatan").

37 Nye 1976, 341.

38 Qtd. in ibid., 342 n. 23.

39 Indeed, Lombroso decided to embark on the study of criminal woman in 1889, the same year as the French attacks at the Second International Congress of Criminal Anthropology. While Lombroso himself had not previously studied female offenders in depth, Pauline Tarnowsky, a Russian physician, had published at least one criminal anthropological book on this population, *Étude anthropométrique sur les prostitutées et les voleuses* (1889), a work with which Lombroso was familiar and one that may have deeply influenced him as he undertook his new project. In fact, Tarnowsky's book may have inspired Lombroso to apply born criminal theory to women. The Russian's 1889 study reaches conclusions very similar to those Lombroso later reached in *La donna delinquente*; it too used photographs to demonstrate offenders' anomalies; and it too started out by using a control group, only to drop the experimental method after a few chapters. The extent to which Lombroso borrowed from Tarnowsky deserves study.

40 See this volume, 107.

41 For the historical context in which Lombroso wrote this passage, see Fee's (1979) useful discussion of the crisis in craniology in the late nineteenth century.

42 See this volume, 108.

43 For information on similar contemporary views, see Fee 1979. Also see Gross [1911] 1968, whose very long section on female criminal psychology simply repeats many of Lombroso's claims and findings, making the same assumptions about female nature.

44 In later years, Ferrero, notwithstanding the fervent pleas of his wife (Lombroso's daughter, Gina), refused to collaborate with her on a book because he considered women inferior to men in ability (Dolza 1990, 151).

45 Ibid., 34 n. 31. The description of Lombroso as the family's pivot comes from Gina Lombroso.

46 Ibid., 61 n. 83.

47 Ibid., 63.

48 Ibid., 10. Also see Gibson 1982, 1990.

49 See this volume, 88.

50 Author's preface, this volume, 37.

51 In Italian, biographies of Lombroso remain surprisingly few. See Villa 1985; Bulferetti 1975; Baima Bollone 1992; and L. Guarnieri 2000. In English, biographical information can be found in articles by Wolfgang 1972 and Pick 1986.

52 Psychiatry was not yet an autonomous discipline in Italy. Lombroso demonstrated his interest in psychiatry by writing a senior thesis on cretinism.

53 This war culminated in the proclamation of the Kingdom of Italy in 1861, under the Piedmontese monarchy. Only Venice and Rome remained outside the new state, and they were annexed in 1866 and 1871, respectively.

54 The phrase is taken from Garin 1980, 4.

55 Villa 1985, 110.

56 On Darwin, see Lombroso 1871.

57 Ibid., 172–73.

58 Ibid., 222.

59 Scientific racists, including Lombroso, misused Darwin's theory, which had never argued that evolution was developing in a positive or progressive direction. Natural selection simply meant that certain creatures were better adapted to specific, local environments. Scientific racists added a teleological bent to Darwinism by assuming that the most complex species were more perfect in a physical, moral, and mental sense.

60 Beccaria [1764] 1963. As we explain in the glossary, the classical school was not so denominated by Beccaria and his group but rather received this label from Lombroso and his followers as they tried to differentiate their own school of thought from it.

61 On moral statistics, see Beirne 1993, chs. 3 and 4.

62 Bénédict Augustin Morel (1809–73) published his famous treatise, *Traité des dégénérences physiques intellectuelles et morales de l'espèce humaine* in 1857. His theory gained popularity in continental Europe, especially in those nations, such as France and Italy, that feared national decline in relation to the military and industrial might of Germany, England, and the United States.

63 Robinson 1976, 27.

64 Nye 1976.

65 Mucchielli 1994.

66 Adam 1912, 22.

67 Ibid., 20.

68 Ibid., 15, 18.

69 Gross's book was translated from the German to become part of the Modern Criminal Science series published by the American Institute of Criminal Law and Criminology.

70 Gross [1911] 1968, 45.

71 Ibid., 410.

72 Ibid., 341.

73 Ibid., 355.

74 Bonger [1916] 1969, 63. Bonger originally produced this work in 1905, but even then, he would have had time to absorb the lessons of Lombroso's work on women had he been interested.

75 Fernald 1920, 3, 246.

76 Ibid., 528.

77 Glueck and Glueck 1934, esp. 310.

78 See, for example, the Gluecks' *Five Hundred Criminal Careers* (1930), a study of male offenders, which concludes with recommendations for greater individuation of treatment.

79 Pollak [1950] 1961, 2, 9.

80 Ibid., 122.
81 Ibid., 129.
82 Heidensohn 1996, 118–19.
83 Konopka 1966, 127.
84 Smart 1976, 27–28.
85 Heidensohn 1968, 160, 171.
86 Klein 1973, 3.
87 Also important in laying this foundation was the work of Marie-Andrée Bertrand of the University of Montreal. For information on her work, and for more information on this history in general, see Rafter and Heidensohn 1995.
88 See, for example, Dalton 1964. For an early critique of this type of reasoning, see Horney 1985.
89 Heidensohn 1996, 114.
90 Also see Horn 1995.
91 L. Guarnieri 2000, 14.
92 Qtd. in Regener 2003, 45.
93 *La donna delinquente* did have predecessors, however, including legal treatises that justified women's fewer liberties and lesser legal standing, relative to men, by discussing women's intellectual incapacities, innate mendacity, and the like. See Graziosi 2000.
94 In some cases we cut a passage in which Lombroso cited his source but then translated a nearby passage based on the same source; in these cases, we moved Lombroso's citation into the passage we translated so readers could follow his own method of documentation.

Author's Preface

1 Lombroso is here referring to the so-called classical school of criminology and distinguishing what he sees as his own empirical and inductive approach from the classical school's deductive attempts to understand criminal behavior. (For more on the classical school, as well as other key concepts in or related to Lombroso's work, see the glossary at the end of this book.)
2 In this paragraph, Lombroso discusses two ways in which his empirical data appear to contradict his overall argument for female inferiority. First, his data indicate that before puberty, human females are equal to human males. But this equality is misleading, Lombroso explains; in truth it is a sign of that premature ("precocious") development that often shows up in inferior beings. Second, Lombroso's data indicate that women have fewer degenerative stigmata or physical signs of abnormality than men. The underlying reason for this relative lack of stigmata, Lombroso explains, is woman's evolutionary inferiority—she is less variable than man. In conclusion, Lombroso gives an example: Among primitive creatures ("monsters"), the two sexes are on a par, but this equality is erased by sexual selection as evolution progresses. Thus, he implies, any example of female equality or superiority is in fact a sign of evolutionary inferiority if not of outright monstrosity.
3 Later Lombroso explains in more detail that despite appearances to the contrary, women are in fact less sensitive than men to pain. They may seem more sensitive be-

cause they react to pain more strongly, but this reaction is a function of their weaker self-control and their tendency to overdramatize in order to elicit sympathy from others.

4 One of Lombroso's central intellectual problems in this book is to explain why women have lower crime rates than men. In *Criminal Man* he had set forth the theory that born criminals are less evolved than "normal" men. Here he argues that women are lower on the evolutionary scale than men. Logically, then, one would expect women to have not lower but higher rates of crime.

5 Lombroso is trying to anticipate a criticism of illogic here; he expects his critics to attack him for saying that women are both less moral than men and less criminal. To deflect this attack, he says that the factors of maternity, weaker intelligence, lesser strength, and lesser variability combine to provide a counterweight, diminishing the criminality of women.

6 Lombroso claims to be founding a new science based on empiricism and logic, and yet here he says that nature is never logical. Ironically, he undermines his own argument. We see him here in a profoundly defensive posture. His defensiveness was brought on, at least in part, by attacks on his theory of the born criminal—most notably from the French—at the Second International Congress of Criminal Anthropology in 1889.

7 Lombroso is here being sarcastic, implying that anthropologists are not good scientists because they equate all groups with tribes and fail to provide an evolutionary framework for comparing them.

8 At the time Lombroso wrote this, Italy had legalized prostitution by licensing brothels, which made women accessible but simultaneously kept them under government regulation. Lombroso favored this type of regulated prostitution. However, there is some contradiction in his thought because while he conceives of the male born criminal as a being who must be removed from society, he argues that the female born criminal, if she is a prostitute, is useful in satisfying male sexual demands.

9 Lombroso here tries to fend off criticism from feminist critics who will attack him for denigrating women.

10 This last phrase refers to Italy, where women could study but not practice law.

11 Lombroso implies that all these women (including Pauline Tarnowsky, the only female criminal anthropologist in Europe) agree with his theory of female inferiority. But at least one of them—Anna Kuliscioff, a socialist feminist and physician—dismissed his views, even though she was a family friend. Moreover, while Tarnowsky believed that both sexes inherited criminality, she explained normal women's weaknesses in social terms (Gadebusch Bondio 1996).

12 Gina Lombroso-Ferrero, daughter of Lombroso and (later) wife of this book's second author, Guglielmo Ferrero.

13 Lombroso wrote this preface, not with his coauthor Guglielmo Ferrero, but rather alone, speaking at times in the first person singular and signing it by himself. Moreover, he identifies his daughter, not Ferrero, as his "steadiest collaborator." Lombroso may here be recognizing the extraordinarily difficult position in which this book, with its insistence on female inferiority, placed his daughter, who did indeed prove to be a steady collaborator (see Lombroso-Ferrero [1911] 1972).

14 Here Lombroso generously acknowledges the contribution of his coauthor, Guglielmo Ferrero, whose role seems, in fact, to have been minimal. For more on Ferrero's role, see the first appendix.

I The Normal Woman

1 Lombroso here refers to the Darwinian idea of an evolutionary scale. In this chapter Lombroso establishes his explanatory framework, which is that of evolutionary biology. He assumes that the ultimate causes of human behavior lie in biology and that biology is determined by the evolutionary process of natural selection. Less directly, in this chapter he establishes his credentials as a scientist by discussing animal evolution in technical terms.

2 The English naturalist Charles Darwin (1809–82) most profoundly influenced nineteenth-century thought with his 1859 book *The Origin of Species*, which was published in Italian in 1864. However, Lombroso's ideas were more deeply affected by Darwin's *Descent of Man and Selection in Relation to Sex* (1871), first published in Italian in 1871. This second work emphasizes human evolution, including man's probable descent from an anthropoid ancestor and sexual selection as a primary factor. Primitive ancestors and the impact of sexual selection on evolution constitute major themes in *Criminal Woman* as well. Professor Mario Portigliatti Barbos, the late-twentieth-century successor to Lombroso's chair in legal medicine at the University of Turin, writes that the 1871 Italian translation of Darwin's *Descent* profoundly influenced Turinese positivist biological research, "orienting it toward work in anthropology and primatology. . . . From this period dates the formation of various collections in comparative anatomy, including Lombroso's own museum" of criminal anthropology (1993, 1444).

3 Herbert Spencer (1820–1903), a British philosopher and social scientist, applied evolutionary theory to the study of society. The most influential evolutionist before Charles Darwin, Spencer may have had an even stronger influence than Darwin on Lombroso's thought. Like Lombroso (and for that matter, Darwin himself), Spencer accepted the Lamarkian theory that acquired characteristics can be inherited. He invented the phrase *survival of the fittest* and is remembered today primarily as a social Darwinist or advocate of allowing "the unfit" to sicken and die without state intervention, a social policy that would (in Spencer's view) enable society to progress "naturally."

4 Lombroso seems here to mean that in primitive creatures, males were inferior to females in size and strength. Their sole superior attribute was their relative structural complexity. Only in recent evolutionary time did males also begin to predominate over females in size and force.

5 In an earlier passage, not translated here, Lombroso cited a Pagliani work titled *Lo sviluppo umano per età, sesso*, ecc., Torino, 1879).

6 Lombroso does not specify his units of measurement in this paragraph.

7 Lombroso seems to have just one "specific practice" in mind, that of carrying infants on the buttocks, a practice to which he attributed the development of the "posterior cushion" in Hottentot women (see figure 1). On the "scientific" construction of a spe-

cific Hottentot woman, and of nonwhite women more generally, see Fausto-Sterling 1995.

8 Presumably, Lombroso is thinking here of grams, although he does not so specify.

9 In table 4, Lombroso does not give specific data on the Capuans, an ancient people who lived south of Rome, but he does refer to them in the textual commentary (the same is true for the Papuans). Here, as in the next table, Lombroso deals simultaneously with the skulls of ancient and contemporary peoples.

10 The supposedly inferior weight of women's brains was central to Lombroso's argument that women as a group were inferior to men. Brain weight was so widely discussed in late-nineteenth-century Europe that early feminists felt they had to refute the evidence. One of their arguments was that body weight had to be factored in (see table 7). They also delighted when, as frequently happened, after the death and autopsy of a famous man, his brain was found to weigh less than that of the average woman.

11 Léonce Manouvrier (1850–1927) and Paul Topinard (1830–1911), a colleague whose name is mentioned later in this paragraph, were leaders of the French school of criminology that forcefully criticized Lombroso's theory of the born criminal. However, Manouvrier and Topinard shared with Lombroso a belief in the importance of heredity as an influence on criminal behavior. For more on Manouvrier, see Mucchielli 1994.

12 Salvatore Ottolenghi (1861–1934) studied medicine under Lombroso at the University of Turin. He is best known for applying Lombroso's theory of the born criminal to police practice. As professor of legal medicine at the University of Rome, he founded a school to train all Italian police administrators in this new field of so-called scientific policing. In 1896, he published a book entitled *La sensibilità della donna* (The sensitivity of women), in which he confirmed Lombroso's views on the inferiority of women to men. For more on Ottolenghi, see Gibson 2002.

13 Lombroso's denial of greater sensitivity in women represents one of the few instances in which he rejects nineteenth-century stereotypes of women. Otherwise, he uses science to "prove" common assumptions about women's physical weakness, low intelligence, vanity, and so on. For a historical analysis of Lombroso's views on women's sensitivity, see Gibson 1990.

14 Presumably, Lombroso made the measurements with an algometer, an instrument whose uses are described more thoroughly in chapter 21. While the figures in the second column add to 100 percent, those of the first column add to only 97 percent, with no explanation of the missing cases.

15 Dante, *The Divine Comedy. The Purgatorio*, 8:76–78.

16 Paolo Mantegazza (1831–1910) was one of the founders of the field of anthropology in Italy. Trained in medicine, he taught at the University of Florence and organized the Society for Anthropology and Ethnography. He wrote on a large variety of topics, including what he called the "physiology of love." While publicly rejecting Lombroso's theory of the born criminal, he shared similar views on the inferiority of women and nonwhite races.

17 Giuseppe Sergi (1841–1936) was one of Italy's leading physical anthropologists. A professor of anthropology first at the University of Bologna, later at the University of

Rome, he founded a museum of anthropology and a laboratory for experimental psychology at Rome. He also published over four hundred books and articles.

18 Lombroso here uses *prostitution* as a synonym for female promiscuity, which he thought was completely acceptable among "savage" peoples. Only as humans evolved did female sexual promiscuity become "a sign of infamy." In the next sentence, he uses *prostitution* to refer to the more modern practice in which men pay women for sex.

19 In these paragraphs, women are compared to both savages and children. Lombroso accepted a widely held nineteenth-century scientific maxim, most famously articulated by Ernst Haeckl, that "ontogeny reproduces phylogeny." According to this biogenetic "law," the human life cycle replicates the evolutionary process, so that children are equivalent to savages. Boys mature into full adulthood, while girls can only hope to reach an intermediary stage, that of normal women.

20 In the original, one of the proverbs is in French and the rest are in dialects from various parts of Italy.

21 This quotation translates as "There is nothing in the mind that is not first in the senses."

22 Lombroso's implication here is that man, due to his more refined sensitivity and greater intelligence, would never be so foolish as to go through childbirth a second time, especially if, like woman, he were indifferent to sex.

23 Lombroso is here trying to establish that women cannot control their impulses, positive or negative, through willpower. This constitutes a theme throughout this chapter. To allow that women have the power to control their feelings would mean admitting the possibility that they are less creatures of biology than Lombroso has previously maintained. Moreover, to allow the possibility that women can make autonomous decisions to be self-sacrificing and compassionate would undermine his claims about female inferiority.

24 Between 1789 and 1870, Europe experienced several waves of revolution, characterized by popular uprisings. Sociologists like Gustave Le Bon (1841–1931) developed early theories of crowd behavior, often depicting the revolutionary crowd as feminine. As Susanna Barrows (1981) has written, crowds were seen as sharing with women the traits of irrationality, impulsiveness, and animal cruelty. Similarly, Charles Dickens chose a woman, Mme. LaFarge, to represent the bloodthirsty ferocity of French revolutionaries in his *Tale of Two Cities*. In Italy, the member of Lombroso's school who wrote most extensively on crowds was Scipio Sighele.

25 Lombroso is here apparently quoting the previously cited work he coauthored with Laschi. No citation to du Camp appears earlier in this chapter.

26 The French novelist Émile Zola authored *Germinal* (1885), *Nana* (1880), and other books cited by Lombroso as scientific evidence. Zola's literary philosophy of naturalism, which called for scientific depictions of brutish depravity, in fact led the novelist to explain human events in terms close to those used by Lombroso.

27 During the 1848 revolution, the Frenchman Ernst Legouvé (1807–1903) advocated expanding women's civil rights and educational opportunities.

28 Following Spencer, in this and the following paragraph Lombroso builds a social Darwinist argument damning women's compassion. Compassion for the weak and the

criminal undermines justice (and, by implication, the process of evolution) by helping the unfit to survive.

29 Lombroso seems to be saying that in the early stages of evolution, males took no part in raising children, a pattern that continued into the early stages of human civilization and that explains why women had to form matriarchies. More recently, men have recognized parental responsibilities, eliminating the need for woman-dominated societies.

30 Lombroso here again expresses the typically social Darwinist idea that existence constitutes a social struggle in which the weak inevitably fail; thus, he implies, it is folly to help them survive. After the turn of the century, Nazis and other eugenicists developed this idea into the doctrine that civilized people, by helping the weak to survive, were harming their societies and that it was thus better to actively prevent the weak from reproducing.

31 In this passage Lombroso touches lightly on themes he develops at greater length in the final chapters: the origins and nature of hysteria and epilepsy as a fundamental cause of criminality.

32 In Lombroso's view, as civilization progresses, women diverge ever more from men, becoming increasingly weak. This contrasts with the position taken by nineteenth-century feminists, who believed that increasing equality for women in law, education, and the workplace would make women mentally, psychologically, and physically stronger.

33 Anticipating the objection that one rarely sees "normal" women being physically cruel, Lombroso argues that today woman's cruelty manifests itself mainly in nonphysical but nonetheless immoral acts. The rest of this paragraph, too, struggles to explain why it is so difficult to detect the fundamental cruelty of woman's nature.

34 Lombroso believed that the evolutionary process is speeding up; see his 1871 *L'uomo bianco e l'uomo di colore* (The white man and the man of color).

35 In this paragraph, too, Lombroso tries to explain why it is so difficult to find examples of woman's fundamental cruelty. Evolution is accelerating, he argues, producing ever more feminine women. Moreover, primitive men killed off the cruelest women, who could thus not reproduce their cruelty for subsequent generations.

36 Here Lombroso is trying to avoid an objection—if evolution selects the fittest, why are women growing progressively weaker and more vaporous?

37 Women are less cruel today than in primitive times, Lombroso reasons, because wicked men no longer want them as mates, a phenomenon that leads to the dilution of purely wicked stock.

38 In a paragraph not translated here, Lombroso gives the full citation to this work as Brehm, *La rita degli animali*, Torino, 1871, vol. III, p. 23.

39 Lombroso's point here is that greenfinch males love more ardently than greenfinch females.

40 Alexandre Dumas (1802–70) was a celebrated French historical novelist and, not incidentally, a famous womanizer.

41 Lombroso implies that only he, as a physician, knew that all three sisters were disgusted sexually by their husbands.

42 The size, number, and complexity of female sexual organs, Lombroso acknowledges, seem to suggest that women were made for love. However, these organs are less sexual than reproductive, he argues in the next paragraph. Thus men are organically superior in sexual love.

43 The French writer Madame de Staël (born Germaine Necker, 1766–1817) was also famous for her political salon. The phrase quoted by Lombroso is one of her most-cited sayings.

44 The French brothers Edmond Louis Antoine Huot de Goncourt (1822–96) and Jules Alfred Huot de Goncourt (1830–70) collaborated as artists, art critics and historians, and novelists.

45 The prolific French novelist George Sand (born Amadine-Aurore-Lucile Dupin, 1804–76) was famous as well for her independence and numerous romantic liaisons, some with leading artists and intellectuals.

46 Today, the nineteenth-century French author Stendhal (born Marie Henri Beyle, 1783–1842) is remembered chiefly for his novels, but Lombroso (to judge from *La donna delinquente*) was especially familiar with Stendhal's *De l'amour*, a collection of thoughts and epigrams, originally published in 1853.

47 Etymological dictionaries disagree with Lombroso, tracing *pudore* to the Latin *pudere*, meaning "to be ashamed."

48 In the chapter entitled "Hysterical Criminals" (this volume, chapter 31), Lombroso states that hysterics are especially prone to make false accusations.

49 Lombroso here argues that women are vain because, unlike men, they have not yet evolved to a level of caring about virtue. This "slowness" explanation is one of the models he uses to account for female inferiority. In other passages, he attributes women's backwardness to a loss of traits they formerly shared with men, such as intelligence, strength, and sexual passion. This "loss" reasoning constitutes a second type of explanation for female inferiority. Elsewhere, Lombroso employs yet a third model, atavism, to account for women's backwardness; but in this passage, he explicitly rejects atavism as an explanation for female vanity.

50 Lombroso is here referring to maternity and compassion, which oblige women to favor their own families and friends and prevent them from understanding more abstract concepts, such as justice.

51 Before writing *La donna delinquente*, Lombroso published *Genio e follia* (Genius and madness), which was in its fourth Italian edition by 1882. This appeared in English as *The Man of Genius* (1891). After completing *La donna delinquente*, Lombroso published yet another book on the topic in 1897, *Genio e degenerazione* (Genius and degeneration).

52 Lombroso's previous Spencer citation, which occurs in a passage not translated here, is to *Introduzione allo studio della sociologia*, cap. xv.

53 The German psychologist Wilhelm Wundt is often recognized as the founder of experimental psychology.

54 Compare part 1, chapter 4, in which Lombroso speaks approvingly of women jurors on the basis of experience in the American West, citing an American source of 1872. Apparently neither he nor Ferrero noticed this contradiction.

55 The reference is to the English novelist George Eliot (born Mary Ann Evans, 1819–80).

56 Earlier in this chapter, in a paragraph not translated here, Lombroso cited Romanes, *L'intelligence des animax*. Paris, 1889, vol. II, p. 43.

57 Anna Kuliscioff (1854–1925) was an early socialist feminist and a friend of Lombroso's daughters, Gina and Paola. Lombroso here misappropriates her argument, which criticized the relegation of women to certain types of work based on their supposedly feminine talents. She also rejected Lombroso's theory of women's inborn inferiority, instead blaming inequalities in education and the workplace for women's failure to become intellectual and political leaders.

2 Female Criminology

1 Pillage by roving outlaw bands was a problem in nineteenth-century Italy. Some of Lombroso's earliest studies of atavism involved the skulls of brigands.

2 Lombroso's conclusion—that females are less criminalistic than males—does not seem to follow from his examples. In any case, his sensational examples of criminality among female animals leave readers with a much more vivid impression than does his anticlimactic conclusion.

3 In late-nineteenth-century Europe, the growing numbers of unmarried women with a college education were called the third sex. These women pursued middle-class professions like teaching, nursing, and social work, which were respectable but usually underpaid. Male commentators ridiculed their masculine intellectual pretensions and compared them unfavorably to "normal" women who devoted themselves to marriage and maternity.

4 The insect order *Hymenoptera* includes bees and wasps.

5 Lombroso does not limit himself to the "crimes of savage and primitive women" announced in the chapter's title, but rather moves freely through time and space, discussing eighteenth-century aristocrats and even savage prosecutions of women.

6 Philippe Pinel (1745–1826), a French physician, is associated with the origins of psychiatry and the humane treatment of the mad. Most famously, he unlocked the chains of the insane in a Parisian lunatic asylum, thus ushering in an era of less punitive and more medicalized treatment of the mentally disturbed.

7 As many passages in this chapter indicate, Lombroso uses *prostitution* as a synonym for any extramarital sexual intercourse on the part of women, regardless of whether money, goods, or favors were exchanged. Similarly, he uses *promiscuity* to describe any type of extramarital sexuality, especially on the part of women.

8 New Britain is an area of Papua New Guinea. We were unable to identify with confidence the location of the New Hanover to which Lombroso refers.

9 In Lombroso's view, human life began in a state of chaos and criminality, with evolution gradually leading to civilization. Thus rape and prostitution (the sexual free-for-all that he considers characteristic of primitives and savages) gave way to marriage, and crime led eventually to the writing of criminal laws. Lombroso's view of humans' original condition echoes that associated with the political philosopher Thomas Hobbes.

10 Lombroso is trying to detect the origins of modern marriage in monogamous relation-

ships among "primitive" people. Early monogamous relationships, he reports, ironically often led to (or were accompanied by) more female promiscuity ("prostitution"). He is also laying a foundation here for his later argument that modern prostitution, involving the exchange of sex for money, should be maintained in legal form (licensed by the state) as an outlet for male lust. Legalization of prostitution, in Lombroso's view, protects marriage, which might break up without this outlet.

11 Lombroso considers these examples to be signs of progress since they indicate a narrowing of the scope in which promiscuous relationships can occur.

12 In this sentence, Lombroso loses his grip on the topic of polyandry, returning to the more engrossing subject of polygamy.

13 A Jew himself, Lombroso is not taking an anti-Semitic stance here. For him, people of all religions evolved from savagery to civilization; see, for example, his reference to Islam in part 2, chapter 1.

14 Solon, known as one of the Seven Wise Men of ancient Greece, provided political leadership to Athens in the early sixth century B.C. He proved particularly significant as a legal reformer.

15 Here again, Lombroso is laying a foundation for his support of government-licensed prostitution in Italy.

3 Anatomy and Anthropometry

1 In this remarkable autobiographical passage, Lombroso critiques his own earlier work, concluding that he overrelied on anthropometry, or the measurement of body parts in general, and on cranial anthropometry, or the measurement of parts of the skull in particular, as guides to the criminal type. He uses religious language—"faith," "ark," "salvation"—suggesting that for him, science is a kind of religion; and he likens himself to a sculptor attempting to create a "new human statue," its proportions to be determined by scientific measurements. Only later (Lombroso says in the next paragraph) did he realize that the differences between criminals and normals are so small as to "defy" measurement. Despite this self-criticism, however, Lombroso does not fully accept responsibility for the "abuse" of anthropometry; one possible interpretation of this paragraph's final sentence is that others were primarily responsible for "the damage that can be caused by excessive confidence."

2 Here Lombroso describes the process by which he came to conclude that not anthropometry but rather "anatomical-pathological investigation" is the true route to discovery of the criminal type. In the next paragraph he laments the way in which anthropometry, becoming popular, eclipsed the study of anatomical abnormalities and lead anthropometrists such as Topinard and Manouvrier to the false conclusion that criminals do not constitute anomalous human types.

3 In 1793, Charlotte Corday, a young woman from the French provinces, traveled to Paris to kill Jean-Paul Marat, the revolutionary leader whom she considered responsible for the Reign of Terror. She stabbed Marat to death in his bath, a political crime for which she was guillotined.

4 Reversing his course, Lombroso here warns against the total rejection of anthropometry, calling such measurements the "symbol" and "flag" of criminal anthropology.

Moreover, he says, whenever anthropometry does reveal a difference between criminals and normal people, we should pay particularly close attention, since such revelations are hard to come by.

5 The place names designating "race" all refer to areas of Italy.

6 The numbers indicate cubic centimeters.

7 Here Lombroso attempts to deal with an embarrassing aspect of his table: the fact that it shows that on the average, criminal women have larger cranial capacity than normal women. He suggests that the data in the table are less trustworthy than those of Mingazzini, who found a much smaller average cranial capacity for criminal women, and he points to other studies that achieved higher results than those shown in his table for the skull capacity of normal women.

8 Continuing his effort to avoid the conclusion toward which his table points—that criminal women have cranial capacity superior to that of normal women—Lombroso shifts the points of comparison to look at the proportion in both groups with a capacity below 1,200 and above 1,400. On the basis of these comparisons he declares "the inferiority of criminals" to be "established."

9 Here Lombroso compares his three groups—criminal women, prostitutes, and normal women—according to the points at which the greatest proportions fall on a preestablished scale. However, without explanation, he uses data on only 52 percent of the normal women. These figures indicate that normal women's range on the scale is greater than that of the other two groups by ten points; thus the normal women rank highest.

10 Here again we find Lombroso excluding data that will disprove his point. He wants to show that prostitutes have heavy jaws, like men, and thus he excludes the two lightest jaws from his average on the grounds that they are "absolutely abnormal."

11 Here Lombroso is referring back to table 12.

12 This last point is the crucial one for Lombroso, who wants to demonstrate that criminal women are more masculine than normal or honest women.

13 This appears as 51 percent in table 17.

14 This appears as 5.4 percent in table 17.

15 This appears as 32.4 percent in table 17.

16 This sentence suggests that Lombroso's criteria for skull normality differed for males and females. If (as seems likely) he defined female abnormality partly in terms of "masculine" traits, he would naturally find what he reports in the next sentence: that the skulls of female criminals are "virile."

17 Lombroso is referring to his own "rule" that criminal women display more cranial anomalies and are therefore more virile than normal women.

18 Usually Lombroso does not deem either political criminals or criminals by passion particularly atavistic, but in the case of Corday he emphasizes the great number of abnormalities in her skull. This suggests considerable concern about women who, by involving themselves in political activity, go beyond the usual sphere of female activity. In contrast, Lombroso ennobles the male political criminal.

19 *Platycephaly* is an anthropological term for flat-headedness.

20 The jugular apophysis is a bony offshoot in the neck.

21 Lombroso usually uses *normal* to identify law-abiding women, but here he uses *healthy* (*sane*), indicating the interpretation of criminality as a physical sickness. Lombroso drew on this interpretation and in turn reinforced it, encouraging acceptance of the idea that crime as an illness infected not only the criminal but also society.

22 This passage provides source information on Lombroso's data and shows that he considered it scientifically important to enumerate his sources so others could check his data. Furthermore, the passage gives readers today a sense of the types and quantity of anthropometrical research on women being done in Europe in the late nineteenth century and the places it was published. However, Lombroso does not critically evaluate his sources or discuss the extent to which their data are comparable.

23 These kilogram weights are equivalent to 200, 215, and 285 pounds, respectively.

24 Lombroso had difficulty forming control groups because few "respectable" women would consent to undress and be measured. Therefore his control groups usually consisted of lower-class women who lacked the freedom to refuse, such as inmates in orphanages and nurses in hospitals.

25 The final figure here seems to be an error. Moreover, here and elsewhere in this chapter, Lombroso does not identify the units of measurement.

26 Here, too, Lombroso does not specify the unit of measurement.

27 Lombroso does not comment further on the data in table 20, nor does he explain why he does not reintroduce here the data on cranial capacity in various female groups that he displayed earlier in table 12.

28 There are racist overtones here in that southern Italians, and Asians and Africans as well, tend to have dark hair.

29 The case of the Old Woman of the Vinegar is analyzed in Fiume 1990.

30 We have not translated Lombroso's text on every item in this table. Lombroso himself did not write text on every item, nor do items in his text always correspond to items listed in the table.

31 The latter number appears as 14 percent in the table.

32 Strabismus is the condition of having a squint or a wandering eye.

33 This appears as 5.5 percent in the table.

34 See editors' notes to author's preface and part 1 n.26.

35 Gurrieri's study seems to have included only prostitutes. It is impossible to tell if the 130 cases mentioned in the next sentence were prostitutes, criminals, or both. When Lombroso specifies a population, we translate the specification; an absence of identifiers indicates the same absence in the original text.

36 Hypospadias is an abnormality of the penis, in which the urethra opens on the undersurface.

37 Alexandre Parent-Duchatelet (1790–1836), whose work Lombroso cites frequently in *Criminal Woman*, was a French physician and public health researcher. His *De la prostitution dans la ville de Paris* (1836) was one of the first studies to identify prostitution as a threat to public hygiene. Parent-Duchatelet himself linked prostitution to the economic hardships of working-class women, but Lombroso was primarily interested in

the French statistics on prostitutes' physical abnormalities, which he used to argue for increases in the social control of female sexuality.

38 Lombroso is discussing these two cases because Parent-Duchatelet reported them as having had extraordinarily developed clitorises. Thus it is puzzling to have Lombroso conclude this discussion by observing their lack of clitoral anomalies.

39 Here Lombroso seems to be claiming that Parent-Duchatelet concluded that female sexual organs varied less than their male counterparts.

40 This appears as 52 percent in the table.

41 On Tarnowsky, see editors' introduction, note 39.

42 By the "pure type" Lombroso means someone who is fully a born criminal. Later he defines the "pure" or "criminal type" as someone with four or more degenerative traits. Those with fewer degenerative characteristics are "half-types" or criminaloids.

43 In the original text, Lombroso refers to specific photographs by number. Despite the numbers, however, it is in many cases impossible to match the text with specific photographs due to mix-ups in the identifications of the photographic plates. Indeed, the index of *La donna delinquente* gives incorrect page references for its own plates, and the plate titles in this index do not always correspond to the labels on the actual images in the text. Nor can *The Female Offender* help straighten out this confusion, for the garbled identifications of *La donna delinquente* were carried over into that translation. It is clear, however, that Lombroso meant the text of this chapter to refer to plates with multiple images, such as those we reproduce here in figures 10–15.

44 Lombroso's *Atlas* (*Atlante*, in Italian) constituted the fourth volume of the fifth and last Italian edition of *Criminal Man*; clearly, he had started to compile it at the time he wrote this. The *Atlas* contains a fascinating mixture of maps and tables of crime, photographs of criminals, and reproductions of art by criminals, including their tattoos.

45 Gabriella (Gabrielle) Bompard, a French prostitute arrested for robbery and murder, was the most sensational female criminal in Europe in the early 1890s, a period that coincided with Lombroso's work on *Criminal Woman*. The case overflowed with riveting details: a mysterious, decomposing body in a trunk; seduction and sex; pioneering forensic work by the French expert in legal medicine Lacassagne; international sleuthing and a fugitive in Havana; false confessions; and mutual accusations by Bompard and Michel Eyraud, her former lover and partner in crime. Lombroso was particularly drawn to Bompard's case by descriptions of her as someone who (like his born criminal) showed total amorality from childhood on. Moreover, the trial raised issues of hypnosis, female suggestibility, and criminal responsibility that dovetailed closely with Lombroso's interests and became themes in *Criminal Woman*.

46 That is, Bompard was about four feet and ten inches tall. Earlier, in a passage not translated here, Lombroso reported that both Salsotto and Marro had found the average height of the honest woman to be 1.55 meters (about five feet) (Lombroso and Ferrero 1893, 302). Thus Bompard was unusually short—a physical anomaly.

47 Lombroso here comes close to undermining his own evidence. He offers photographs for proof that female criminals are marked by degenerative traits, but—to fend off arguments that the criminals look fairly normal—he argues that the images may fool us.

48 Lombroso suggests that prostitutes evolved with attractive traits because these helped them survive in the struggle of the fittest.

49 At the time Lombroso wrote, Italian prisons were analogous to American jails, places were women were held before trial and on short sentences; penitentiaries, in contrast, were institutions for women found guilty of more serious crimes and serving longer sentences. Lombroso's point here is that his sample includes diverse cases.

50 Lombroso here shows that he is aware that regional physical differences could be confused with anomalies, and he claims to be able to separate the two when classifying. However, because he does not describe his method of making the distinction, the criteria for anomaly remain vague.

51 Here again Lombroso inadvertently raises the problem of lack of well-defined criteria for identifying anomalies, and hence for identifying the full criminal type and full prostitute type.

52 Lombroso here combines his two samples of 52 women in the Turin prison and the 234 penitentiary cases. However, he does not explain why he considers these groups "homogeneous," and indeed at the start of the chapter he stated that the two differed in ethnic composition.

53 This appears as 18.7 percent in table 23.

54 This appears as 35.2 percent in table 23.

55 That is, 2 percent of normal (nonoffender) women have four or more degenerative traits, thus qualifying as complete types or born criminals. Lombroso does not attempt to explain this phenomenon.

56 This appears as 25.7 percent in table 23.

57 Evidently this difference in frequency of the full type makes for the only difference between born criminals and born prostitutes, since Lombroso identifies both in terms of degenerative traits.

58 Lombroso uses the term *occasional criminals* to refer to lawbreakers pushed into crime more by circumstance than by defective biology and who are, therefore, reformable. However, because he identifies occasional criminals by their relative lack of anomalies, this sentence proves circular in its reasoning.

59 Lombroso means that these deformities are due to prenatal damage rather than atavism.

60 Lombroso is arguing that in all groups—animals, criminals, and the law-abiding—females exhibit fewer anomalies than males because they are less variable. This lesser variability provides yet another reason for the lower frequency of anomalies in female deviants.

61 In this paragraph—one of the most garbled and strained in the entire book—Lombroso attempts to reconcile a basic contradiction between his theory and his data. His theory would predict that women, being lower on the evolutionary scale, would have more anomalies than men, but his data show them to have fewer. Lombroso continues to struggle with this contradiction in the next few paragraphs.

62 In this paragraph, too, Lombroso's logic becomes particularly convoluted and strained.

63 Lombroso seems to be saying that the cerebral cortex—an organ he views as the true

seat of the nervous system and intelligence—is less sensitive and therefore less active in women than men, a difference that pushes women more rapidly into epilepsy and sexually deviant behavior than into serious crime.

64 In the previous section, Lombroso was primarily concerned with the relative infrequency of the female criminal type, and while he did occasionally refer to atavism, he drew mainly on the slowness explanatory model, according to which women evolve less rapidly than men. In this section, he mainly employs the atavism explanatory model, according to which women are inferior through reversion to a more primitive evolutionary stage.

65 Two kilograms equal about four and a half pounds.

66 In fact, 13 amounts to 1 percent of 1175.

67 In fact, 36 is 1.6 percent of 2161.

68 In the 1895 translation (*The Female Offender*), this chapter in particular is marked by omissions and deliberate mistranslations designed to eliminate sexual references, especially to lesbianism and other sexual practices among women. Seven passages were dropped entirely, while in others the sexual content was concealed. The excised passages are restored in this edition.

4 Biology and Psychology

1 Lombroso's reference here may be to the 1887 work by Salsotto cited in part 3, chapter 4, note g.

2 A related thesis was developed in the late twentieth century by Katharina Dalton in *The Premenstrual Syndrome* (1964).

3 Lombroso here seems to be contradicting his earlier data, which showed menstruation to start at a slightly later age in criminal women. This sentence concurs, however, with his earlier statements about prostitutes.

4 Lombroso does not here give an average number of children for noncriminal women.

5 Lombroso offers this piece of folk wisdom as evidence that criminal women have unusual muscular power.

6 The figures on normal women add to almost 100 percent (97 percent), but those on criminals and prostitutes add to only 79.5 percent.

7 Lombroso does not specify the scale of measurement he uses for comparisons in this section and the next.

8 Lombroso here uses *culture* (*cultura*) to denote social class. In what follows, he assumes that lower-class women are less well evolved than middle-class or upper-class women and thus closer to savages.

9 Lombroso is trying to explain data that do not support his preconceived theory, according to which prostitutes should have a duller sense of touch than honest women. He argues that some prostitutes might have tested as more sensitive than normal women because they were compared with honest women who were relatively crude (peasants), or older, or themselves somewhat anomalous.

10 An algometer or pain-threshold meter, is a handheld instrument used to measure sensations of pain caused by pressure. It consists of a piston rod with a rounded tip which presses against the skin. Lombroso devised his own variant on the standard algometer,

consisting of "an induction coil, put into action by a bichromate battery. The poles of the secondary coil are placed in contact with the back of the patient's hand and brought slowly up behind the index finger, when [*sic*] the strength of the induced current is increased until the patient feels a prickling sensation in the skin (general sensibility) and subsequently a sharp pain (sensibility to pain)" (Lombroso-Ferrero [1911] 1972, 246–47).

11 Lombroso viewed left-handedness as an abnormality.

12 Lombroso considered most lesbians to be a subset of prostitutes. Lesbianism was only one of the many, sometimes contradictory, types of sexual deviancy that he ascribed to prostitutes; these included frigidity, nymphomania, sadism, and lust murder. Lombroso believed that "born lesbians" recruited heterosexual women in brothels and turned them into "occasional lesbians."

13 Lombroso here uses the French for *girls of marble*.

14 Lombroso reasons that prostitutes who have had children are somewhat closer to normal women than are childless prostitutes—and thus naturally more sensitive to pain.

15 Lombroso here contradicts an earlier statement in this paragraph about tongue sensitivity.

16 Throughout this chapter, Lombroso is vague in pronoun referents, so that it is sometimes impossible to determine whether he is referring to female criminals, prostitutes, all female sexual deviants, normal women, or all women. We have perforce left the referents vague in the translation as well.

17 Valeria Messalina, who married the Roman emperor Claudius in 39 or 40 A.D., was famous for her promiscuity and cruelty. For Lombroso, she signified nymphomania and moral depravity.

18 After the emperor Claudius approved the murder of Messalina in 49 A.D., he married his niece Agrippina; together they produced Nero, who eventually succeeded his father and became infamous for his lusts and depravity. Agrippina was rumored to have worked behind the scenes to ensure Nero's succession, and she may in fact have poisoned Claudius to that end. Later, Nero had her killed. In Lombroso's view, Agrippina committed incest and murder; he also considered her to have been guilty of abortion and theft.

19 Lombroso began discussing the Bompard case in this volume, 139.

20 We have been unable to identify a novel by Meunier with this title. However, Lombroso may have been thinking of a novel by Catulle Mendès titled *La femme-enfant* and published in 1892, while the physician was working on *Criminal Woman*.

21 Lombroso seems to have forgotten that in chapter 20 (this volume, 159–60), he reports that prostitutes tend to menstruate prematurely.

22 It is not clear whether the comparison here is with normal women or female criminals.

23 Lombroso here defines sexual intercourse as heterosexual intercourse. In the next sentence, he uses *frigid* to mean "frigid with males." Through such usages, Lombroso defines heterosexual intercourse as the standard for normality in sexual relations.

24 For more on Krafft-Ebing, see the introduction to this volume.

25 Epilepsy is key to Lombroso's theories of criminality. For more on this see the entry on "epilepsy" in the glossary to this volume.

26 The concept of masochism was relatively new at the time Lombroso wrote *Criminal Woman*. The evolution of the term began in the 1890s with publication of Leopold von Sacher-Masoch's novel *Venus im Pelz* (Venus in furs; the specific year of the original publication is unknown). Krafft-Ebing, the German psychologist and sexologist, derived the term *masochism* from Sacher-Masoch's name. Sigmund Freud and Havelock Ellis later elaborated on the concept. Lombroso seems to have picked up the term from Krafft-Ebing (see his note later in this chapter on novels about lesbianism). Of course, the concept of female masochism fit well with Lombroso's own interest in justifying female subordination.

27 Lombroso cites Schiller's play as *Kabul und Liebe*, not (as it should be) *Kabale und Liebe*, but it is impossible to know whether this was a typographical error or a lapse in his German.

28 Lombroso is referring to the journal entitled *Archives of Criminal Anthropology, Psychiatry, and Legal Medicine*, which he founded in 1880. The leading journal of Italian criminal anthropology, the *Archives* published cutting-edge research by a large group of criminologists including Ferri, Ottolenghi, Marro, and Sergi. It featured a large number of articles on female crime and prostitution in the years 1889–1895.

29 Earlier in this chapter, Lombroso cited Parent-Duchatelet as believing that nearly all elderly prostitutes are lesbians.

30 Scipio Sighele (1868–1913) was a lawyer, sociologist, and follower of Lombroso. He was best known for his studies of crowd psychology, juvenile delinquency, female crime, and criminal couples.

31 Women's prisons in Italy, France, and other Catholic countries were staffed by nuns in the late nineteenth and early twentieth centuries.

32 The heroine of Zola's novel *Nana*.

33 Like other degenerationists, Lombroso believed that once degeneration begins, it involves mental, moral, and physical decay. Thus "naturally" a criminal tends to take on characteristics of the opposite sex, and epileptics and morally insane people can be expected to practice sexual perversions.

34 Lombroso considers this prisoner's aggressive courting of other women and the explicitly erotic tone of her letters to be more typical of men than women, and hence more masculine.

35 In this paragraph, Lombroso uses the terms *urninga* and *urningo* to denote, respectively, the feminine and masculine partners of lesbian couples. The term *urnings* was invented in 1864 by Karl Ulrichs, in a pamphlet titled *Vindex*, to denote effeminate men who seek other men as sexual partners. Lombroso may have picked the term up from Krafft-Ebing, who defined *urningism* as a mental illness.

36 Lombroso means that criminals, as atavistic throwbacks to an earlier evolutionary stage, are exceptions among well-evolved, civilized people.

37 Here Lombroso is referring to the case of the soldier Misdea, who in 1884, unhinged by what seemed to him unfair treatment by a corporal, opened fire in a barracks in Naples, killing and wounding many fellow soldiers. Called in to examine Misdea, Lombroso concluded that his underlying problem was epilepsy.

38 Lombroso here anticipates the late twentieth-century "control" theory of crime, ac-

cording to which people who are bonded to society through relationships, religion, commitment to work, and so on are less likely than poorly bonded people to commit crimes.

39 The woman to whom Lombroso refers may have been the Madame Lafarge who was put on trial in 1840 for poisoning her husband with arsenic. This famous trial, in which experts battled over the physical evidence, is today cited as the origin of forensic toxicology. Madame Lafarge's memoirs, published in 1841 and frequently reprinted thereafter, provided one of the few first-person accounts by a notorious woman offender.

40 Similarly, a twentieth-century study identified a group of shoplifters who steal not out of dire necessity but because they are too poor to afford small luxuries for themselves. They feel obligated to spend the family's income on other family members; with nothing left over, the only way they can treat themselves to small "extras" is by pilfering. See Cameron 1964. However, Cameron does not draw biological conclusions from her findings.

41 Although Lombroso uses the outlaw Bell-Star to exemplify the moral ghastliness of the female born criminal, he is clearly captivated by her as a romantic, adventurous, cross-dressing hero.

42 One might expect Lombroso here to mean that 54 percent of occasional criminals lack anomalies, but what he explicitly says is that 54 percent of all female criminals are anomaly free.

43 Lombroso cites no source for these quotes from Adolphe Guillot (1836–1905). They may be from his exposé of Parisian jails and morgues, *Paris qui souffre: La basse geôle du Grand Châtelet et les morgues modernes* (Paris: P. Rouquette, 1887).

44 According to Lombroso, suggestion works only when one of the two parties is much more dominant and authoritative than the other.

45 An example can be found in the field of law: In the late nineteenth century, in both Italy and the United States, women were sometimes allowed to study law, but they were forbidden to practice it.

46 Henri Joly (1839–1925), a French psychologist, wrote extensively on crime, prostitution, and public hygiene.

47 On women, shoplifting, and kleptomania, see O'Brien 1983 and Abelson 2000.

48 Lombroso began this list, starting with "Suggestion," to enumerate the causes of crime in female occasional offenders, but here he starts to refocus on the nature of female occasional crime.

49 While critics have often assumed that Lombroso had but one criminological idea—his theory of the born criminal—he in fact had many ideas about the causes of crime and foreshadowed a number of later etiological concepts, albeit without weaving these together logically. Here he anticipates what is today called the "opportunity theory" of criminal behavior.

50 Lombroso was not accurate in his view of American attitudes toward abortion at the turn of the twentieth century. While many common people did not consider abortion wrong, by 1900 the medical profession had supported successful campaigns at the state level to criminalize most abortions. See Tone 1997.

51 Lombroso seems to be referring here to the popular belief that women, because they are supposedly more emotional than men, commit more crimes of passion.

52 In this chapter, Lombroso uses over thirty-five cases to illustrate his points, but he also uses a few of these cases repeatedly (Vinci, Provensal, Jamais, Daru, Noblin, and several others not named in the list of age at offense). Our translation concentrates on the examples that turn up over and over again. Lombroso does not identify the cases further than indicated here; some must have been well-known in his day.

53 Lombroso does not specify the comparison group here. He may be comparing crimes-of-passion offenders with other criminals, or the comparison may be with women in general.

54 Oddly, Lombroso says very little about political offenders in this chapter, after noting here that female crimes-of-passion offenders are often passionate politically. In *Criminal Man*, he spends a great deal of time on the male political offender, devoting a full chapter to criminals of this type. Lombroso may have shied away from the topic here due to the difficulty of reconciling examples of intelligent and deliberate female political crime with his other ideas about female criminality.

55 Heloise (1101–64), famous for her devotion to Pierre Abelard, helped initiate the concept of romantic love.

56 Earlier, Lombroso wrote that Noblin strangled a rival.

57 In this passage, Lombroso actually goes beyond arguing that public opinion and prejudice can push people into crime. He makes the radical argument that law itself, in some circumstances, can be said to cause crime.

58 Lombroso here perceives a logical dilemma: He has declared that maternal feelings are women's strongest sentiments, but he has also reported that women commit few crimes out of maternal feeling and that these feelings work as a kind of brake on women's criminalistic tendencies. Thus, in the next few paragraphs, he attempts to reconcile these seemingly contradictory positions.

59 Parts of this paragraph anticipate the late-twentieth-century control theory of criminal behavior, according to which social bonds such as close personal relationships restrain people from committing crimes.

60 In this section, Lombroso gives examples only to illustrate the exceptions, not the rule.

61 This example anticipates current debates over partner killings by battered women. Lombroso notes that women retaliate more slowly than men, a phenomenon that, in current interpretations, relates to women's lesser physical strength. The lag between the abuse and retaliation should not be legally deemed premeditation, feminist theorists argue today, for it is in fact a function of biological sex differences. Whereas Lombroso insists on comparing women to a male standard, today many legal theorists insist that different standards for the two sexes are necessary in some cases.

62 The Romania-born Max Nordau (1849–1923), a philosopher, author, and physician, won Lombroso's admiration with his study *Degeneration*, first in German about 1893 (*Entartung* [Berlin: C. Duncker, 1893?]). Lombroso may here be referring to Nordau's earlier work, *De la castration de la femme* (Paris, A. Delahaye et É. Lecrosnier, 1882).

63 *Indiana*, a novel published by George Sand in 1832, focuses on a much-victimized woman who is mistreated by both her elderly husband and her caddish lover.

64 Lombroso's explanation here is meant to be biological, but it verges on the mystical.

65 Here Lombroso is returning to his assertion at the beginning of the chapter that women commit suicide much less frequently than men. The exception is suicide for love, where women predominate because of the biological influence of their reproductive organs.

66 See table 28.

67 In the Italian, Lombroso here uses *stigmata*, a term that, like *anomaly*, indicates that he considers the trait a sign of degeneration.

68 *Scudo* and *luigi* refer to types of coins.

69 While this example somewhat undercuts Lombroso's point, he offers it to show that prostitution satisfies its practitioners' greediness.

70 Again, etymological dictionaries disagree with Lombroso on this point by tracing *pudore*, the Italian word for "modesty," to the Latin *pudere*, "to be ashamed."

71 Lombroso here uses the term in English.

72 This list of secondary traits of the born prostitute is introduced by a paragraph suggesting that Lombroso will be pointing to similar traits in morally insane women. However, he does not always carry through on the comparison, instead concentrating on prostitutes' characteristics.

73 Like many other authors who through the centuries have written about moral insanity or psychopathy, Lombroso here attributes to the morally insane short attention spans and restlessness. For a more recent but similar diagnosis, see Eysenck 1979.

74 In the original this reads, "*Piccole inginocchiate* le piccole fioraie saffiche." The first phrase means "little kneeling girls" and the second means, literally, "little lesbian flower girls."

75 This and other references to prostitutes' low intelligence contradict what Lombroso said earlier about the "extreme variation" in prostitutes' intelligence.

76 This passage reveals a typical habit in Lombroso's thinking, his assumption that things must balance out or compensate for one another. He often assumes, for instance, that if one thing withers, another must flourish—and this sort of assumption then becomes the basis for an explanation. This habit of thought was not idiosyncratic to Lombroso, but rather widespread in late-nineteenth- and early twentieth-century thought. Freud, for example, used similar hydraulic metaphors in his characterization of the libido as a finite source of energy. Libido could be utilized by the id, the ego, or the superego, but only at the expense of the other two.

77 This kind of reasoning, too, is typical of Lombroso. He assumes that in evolution, the most recent development will be the first to degenerate. More "primitive" traits, in contrast, are more fundamental and difficult to erase.

78 Although Lombroso considered prostitutes and female born criminals to be theoretically equivalent, he proposed different methods of control for the two groups. Like male born criminals, female born criminals were to be sent to prisons or executed. On the other hand, prostitutes, because they served a useful social function as a safely valve for the male sex drive, were to be enclosed in state-licensed brothels.

79 Lombroso is probably referring to the French writer and photographer Maxime du Camp (1822–94).

80 In Italy and most other European nations in the late nineteenth century, prostitutes could practice their profession legally if they registered with the police. See Gibson 1986.

81 In late-nineteenth-century and early twentieth-century Europe and America, the international traffic in women was called "the white slave trade," in deliberate reference to the recently abolished black slave trade.

82 Lombroso's point, which he does not fully articulate here, is that while there are few female criminals relative to male criminals, the proportion of female insane criminals to male insane criminals is even smaller. Lombroso does not formally define *insanity*, but material later in this chapter indicates that he includes under this heading at least some cases involving alcoholism, delusions, epilepsy, hysteria, megalomania, melancholy, mental retardation (imbecility and idiocy), moral insanity, religious mania, and suicidal impulses. He does not distinguish (as we do today) between the criminally insane (those afflicted by mental disorder at the time of their crime) and insane criminals (those who become mentally disordered while serving their prison sentences), but rather treats both groups as part of the same phenomenon.

83 In Italy as in other European countries and the United States in the late nineteenth century, there was considerable debate as to whether mental retardation should be considered a form of insanity or an entirely separate category of mental affliction. There was also debate as to whether mental retardation should serve as a defense against criminal prosecution or punishment. In Italy, followers of Lombroso grouped mental retardation with other types of insanity that should exempt criminals from moral responsibility for their crimes, and therefore from prison. The psychiatrist Enrico Morselli used this Lombrosian argument as a defense expert witness in the trial of Callisto Grande, a man accused in 1875 of killing four children. See P. Guarnieri 1993.

84 Lombroso titles the rest of this chapter "Premeditation," but he gives few examples to illustrate elaborate criminal planning by women, instead discussing biological factors that he believes lead women to madness and hence crime. Lombroso may have been thinking of criminal irresponsibility as the opposite of premeditation, and thus a topic appropriate for treatment here, but he does not explicitly say so. Another explanation for the incoherence of this section, one supported by the brevity of the chapter and Lombroso's reliance in it on other authorities, is that he was not particularly interested in criminal insanity at this point in the writing of *Criminal Woman*. He was more excited about his newest theory, first enunciated in 1889 in the fourth edition of *Criminal Man*, that saw epilepsy as an underlying cause of criminal behavior, and he was perhaps anxious to move on to the next chapter, which deals with that topic.

85 In 1890, Séverin Icard published a book titled *La femme pendant la période menstruelle: Étude de psychologie morbide et de médicine légale* (Paris: Alcan).

86 The first characteristic of insane women, according to Lombroso, is the association of insanity with aspects of the female life cycle: pregnancy, nursing, menopause. The second is heightened sexuality.

87 Lombroso spells out his ideas on the relationships among epilepsy, criminality, and

moral insanity only sketchily in this chapter, referring readers several times to *Criminal Man* for more detail. He associated all three types of disability with degeneration, but he seems to be moving (at least in this chapter) toward a view of epilepsy as even more fundamental than degeneration, rather than one of its signs. As part of this theoretical shift (which, again, is only partly accomplished here), Lombroso tries to expand the definition of epilepsy to include not only motor epilepsy but also psychological epilepsy. As Portigliatti Barbos (1993) points out, in the late nineteenth century other authors were similarly expanding the definition of epilepsy. Portigliatti Barbos further observes that by using epilepsy as an explanation for criminality, Lombroso was aligning himself with psychiatry and making criminality an even more pathological phenomenon than it had been earlier.

88 It is unclear how Lombroso's finding of low rates of epilepsy in criminal women confirms his theory of the close relationship between epilepsy and innate criminality. But it does help him explain away women's puzzlingly low rates of crime.

89 Five or six liters is equivalent to six or seven quarts.

90 Here Lombroso explains the very low rate of epilepsy among prostitutes—whom his theory would suggest have high rates—by referring back to the fundamentally sexual nature of female atavism.

91 On the history of hypnotism in modern Italy, including its place in criminal law, see Gallini 1983.

92 Jean-Marie Charcot (1825–93), a French neurologist, investigated parallels between hysteria and epilepsy. His work on hypnotism would also have interested Lombroso.

93 Here the comparison group seems to be children.

94 It is unclear why Lombroso created a section on calumny in this chapter when he had an earlier section on false accusations, almost the same thing.

Appendices 1 and 2

1 It is difficult to get clear information on the various early editions and reprints of Lombroso's work. We have derived our data from a combination of sources: The National Union Catalog, the Library of Congress's WorldCat listing, and, especially, Renzo Villa's 1985 study of *Il deviante e i suoi segni*.

2 Dolza 1990, 141.

3 Ibid.

4 Page xiii of the preface to the French edition of 1896, as quoted and cited by Horn 1995, 124 n. 16.

5 Lombroso and Ferrero [1895] 1915, 198.

6 Lombroso and Ferrero 1893, 475.

7 The title reads exactly, *Basic Characteristics of Women Criminals* by Cesare Lombroso [*sic*], new and exp. ed. (Albuquerque, N.M.: Foundation for Classical Reprints, 1983), and has 102 pages.

8 *The Female Offender* here omits Lombroso's citation.

9 This image is captioned "Old Woman of the Vinegar" in this new edition.

10 Note that the TFO caption identifies these women as "fallen women," not "criminals," as in LDD, and that it further identifies them only as Russians, not "French, Germans,

and Russians," as in LDD. Some evidence suggests that the TFO identification is more likely to be accurate; thus we have captioned our reproduction, "Physiognomy of Russian prostitutes."

11 Note that the third national group, identified as "Italiane" in LDD, is called "Russian" in TFO.

12 TFO gives two views (one a profile, the other frontal) of Bompard, whereas LDD presents a single, three-quarter profile.

13 The Italian caption means "Patagonian girl," not "Red Indian woman."

Glossary

This glossary is designed to guide readers to the meanings of Lombroso's key terms and concepts.

abnormality A term Lombroso uses in several different ways, to refer to (1) a deviation from a statistical average; (2) a deviation from law-abiding behavior; (3) a degenerative trait and therefore sign of criminality. Applied to women, *abnormal* can also refer to (4) extramarital sexual intercourse or "precocious" (premature) sexuality.

anatomico-pathological method A criminal anthropological method of studying the human body for signs of criminality through measurement (anthropometry) and through a supplemental physical examination that measurement might miss. In *Criminal Woman* (chapter 11), Lombroso claims that he now follows this method in preference to his earlier exclusive reliance on anthropometry.

anomaly A sign of deviance and hence of potential criminality. Originally Lombroso used this term to refer to an atavism, but in *Criminal Woman*, he also applies it to any degenerative trait. For Lombroso, an anomaly can be biological, intellectual, or psychological, and it can be detected through physical examination, an interview, visual inspection, or hearsay. *Anomaly* is a synonym for *stigma*, as in Lombroso's famous phrase "the stigmata of degeneration."

anthropometry Scientific measurement of the human body, body parts, and capacities for the purpose of establishing physical types (such as the criminal type) and identifying anomalies. As anthropology became established as a scientific field of study in the mid-nineteenth century, anthropologists relied increasingly on anthropometry to bring precision to their studies of human types.

atavism A primitive form of humanity; a throwback to an earlier evolutionary stage in which humans were more savage, animalistic, and criminalistic than today.

born criminal A pure or natural offender; someone with four or more degenerative characteristics and who can thus be defined as belonging to the full criminal type. Lombroso thinks of born criminality as a pathology present from birth. In his view, born criminals cannot avoid committing criminal acts; they are biologically destined to do so.

born prostitute A woman who is hopelessly doomed to sexual promiscuity. Lombroso believes that in women, atavism is more likely to express itself through illegitimate sexual activity than through criminal behavior; thus he identifies the born prostitute, not the female born criminal, as the counterpart of the male born criminal. The born prostitute is even more atavistic and anomalous than the female born criminal, and lower on the evolutionary scale.

brachycephaly Short- or broad-headedness. Like physical anthropologists, Lombroso classified human skulls into brachycephalic and dolichocephalic groups.

classical school A philosophical approach to the analysis of crime and punishment based on Enlightenment beliefs about humans' capacity for rational behavior. The classical school is often traced back to Cesare Beccaria's 1764 *Essay on Crimes and Punishments*, a book that used deductive logic to argue for rationality and proportionality in criminal sentencing. While the classical school was in fact not a distinct group but rather an international philosophical orientation toward issues of crime and punishment, Lombroso and his followers identified it as a "school" in order to distinguish themselves from it. Their newer school of criminal anthropology called for science, not logic, induction, not deduction, and a focus on the criminal, not the crime or its punishment. See also criminal anthropology.

cranial capacity The volume inside the human braincase or skull. Lombroso assumes that cranial capacity is a sign of brain size and that brain size correlates positively with intelligence and other desirable traits. To estimate the cranial capacity of living subjects, Lombroso used head measurements. For the dead, he probably followed physical anthropologists' practice of pouring grapeshot or pepper seeds inside a skull and then weighing the amount.

criminal In Lombroso's vocabulary, anyone who (1) has committed a crime or is capable of doing so; (2) has been convicted of a crime; (3) is in prison; or (4) bears four or more anomalies. When Lombroso applies *criminal* to plants and animals, he uses the term to denote lower organisms that have transgressed the moral codes of nineteenth-century Europeans. Thus confidently anthropomorphizing, Lombroso writes about polygamous llamas and the jurisprudence of ants. *Criminal* is synonymous with the Italian *delinquente* in Lombroso's vocabulary (but not equivalent to the softer English term delinquent, into which it is sometimes mistranslated).

criminal anthropology An approach to the study of crime that adopts the methods of physical anthropology and begins from the premise that science can discover the causes of crime by using the human body as fundamental data. Advocates of this approach—known as the positivist school, the Italian school, or the criminal anthropological school—defined themselves in opposition to the classical school. Whereas advocates of the classical approach focused on crime and (especially) punishment, criminal anthropologists called for a study of criminal types. Criminal anthropology was founded by Ceasare Lombroso, who was also its main exponent; from about 1870–1900, he and his followers were generally recognized as the world's authorities on criminal behavior. During this period, in which there was no other scientific approach to the study of lawbreaking, *criminal anthropology* was also used as a synonym for what is now called *criminology* or the study of the causes of crime.

criminal by passion Someone who breaks the law through a sudden outburst of emotion, usually one brought on by difficulties in love or politics. Unlike the born criminal, the criminal by passion has few or no anomalies.

criminal type Someone with four or more degenerative traits; a synonym for *born criminal*.

criminaloid An offender halfway between the born criminal and the occasional criminal; a lawbreaker with just a few anomalies.

degeneration A condition analogous to illness in which the human organism is said to exist in a state of silent and for the most part invisible decay. In his early work, Lombroso tends to explain criminality in terms of atavism, a condition with which the criminal is born; later, Lombroso also explains criminality in terms of degeneration, a heritable or acquired condition in which one gradually slips backward down the evolutionary scale. For Lombroso as for other degenerationists, the deterioration can be physical, intellectual, psychological, or all three at once. Moreover, the signs of degeneration are fluid and interchangeable, for they are merely outward manifestations of the inner process of decay. At first associated with the work of Bénédict Auguste Morel (1857), degeneration became a leading explanation of crime and other social problems in the late nineteenth century in both the United States and Europe, laying the foundation for later, gene-based theories of criminality. See also heredity.

delinquent See criminal.

dolichocephaly Long-headedness. See brachycephaly.

epilepsy Technically, a chronic nervous disorder associated with changes in consciousness and with convulsions. Using the term very loosely, in his later work Lombroso often speaks of epilepsy as an equivalent to or cause of inborn criminality. In *Criminal Woman*, he is not clear about the relationship of epilepsy to crime, although he does state that epilepsy is a form of degeneration and that it is more likely to afflict men than women.

evolution The most significant of all natural processes, in Lombroso's view, because it is the one through which organisms become steadily more differentiated, complex, and civilized. Lombroso adopts Darwin's concept of evolution but, like many of his contemporaries, he gives Darwin's ideas a teleological twist, arguing that whatever is must be the result of evolution and that it must therefore be socially useful and good. This sort of reasoning has given Lombroso a reputation for being a political conservative but, he in fact reasons this way inconsistently and only when it suits his broader purposes to do so.

heredity The process by which traits are passed through the generations. Writing in a period before the discovery of the gene, Lombroso is vague about how heredity might operate; nor does he show much curiosity about the process itself. Like other scientists of his generation, he assumes that degeneration is a heritable affliction. However, and again typically, Lombroso also adopts the Lamarckian position that acquired traits can become permanent and heritable. Thus he believes that an individual who is lazy, or impoverished, or habitually drunken can acquire the degenerative tendency and pass it on through heredity to his or her children, in whom it might manifest itself in prostitution or criminality.

honest woman See normal woman.

hysteria A psychological condition characterized by excitability and sudden mood changes. Perpetuating a long tradition, Lombroso associates hysteria with women in particular; in his view, as in that of many of his contemporaries, women generally lack rationality and self-control, which makes them more inherently emotional than men and thus more susceptible to hysteria. Lombroso regards hysteria as a form of insanity typified by lack of self-restraint, suggestibility, and a tendency to make false accusations.

lesbianism Sexual relationships between women. Lombroso's usual term for such relationships is *tribadismo*, which technically denotes a relationship in which one female partner simulates the male role; however, Lombroso uses *tribadismo* more broadly to refer to any homosexual relationship between or among women. Less frequently, he uses another synonym, *saffismo*. He finds that lesbianism is particularly common among prostitutes and female prisoners, and he considers it a degenerative trait.

median occipital fossetta (fossetta occipitale mediana) An anatomical peculiarity of the cranium that Lombroso interpreted as evidence for the atavistic nature of the criminal. Lombroso first detected this anomaly in 1872, while dissecting the corpse of a brigand named Villela. At a midway point in the base of the skull, where a "normal" person would have a small bony crest, Villela's skull was indented, an abnormality that reminded Lombroso of the skulls of monkeys and lemurs. He instantly grasped (or so he said later) that the criminal must be a throwback to an earlier evolutionary type. For Lombroso, the median occipital fossetta became a key biological sign of the born criminal.

moral insanity A condition in which an individual remains normal intellectually but nonetheless lacks a conscience or moral sense; an early term for the state today termed *psychopathy*. Lombroso views moral insanity as an atavism or form of degeneration, and he associates it with born criminals and epileptics in particular. The subject of a book published in 1835 by the Englishman James Cowles Prichard, moral insanity was a widely recognized and much-discussed phenomenon throughout the nineteenth century. Combining this popular concept with his notion of the born criminal, Lombroso helped prepare the ground for subsequent studies of psychopaths and sociopaths. The association also contributed to a reconceptualization of criminality as a kind of disease or mental pathology.

normal woman A term Lombroso uses to denote a woman (1) with two or fewer anomalies; (2) who has not been convicted of a crime or is not in jail or prison; (3) who is sexually frigid and engages in sexual activity only in the context of marriage. In the case of women, Lombroso equates law-abiding behavior with chastity. Even though he is aware of nondetected offenders in the general population, Lombroso constructs tables comparing honest or normal woman with criminal women, treating the two categories as dichotomous variables.

occasional criminal An offender with few or no anomalies who is pushed into criminal behavior by environmental circumstance (poverty, bad family, misfortune) or (in the case of women) by an evil man. Occasional criminals, because they are less degenerate than born criminals, can be reformed.

precocity Premature development, signaling abnormality. In *Criminal Woman*, Lombroso first uses the term to indicate early developmental advantages among females that later disappear. Starting with the assumption (part 1, chapter 2) that "the more superior the animal, the later its development," he dismisses examples of early female developmental superiority as precocious and misleading. A second and related context in which Lombroso draws on the idea of precocity is that of sexuality. When girls mature sexually before boys, or begin sexual activity earlier, Lombroso condemns these developments as examples of precocity. That is, he uses male development as the norm, labeling deviations from it precocious and hence abnormal. At other times, when comparing bad women with good or normal women, he uses the latter as the standard; thus bad women, if they show signs of earlier development, are precocious and dangerously different.

primitive women See savage women.

prostitute A term that denotes (1) a woman who exchanges sex for money; or (2) any woman, but particularly one who belongs to the lower classes, who has sexual experience outside of marriage.

race A group defined by skin color, nationality, or ethnicity. Using the term very loosely, Lombroso associates racial categories with ranks on the evolutionary scale and therefore (in his logic) with degrees of criminality as well. In one of his first books, *L'uomo bianco e l'uomo di colore* (The white man and the man of color), written in 1871, Lombroso explains that in the earliest evolutionary stages, everyone was black, and that blacks today remain closer than other races to monkeys. As evolution progressed, it produced people with yellow skins and later whites. The European races are the most highly evolved and therefore most civilized. In phrases such as "the European races" and "the Italian races," Lombroso also uses *race* as a synonym for *nationality* and *ethnicity*. He considers southern Italians inferior to northern Italians because the former have African and Arab blood. *Race* for him is both a descriptive and an explanatory term. Using the concept imprecisely, he can call on it to explain a wide range of phenomena.

regression A process similar to that of degeneration, in which a human organism slides backward and downward on the evolutionary scale. Also termed *reversion*.

saffism See lesbianism.

savage women Primitive women; women in an earlier state of evolution than European women. Conceiving of savage women as the ancestors of contemporary European women, Lombroso pictures them as dark-skinned, uncivilized, and animalistic in their desires and habits. In the same category he places contemporary women—Australian Aborigines, Africans, some Asians, and Native Americans—who in his view continue to exhibit these primitive traits. In *Criminal Woman*, Lombroso projects sexual fantasies onto these women and their "primitive" life, which he depicts as a state of continuous promiscuity for both sexes.

stigmata of crime See anomaly.

tribadism See lesbianism.

variation A Darwinian term denoting natural evolutionary changes. Lombroso frequently uses *variation* to explain gender differences. In his view, men are more mobile than women and hence more variable and rapid in their evolution. Women, on the other hand, are sedentary and conservative physiologically; hence they are less variable, slower in their evolution, and inferior to men.

References

Abelson, Elaine S. 2000. "Shoplifting and Kleptomania." Pp. 243–44 in *Encyclopedia of Women and Crime*, ed. Nicole Hahn Rafter. Phoenix, Ariz.: Oryx.

Adam, Hargrave L. 1912. *Woman and Crime*. London: T. W. Laurie.

Adler, Freda. 1975. *Sisters in Crime: The Rise of the New Female Criminal*. New York: McGraw-Hill.

Aschaffenburg, Gustav. 1913. *Crime and Its Repression*. Trans. Adalbert Albrecht. Boston: Little, Brown.

Baima Bollone, Pierluigi. 1992. *Cesare Lombroso: Ovvero: Il principio dell'irresponsabilità*. Turin: Societa editrice internazionale.

Barrows, Susanna. 1981. *Distorting Mirrors: Visions of the Crowd in Late Nineteenth-Century France*. New Haven, Conn.: Yale University Press.

Beccaria, Cesare. [1764] 1963. *On Crimes and Punishments*. Trans. Henry Paolucci. Indianapolis: Bobbs-Merrill.

Becker, Peter, and Richard F. Wetzell, eds. 2004 [forthcoming]. *Criminals and Their Scientists: The History of Criminology in International Perspective*. Cambridge: Cambridge University Press.

Beirne, Piers. 1993. *Inventing Criminology: Essays on the Rise of Homo Criminalis*. Albany: State University of New York Press.

Bonger, Willem Adriaan. [1916] 1969. *Criminality and Economic Conditions*. Bloomington: Indiana University Press.

Bulferetti, Luigi. 1975. *Cesare Lombroso*. Turin: Unione tipografico-editrice torinese.

Chen, Xingliang. 1992. *Yi chuan yu fan zui*. Beijing: Jun zhong chu ban she.

Cameron, Mary Owen. 1964. *The Booster and the Snitch: Department Store Shoplifting*. New York: Free Press of Glencoe.

Colombo, Giorgio. [1975] 2000. *La scienza infelice: Il museo di antropologia criminale di Cesare Lombroso*. Turin: Bollati Boringhieri.

Dalton, Katharina. 1964. *The Premenstrual Syndrome*. Springfield, Ill.: C. C. Thomas.

Dolza, Delfina. 1990. *Essere figlie di Lombroso: Due donne intellettuali tra '800 e '900*. Milan: F. Angeli.

Drapkin, Israel. 1977. *Cesare Lombroso: El creador de la moderna criminología científica*. Buenos Aires: Congreso Judío Latinoamericano.

Dugdale, Richard L. 1877. *The Jukes: A Study in Crime, Pauperism, Disease, and Heredity*. New York: Putnam's Sons.

Ellis, Havelock. 1890. *The Criminal*. London: Walter Scott.

——. [1906] 1936. *Sex in Relation to Society*. New York: Random House.

Ellis, Havelock, and John Addington Symonds. [1897] 1994. *Sexual Inversion*. United States: Ayer Company Publishers.

Erony, Susan, and Nicole Hahn Rafter. 2000. *Searching the Criminal Body: Art/Science/Prejudice*. Albany: University Art Museum, University of Albany.

Eysenck, H. J. 1979. *Crime and Personality*. 3d. ed. London: Routledge and Kegan Paul.

Fausto-Sterling, Anne. 1995. "Gender, Race, and Nation: The Comparative Anatomy of 'Hottentot' Women in Europe, 1815–1817." Pp. 19–48 in *Deviant Bodies: Critical Perspectives on Difference in Science and Popular Culture*, ed. Jennifer Terry and Jacqueline Urla. Bloomington: Indiana University Press.

Fee, Elizabeth. 1979. "Nineteenth-Century Craniology: The Study of the Female Skull." *Bulletin of the History of Medicine* 53: 415–33.

Feinman, Clarice. 1980. *Women in the Criminal Justice System*. New York: Praeger.

Fernald, Mabel Ruth. 1920. *A Study of Women Delinquents in New York State*. New York: The Century Company.

Fiume, Giovanna. 1990. *La vecchia dell'aceto: Un processo per veneficio nella Palermo di fine Settecento*. Palermo: Gelka.

Gadebusch Bondio, Mariacarla. 1995. *Die Rezeption der kriminalanthropologischen Theorien von Cesare Lombroso in Deutschland von 1880–1914*. Ed. Rolf Winau and Heinz Müller-Dietz. Husum: Matthiesen.

——. 1996. "La tipologizzazione della donna deviante nella seconda metà dell'ottocento: La prostituta, la criminale e la pazza." Pp. 283–314 in *Per una storia critica della scienza*, ed. Marco Beretta, Felice Mondella, and Maria Teresa Monti. Bologna: Cisalpino.

Gallini, Clara. 1983. *La sonnambula meravigliosa: Magnetismo e ipnotismo nell'Ottocento italiano*. Milan: Feltrinelli.

Garin, Eugenio, 1980. "Il positivismo italiano alla fine del secolo XIX fra metodo e concezione del mondo." *Giornale critica della filosofia italiana* ser. 5, vol. 1: 1–27.

Gibson, Mary. 1982. "The *Female Offender* and the Italian School of Criminal Anthropology." *Journal of European Studies* 12: 155–65.

——. 1990. "On the Insensitivity of Women: Science and the Woman Question in Liberal Italy, 1890–1910." *Journal of Women's History* 2, no. 2: 11–41.

——. [1986] 1999. *Prostitution and the State in Italy, 1860–1915*. Columbus: Ohio State University Press.

——. 2002. *Born to Crime: Cesare Lombroso and the Origins of Biological Criminology*. Westport, Conn.: Praeger.

Glueck, Sheldon, and Eleanor T. Glueck. 1930. *Five Hundred Criminal Careers*. New York: Knopf.

——. 1934. *Five Hundred Delinquent Women*. New York: Knopf.

Goring, Charles Buckman. [1913] 1972. *The English Convict: A Statistical Study*. Montclair, N.J.: Patterson Smith.

Gould, Stephen Jay. 1981. *The Mismeasure of Man*. New York: Norton.

Graziosi, Marina. 2000. "Women and Criminal Law: The Notion of Diminished Responsibility in Prospero Farinaccio (1544–1618) and Other Renaissance Jurors." Pp. 166–81 in *Women in Italian Renaissance Culture and Society*, ed. Letizia Panizza. Oxford, U.K.: Leganda.

Gross, Hans. [1911] 1968. *Criminal Psychology: A Manual for Judges, Practitioners and Students*. Montclair, N.J.: Patterson Smith.

Guarnieri, Luigi. 2000. *L'atlante criminale: Vita scriteriata di Cesare Lombroso*. Milan: Mondadori.

Guarnieri, Patrizia. 1993. *A Case of Child Murder: Law and Science in Nineteenth-Century Tuscany*. Cambridge, U.K.: Polity.

Guillot, Adolphe. 1889. *Paris qui souffre: La basse geôle du Grand Châtelet et les Morgues Modernes*. Paris: P. Rougualte.

Harrowitz, Nancy A. 1994. *Antisemitism, Misogyny, and the Logic of Cultural Difference: Cesare Lombroso and Matilde Serao*. Lincoln: University of Nebraska Press.

Healy, William. 1915. *The Individual Delinquent: A Textbook of Diagnosis and Prognosis for All Concerned in Understanding Offenders*. Boston: Little, Brown.

Heidensohn, Frances. 1968. "The Deviance of Women: A Critique and an Enquiry." *British Journal of Sociology* 19, no. 2: 160–75.

——. 1996. *Women and Crime*. 2d ed. Houndmills, U.K.: Macmillan.

Horn, David G. 1995. "This Norm Which Is Not One: Reading the Female Body in Lombroso's Anthropology." Pp 109–28 in *Deviant Bodies: Critical Perspectives on Difference in Science and Popular Culture*, ed. Jennifer Terry and Jacqueline Urla. Bloomington: Indiana University Press.

Horney, Julie. 1985. "Menstrual Cycles and Criminal Responsibility." 1978. Pp. 159–75 in *Biology, Crime, and Ethics: A Study of Biological Explanations for Criminal Behavior*. Cincinnati, Ohio: Anderson.

Kellor, Frances Alice. 1901. *Experimental Sociology, Descriptive and Analytical: Delinquents*. New York: Macmillan.

Klein, Dorie. 1973. "The Etiology of Female Crime." *Issues in Criminology* 8, no. 2: 3–30.

Konopka, Gisela. 1966. *The Adolescent Girl in Conflict*. Englewood Cliffs, N.J.: Prentice-Hall.

Krafft-Ebing, Richard von. 1892. *Psychopathia sexualis*. Stuttgart: F. Enke.

Leschiutta, Pierpaolo. 1996. *Palimsesti del carcere: Cesare Lombroso e le scritture proibite*. Naples: Liguori.

Lombroso, Caesar, and William Ferrero [*sic*]. [1895] 1915. *The Female Offender*. New York: D. Appleton and Company.

Lombroso, Cesare. 1871. *L'uomo bianco e l'uomo di colore: Lettere sull' origine e le varietà delle razze umane*. Padova: F. Sacchetto.

——. 1876. *L'uomo delinquente studiato in rapporto alla antropologia, alla medicina legale ed alle discipline carcerarie*. Milan: Hoepli.

——. 1882. *Genio e follia: In rapporto alla medicina legale, alla critica ed all storia*. 4th ed. Rome: Bocca.

——. 1891. *The Man of Genius*. New York: Scribner's.

——. 1897. *Atlante*. Vol. 4 of the 5th edition of *L'uomo delinquente*. Fratelli Bocca Editori.

——. 1897. *Genio e degenerazione: Nuovi studi e nuove battaglie*. Palermo: Sandron.

——. 1983. *Basic Characteristics of Women Criminals*. New and exp. ed. Albuquerque: Foundation for Classical Reprints.

Lombroso, Cesare, José Luis Peset Reig, and Mariano Peset Reig. 1975. *Lombroso y la escuela positivista italiana*. Madrid: C.S. de I.C.

——. 1995. *Delitto, genio, follia: Scritti scelti*. Ed. Delia Frigessi, Ferruccio Giacanelli, and Luisa Mangoni. Turin: Bollati Boringhieri.

——. 2005 [forthcoming]. *Criminal Man*. Trans. Mary Gibson and Nicole Hahn Rafter. Durham, N.C.: Duke University Press.

Lombroso, Cesare, and Guglielmo Ferrero. 1893. *La donna delinquente, la prostituta e la donna normale*. Turin: Roux.

Lombroso-Ferrero, Gina. [1911] 1972. *Criminal Man According to the Classification of Cesare Lombroso*. Montclair, N.J.: Patterson Smith.

Lydston, G. Frank. 1904. *The Diseases of Society (The Vice and Crime Problem)*. Philadelphia: J. B. Lippincott.

Mazzarello, Paolo. 1998. *Il genio e l'alienista: La vista di Lombroso a Tolstoj*. Naples: Bibliopolis.

McKay, Carol. 1996. "'Fearful Dunderheads': Kandinsky and the Cultural Referents of Criminal Anthropology." *Oxford Art Journal* 19, no. 1: 29–41.

Mella, Ricardo, Antón Fernández Álvarez, and Valentín Arias. 1999. *Lombroso e os anarquistas*. Vigo: Edicións Xerais de Galicia.

Morel, Bénédict Auguste. 1857. *Traité des dégénérescences physiques, intellectuelles et morales de l'espèce humain*. Paris: J. B. Baillière.

Mucchielli, Laurent, ed. 1994. *Histoire de la criminologie française*. Paris: Editions L'Harmattan.

Nye, Robert A. 1976. "Heredity or Milieu: The Foundations of Modern European Criminological Theory." *Isis* 47, no. 238: 335–55.

O'Brien, Patricia. 1983. "The Kleptomania Diagnosis: Bourgeois Women and Theft in Late Nineteenth-Century France." *Journal of Social History* 17: 65–77.

Parent-Duchatelet, A.-J.-B. 1836. *De la prostitution dans la ville de Paris: Considérée sous le rapport de l'hygiène publique, de la morale et de l'administration*. Paris: J.-B. Ballière.

Parmelee, Maurice. 1911. "Introduction." Pp. xii–xxxii in *Crime: Its Causes and Remedies*, by Cesare Lombroso. Trans. Henry P. Horton. Boston: Little, Brown.

Pick, Daniel. 1986. "The Faces of Anarchy: Lombroso and the Politics of Criminal Science in Post-unification Italy." *History Workshop* 21: 60–81.

Pollak, Otto. [1950] 1961. *The Criminality of Women*. New York: Barnes.

Portigliatti Barbos, Mario. 1993. "Cesare Lombroso e il museo di antropologia criminale." Pp. 1441–60. in *Storia illustrata di Torino*, ed. Valerio Castronovo. Milan: Elio Sellino.

Quiroz Cuarón, Alfonso. 1977. *Homenaje a César Lombroso*. Mexico City: Segretaria de Gobernación.

Rafter, Nicole Hahn. 1992. "Criminal Anthropology in the United States." *Criminology* 30, no. 4: 525–45.

——. 1997. *Creating Born Criminals*. Urbana: University of Illinois Press.

——. 2001. "Looking at Lombroso: Space, Gender, and Representation in *La donna delinquente*." Paper presented at Workshop on Urban Space and Criminological Discourse, 15 December 2001, Vienna, Austria.

Rafter, Nicole Hahn, and Frances Heidensohn, eds. 1995. *International Feminist Perspectives in Criminology: Engendering a Discipline*. Buckingham, U.K.: Open University Press.

Regener, Susanne. 1999. *Fotografische Erfassung: Zur Geschichte medialer Konstruktionen des Kriminellen*. Munich: Fink.

——. 2003. "Criminological Museums and the Visualization of Evil." *Crime, History, and Societies* 7, no. 1: 43–56.

Robinson, Paul. 1976. *The Modernization of Sex: Havelock Ellis, Alfred Kinsey, William Masters, and Virginia Johnson*. New York: Harper and Row.

Rondini, Andrea. 2001. *Cose da pazzi: Cesare Lombroso e la letteratura*. Pisa: Istituti Editoriali e Poligrafici Internazionali.

Sacher-Masoch, Leopold von. [n.d.] 2000 *Venus in Furs*. Trans. Joachim Neugroschel. New York: Penguin.

Smart, Carol. 1976. *Women, Crime, and Criminology: A Feminist Critique*. London: Routledge and Kegan Paul.

Tarnowsky, Pauline. 1889. *Étude anthropométrique sur les prostitutées et les voleuses*. Paris: E. Lecrosnier et Babé.

Tone, Andrea, ed. 1997. *Controlling Reproduction: An American History*. Wilmington, Del.: Scholarly Resources.

Villa, Renzo. 1985. *Il deviante e i suoi segni: Lombroso e la nascita dell' antropologia criminale*. Milan: F. Angeli.

Wetzell, Richard F. 2000. *Inventing the Criminal: A History of German Criminology, 1880–1945*. Chapel Hill: University of North Carolina Press.

Wines, Frederick Howard. 1895. "Criminal Anthropology." Pp. 229–65 in *Punishment and Reformation: A Historical Sketch of the Rise of the Penitentiary System*. New York: Crowell.

Wolfgang, Mavin E. 1972. "Cesare Lombroso, 1835–1909." Pp. 232–91 in *Pioneers in Criminology*, ed. Hermann Mannheim. 2d enl. ed. Montclair, N.J.: Patterson Smith.

Index

CESARE LOMBROSO (1835–1909) is widely considered the founder of criminology. His book *La donna delinquente* was first published in Italy in 1893.

GUGLIELMO FERRERO (1871–1942) was a young law student when Cesare Lombroso invited him to help with the research on *Criminal Woman*. He married Lombroso's daughter Gina in 1901.

NICOLE HAHN RAFTER teaches at Northeastern University in the Criminal Justice and the Law, Policy, and Society programs. She is the author and editor of many books on crime, law, and gender, including *Creating Born Criminals* (1997) and *Shots in the Mirror: Crime Films and Society* (2000).

MARY GIBSON is a professor of history at John Jay College of Criminal Justice at the City University of New York. She is the author of *Born to Crime: Cesare Lombroso and the Origins of Biological Criminology* (2002) and *Prostitution and the State in Italy, 1860–1915* (1986).

Library of Congress Cataloging-in-Publication Data
Lombroso, Cesare, 1835–1909.
[Donna delinquente. English]
Criminal woman, the prostitute, and the normal woman /
by Cesare Lombroso and Guglielmo Ferrero ; translated and
with a new introduction by Nichole Hahn Rafter and Mary Gibson.
Includes bibliographical references and index.
ISBN 0-8223-3207-8 (cloth : alk. paper)
ISBN 0-8223-3246-9 (pbk. : alk. paper)
1. Female offenders. 2. Criminal anthropology. 3. Prostitutes.
I. Ferrero, Guglielmo, 1871–1942. II. Rafter, Nicole Hahn, 1939–
III. Gibson, Mary. IV. Title.
HV6046.L7813 2004 364.3′74—dc22 2003015046